ASPECTS OF DISTRIBUTION OF WEALTH AND INCOME

THE JEROME LEVY ECONOMICS INSTITUTE SERIES

General Editor: Dimitri B. Papadimitriou, Levy Institute Professor of Economics, Bard College, Annandale-on-Hudson, New York

Geoffrey Harcourt, Alessandro Roncaglia and Robin Rowley (*editors*)
INCOME AND EMPLOYMENT IN THEORY AND PRACTICE

Dimitri B. Papadimitriou (*editor*)
ASPECTS OF DISTRIBUTION OF WEALTH AND INCOME

Dimitri B. Papadimitriou and Edward N. Wolff (*editors*)
POVERTY AND PROSPERITY IN THE USA IN THE LATE
TWENTIETH CENTURY

Aspects of Distribution of Wealth and Income

Edited by

Dimitri B. Papadimitriou

Levy Institute Professor of Economics
Bard College, Annandale-on-Hudson, New York

St. Martin's Press

First published in Great Britain 1994 by
THE MACMILLAN PRESS LTD
Houndmills, Basingstoke, Hampshire RG21 2XS
and London
Companies and representatives
throughout the world

A catalogue record for this book is available
from the British Library.

ISBN 0–333–56696–3

Printed in Great Britain by
Ipswich Book Co Ltd
Ipswich, Suffolk

First published in the United States of America 1994 by
Scholarly and Reference Division,
ST. MARTIN'S PRESS, INC.,
175 Fifth Avenue,
New York, N.Y. 10010

ISBN 0–312–12101–6

Library of Congress Cataloging-in-Publication Data
Aspects of distribution of wealth and income / edited by Dimitri B.
Papadimitriou.
p.   cm.
Includes index.
ISBN 0–312–12101–6
1. Income distribution—United States.   2. Income distribution.
3. United States—Economic conditions.—1981–   4. Economic
history—1971–1990.   I. Papadimitriou, Dimitri B.
HC110.I5A78   1994
339.2'0973—dc20   93–40402
                                                      CIP

Contents

Contents

The Jerome Levy Economics Institute of Bard College

Founded in 1986, The Jerome Levy Economics Institute of Bard College is an autonomous, independently endowed research organization. It is nonpartisan, open to the examination of diverse points of view, and dedicated to public service.

The Institute believes in the potential for economic study to improve the human condition. Its purpose is to generate viable, effective public policy responses to important economic problems. It is concerned with issues that profoundly affect the quality of life in the United States, in other highly industrialized nations, and in countries with developing economies

The Institute's present research agenda includes such issues as financial instability, poverty and problems associated with the distribution of income and wealth. Other research interests include the issues of public and private investment and their relationship to productivity, competitiveness, and the prospects for growth and employment. In all its endeavors, the Institute places heavy emphasis on the values of personal freedom and justice. The opinions expressed in this volume are those of the authors and do not necessarily represent those of The Jerome Levy Economics Institute of Bard College.

Acknowledgements

I would like to most sincerely thank the Board of Governors of The Jerome Levy Economics Institute of Bard College for sponsoring the Conference on 'Aspects of Distribution of Wealth and Income' from which this collection of essays is drawn. I want to thank the contributors for their promptness and their readiness in carrying out revisions, Linda Christensen and Deborah C. Wizeman for their hard work in preparing this manuscript, Tim Farmiloe, our publishing editor, for his cooperation and encouragement, and Keith Povey for his editorial assistance. Needless to say, however, I am indebted as always to my assistant Susan Howard, for her skill, loyalty, devotion and good humor without which this book would not have been possible. To her, my warm and sincere thanks.

DIMITRI B. PAPADIMITRIOU

Notes on the Contributors

Robert B. Avery is Professor in the Department of Consumer Economics at Cornell University and a Research Associate at the Federal Reserve Bank of Cleveland. Prior to his arrival at Cornell, Dr Avery was Senior Economist at the Board of Governors of the Federal Reserve System (1981–8) and Assistant Professor of Economics in the Graduate School of Industrial Administration at Carnegie Mellon University (1975–81). While at the Federal Reserve Board, he served as Project Director of the 1983, 1986 and 1989 Surveys of Consumer Finances.

Rebecca Blank is Associate Professor of Economics and Education at the School of Education and Social Policy, Northwestern University. Dr Blank also taught at Princeton University, and until recently was with the Council of Economic Advisers in Washington, DC.

Alan S. Blinder is the Gordon S. Rentschler Memorial Professor of Economics, Princeton University. Dr Blinder is a regular contributor to *Business Week*, and on the editorial boards of the *Journal of Economic Literature*, and the *Journal of Monetary Economics*, and is associate editor of the *Journal of Public Economics*. His publications include *Toward an Economic Theory of Income Distribution; General Equilibrium Systems: Essays in Memory of Rafael Lusky* (ed. with P. Friedman); *Economics: Principles and Policy* (with W. J. Baumol); *Economic Policy and the Great Stagflation*, and *Hard Heads and Soft Hearts*.

John Coder is staff assistant in the Census Bureau's Housing and Household Economic Statistics Division. Mr Coder has been employed at the Bureau of the Census since 1970, working throughout his career in the income statistics area, and served from 1980 through 1988 as Chief of the Income Statistics Branch before accepting a special 18-month assignment with the Luxembourg Income Study. He is currently leading the Bureau's research program concerning nonsampling errors in the March Current Population Survey and Survey of Income and Program Participation income data.

Gordon W. Green, Jr is Assistant Division Chief in the Census Bureau's Housing and Household Economics Statistics Division. Dr Green is in charge of the preparation of socioeconomic statistics and he oversees work in the subject areas of income distribution, poverty, wealth, and labor force statistics. Dr Green has worked at the Census Bureau since 1973, and has written many reports and papers on the relationship between demographic and economic variables and changes in income and poverty statistics. His publications include: *Getting Straight A's*, and *Getting Ahead at Work*.

F. Thomas Juster is Director, Institute for Social Research and Professor of Economics, University of Michigan. Dr Juster also taught at Amherst College, and held positions of Senior Research Analyst for the CIA and Senior Research Staff of the NBER. His publications include: *Consumer Expectations, Plans and Purchases: A Progress Report; Anticipations and Purchases: An Analysis of Consumer Behavior; Household Capital Formation and Financing: Growth and Cyclical Behavior, 1897–1962; Education, Income and Human Behavior* (ed.); *The Distribution of Economic Well-being* (ed.); *Social Accounting Systems: Essays on the State of the Art*, authored with K. Land.

Thomas Karier is Professor of Economics, Eastern Washington University and was Visiting Professor of Economics, Bard College and Resident Scholar, Jerome Levy Economics Institute. Dr Karier's recent articles include: 'The Unions and the U.S. Comparative Advantage,' *Industrial Relations*; Labor Relations and the Composition of U.S. Foreign Trade,' and 'New Evidence on the Effect of Unions and Imports on Monopoly Profits: A Rejoinder,' *Journal of Post-Keynesian Economics*.

James N. Morgan is Professor of Economics, University of Michigan and Resident Scientist, Institute for Social Research. Dr Morgan's publications include: *Income and Welfare in the United States; The Economic Behaviour of the Affluent* (with R. Barlow and H. Brazer); *Productive Americans* (with I. Sirageldin and L. Baerwaldt); *The Economics of Personal Choice* (with G. Duncan) and *Five Thousand American Families: Patterns of Economic Progress* 10 volumes (ed. and co-author).

Dimitri B. Papadimitriou is Executive Vice President and the Levy Institute Professor of Economics, Bard College; Executive Director of the Jerome Levy Economics Institute and the Bard Center.

Dr Papadimitriou was a visiting Scholar, Center for Economic Planning and Research (Athens, Greece); Wye Fellow, Aspen Institute. He is the general editor of the Levy Economics Institute Series, editor of *Profits, Deficits and Instability; Financial Conditions and Macroeconomic Performance: Essays in Honor of Hyman P. Minsky* (with Steven Fazzari); and *Poverty and Prosperity in the USA in the Late Twentieth Century* (with Edward N. Wolff).

Edmund S. Phelps is the McVickar Professor of Political Economy, Columbia University. Dr Phelps is the author of many books and articles including: *Fiscal Neutrality toward Economic Growth; Inflation Policy and Unemployment Theory; Individual Forecasting and Aggregate Outcomes: Rational Expectations Examined.* Dr Phelps is a fellow of the American Academy of Sciences, the Guggenheim Foundation and the National Academy of Sciences; was President of the Atlantic Economic Society in 1984 and Vice President of the American Economic Association.

Leonard A. Rapping was Professor of Economics, University of Massachusetts-Amherst. Dr Rapping's contributions include: 'The Great Recession of the 1970's: Domestic and International Considerations,' in *Alternative Directions in Economic Policy*; 'The Domestic and International Aspects of Structural Inflation,' in *Post-Keynesian Theories of Inflation*; 'Bureaucracy, the Corporation and Economic Policy,' *Journal of Post-Keynesian Economics*.

Joan R. Rodgers is Assistant Professor of Economics, University of North Carolina-Greensboro. Dr Rodgers was resident scholar, Jerome Levy Economics Institute. Her publications include: 'Poverty and Choice of Marital Status: A Self-Selection Model,' *Popular Research and Policy Review*; 'Measuring the Intensity of Poverty among Subpopulations, with Application to the United States' (with John L. Rodgers), *Journal of Human Resources*; 'Does the Choice of Poverty Index Matter in Practice?,' *Social Indicators Research*.

Paul Ryscavage is Senior Labor Economist in the Census Bureau's Housing and Household Economic Statistics Division. He serves as a staff assistant to the Assistant Division Chief of that Division and conducts research on the nation's labor force and income distribution. Mr Ryscavage has worked at the Census Bureau since 1983 and prior to that, at the US Bureau of Labor Statistics since 1962.

Paul S. Sarbanes is US Senator from Maryland; Chairman, Joint Economic Committee and member of the Banking, Housing and Urban Affairs and Foreign Relations Committees of the US Senate. Senator Sarbanes was educated at Princeton University, Phi Beta Kappa and holds the LL.B., cum laude from Harvard Law School. He was a Rhodes scholar, Balliol College, Oxford University and is admitted to practice by the Maryland Court of Appeals. Senator Sarbanes was assistant to Walter Heller, Chairman of the Council of Economic Advisers.

Isabel V. Sawhill is Senior Fellow and Program Director, Urban Institute. Dr Sawhill is a former Director, Commission for Employment Policy and her publications focus on macroeconomic policy, employment and income distribution.

Erik Thorbecke is the H.E. Babcock Professor of Economics and Food Economics, Cornell University. Dr Thorbecke spent two years with USAID in Washington as Chief of the Sector Analysis Division (PPC) and Associate Assistant Administrator for Program Policy, and from 1975 was a member of AID's Research Advisory Committee. He is currently Senior Research Fellow of AID's Institute for Policy Reform. Dr Thorbecke is also Director of the Program on comparative Economic Development, Cornell University. He has been consultant to the World Bank, FAO, ILO, IFAD and other agencies.

Howard M. Wachtel is Professor of Economics, the American University. His publications include *The Money Mandarins*.

Sourushe Zandvakili is Assistant Professor of Economics, University of Cincinnati and was Resident Scholar, Jerome Levy Economics Institute. Dr Zandvakili's contributions include: 'A Class of Generalized Measures of Mobility with Applications,' *Economic Letters*; 'Mobility Profiles and Time Aggregates of Individual Incomes,' *Research on Economic Inequality*; and 'Generalized Entropy Measures of Mobility for Different Sexes and Income Levels,' *Journal of Econometrics* (all with E. Maasoumi).

1 Introduction

Dimitri B. Papadimitriou

The primary fact of economics is the production of wealth. The division of the product among those who create it is secondary in logical order and, in a sense, in importance. Yet, the most important subject of thought connected with social economy is distribution. If the term be used broadly enough it designates all of the economic process that presents moral problems for solution. On the settlement of the ethical questions concerning the division of the social income depends not only the peace of society but the fruitfulness of industry (J. B. Clark, *Palgrave's Dictionary of Political Economy*).

The study of income and wealth disparity has always occupied the centre stage in economics, and has been the subject of considerable research and scrutiny of late, in light of the last decade's deepening of inequality, especially in the United States. In the 1960s and early 1970s, periods of sustained growth and high employment in the United States and other industrialized countries, the distribution of income and wealth improved. Research documenting such improvement became the focus of interest to academicians and policy-makers. The United States poverty rate in 1960 was 22 percent, and had declined by 50 percent in 1973, as reported in the US Census *Current Population Reports*. Correspondingly, wealth disparity improved by 40 percent, from the 32 percent share of the top 1 percent in the distribution ladder in 1962, down to 18 percent in 1976. These trends, however, were reversed in the decade of the 1980s, in which the poverty rate increased to 14 percent in 1990, and wealth inequality, similarity, rose to 32 percent again in 1986 (Gittleman and Wolff, 1993).

Customary measures of income have shown that there has been an erosion in the growth of real incomes in 1973–90 – 0.3 percent per year, as opposed to the 2.7 percent per year in 1947–73 (Nelson, 1992). In addition, the income disparity in 1973–90 showed higher dispersion, especially along gender lines, in that year-round, full-time, real median earnings for males declined by 10.6 percent, while correspondingly for female earners they increased by 13 percent. The male–female earnings ratio thus showed an increase from 0.60 in 1980 to 0.72 in

1990 reflecting the gains in women's earnings, but still showing significant differences *vis-à-vis* those of their male counterparts (Nelson, 1992). The differences relate closely to those estimated by Joan R. Rodgers in Chapter 3, in which they are contrasted in terms of male- and female-headed households.

There are other aspects of inequality that are associated with variables which, when measured, reflect the changing demography and geography of income. Estimates of variables such as race, schooling, experience, health, size of household, and location can trace how the members of each of these groups progress. An attempt of this sort is made in Chapter 3, in which an estimation of these variables provides valuable insights into the anatomy of income inequality. For white–nonwhite, skilled–nonskilled, experienced–new entrant, healthy–disabled, male–female-headed or large–small household, and city–suburban income and wealth distinctions, describe not the economy of the 1960s, but of the late 1980s. During the Eisenhower and the Kennedy–Johnson years, there were fewer women in the labor force – 24.6 percent in 1960 compared to 39.2 in 1990 (Nelson, 1992) – and fewer female-headed families. The industrial sector – skilled labor – commanded a greater percentage of the hired hands, then, than the service sector that dominates the American economy does today (Bluestone and Harrison, 1988). Finally, in the 1980s foreign competition, especially for automobile imports – a concentrated goods market – had a significant impact in earnings inequality (Borjas and Ramey, 1992).

Studies in the distribution of wealth show, in general, a pattern related to the distribution of income. Inequality of wealth follows that exhibited by income, but in a much more pronounced way. From the Federal Reserve Board's Survey of Consumer Finances (SCF), in 1983 the top 1 percent of the population in the United States owned 28.3 percent of household wealth, while the bottom 80 percent owned 25.3 percent. Even though the data collection on wealth from survey research is prone to error because of the respondents' desire to maintain confidentiality, the data do show who owns how much of the wealth in the United States. Furthermore, a major study tracing the changes in the type of assets over time showed that in 1988, housing assets constituted 20.6 percent of US household wealth, followed by pension assets of 14.5 percent, while unincorporated business assets were at 7.6 percent (Wolff, 1989). A more in depth examination of the distribution of wealth reveals even more startling inequalities. According to the US Census Bureau, for example, in 1984 the median household net worth for whites was $39 135, while for Hispanics and blacks it was \$4913 and \$3397, respectively. Along the same line, the distribution of assets is even more unequal, as indicated in a study by Oliver and Shapiro (1990). Using data for 1984 from the Survey of Income and Program Participation (SIPP), they report that 30 percent of white households, 67 percent of black households and 68 percent of single-parent households have zero or negative net financial assets –'assets that are available for use' and which exclude equity in homes and automobiles (quoted in Sherraden, 1991). Finally, and in concert with economists' use of a yardstick, the Gini coefficients of inequality, calculated by Wolff (1987) for a number of wealth categories, are: (i) for all wealth: 0.72, (ii) fungible wealth (wealth net of consumer durables and household inventories): 0.80, (iii) financial wealth (fungible wealth net of owner-occupied housing equity): 0.91, and (iv) capital wealth (financial wealth net of savings and cash values of pension funds and insurance): 0.94. Since a Gini coefficient of 1 denotes perfect inequality, the Wolff calculated coefficients, especially those of financial and capital wealth, are the most disturbing. Given that the asset distribution changes gradually from year to year, there is no reason to assume that the distribution for later years is more encouraging (Sherraden, 1991).

Measurements of net worth inevitably raise questions relating to measurement of saving, saving rates, saving behavior, and their trends. A survey of the literature and continuous research on savings measurements show that the estimates vary dramatically. This despite the agreement by policy-makers and economists alike on the importance of consistency in the estimates that reflect the various concepts of saving, i.e., private, personal, household, corporate, government, etc. Macroeconomic measurements of saving customarily rely on the estimates derived from the national income and product accounts (NIPAs) – gross private and personal saving – from current income. Another macroeconomic measurement of nontangible saving used is calculated from the sectoral flow of funds (FFAs) analysis that estimates capital accounts changes of net worth (Lipsey and Tice, 1989, p. 2). On the microeconomic side, household saving behavior and measurement have relied on microdata sets primarily from the SIPP and SCF. The serious discrepancies in the measurements, both on the macro and micro levels, have been attributed to conceptual reasons, specifically in the difficulty of defining clearly what saving is, and whether consumer durables, capital assets – private and public – human capital investment and pension funds are saving or wealth. In addition, discrepancies in the balance of payments also affect the international savings estimates (Lipsey and Tice, 1989, p. 3). In Chapter 2 of this volume, James N. Morgan and F. Thomas Juster, using a different household survey, the Panel Study of Income Dynamics (PSID), examine a number of factors affecting saving behavior. Over the 1984–9 period, they assess estimates of saving, and investigate the behavior that actively promotes saving – self-employment, early retirement, life-cycle motives – as well as inactive saving behavior that results from exogenous events – changes from capital gains and losses, inheritances, and household structure. The conceptual and measurement problems pointed out by Robert B. Avery in his commentary to the chapter notwithstanding, Morgan and Juster's analysis reveals a number of interesting aspects of saving behavior that differ significantly from previous studies. The authors' striking results, and the inferences drawn from them, show how behavior characteristics for the groups of individuals examined relate to several variables that include race, gender, age and education.

The customary measures of inequality that have been and are being used include both ordinal approaches to welfare comparisons, and comparable cardinal utility functions. The most frequently used measure of inequality that axiomatically corresponds to the ordinal approach to measuring inequality is the well known Gini coefficient (Sen, 1982). Even though the Gini coefficient is widely used, including its use in Chapter 4 of this book, it has been much criticized as being a summary statistic that is not accurately estimated, being insensitive in not weighing the tails of the distribution equally, and, thus, being primarily meaningful only when the means of the distributions of income are equal. Its popularity is mostly attributed to the fact that it lends itself to graphical representation by the Lorenz curve, as shown in Figure 4.1 in Chapter 4. Other commonly used measures of inequality include the Theil and Atkinson measures (Chapter 4), also not without criticism.

The Lorenz curves have also been used in recent theoretical advances in measuring the distribution of income within the framework of dominance techniques. Dominance methods have been used in investigating income inequality for the United States and other countries (Bishop, Formby, and Smith, 1991), changes in the level of well-being during periods of growth and recessions (Bishop, Chow and Formby, 1991) and numerous other applications involving statistical distributions.

Both the Gini coefficient and dominance methodologies of measuring inequality have been criticized for being inconsistent when used in comparing economic inequality across several countries. Furthermore, they rely on aggregated data which omit valuable information and, in addition, assume consistency in methodology of aggregating across countries. As data became available in microeconomic form, new methods for income inequality measurements were developed. One such method is that of the Generalized Entropy family of measures employed by Sourushe Zandvakili (Chapter 5) in his attempt to estimate and compare the income inequalities in twelve countries using micro data sets available from the Luxembourg Income Study (LIS). The Generalized Entropy family of measures has been shown to satisfy all important and fundamental welfare axioms, and Theil's (1967) additive decomposability property (p. 121).

International comparisons are, for the most part, invaluable intellectual exercises, since they provide opportunities for lessons to be learnt, especially when public policy evaluation is involved. Zandvakili's contribution in Chapter 5 of this book provides an illustration of how significant such comparisons can be in assessing other countries' public policies and their effect on household inequalities, and contrasting them with those in the United States. This comparability becomes even more crucial when estimations isolate the effects of a number of demographic variables, such as age, gender, ethnicity, education level, and size of household. Along the same line of reasoning, the contribution by Gordon W. Green, John Coder and Paul Ryscavage (Chapter 4) provides important insights into earnings disparities for men in five countries of the industrialized world in the 1980s. Their conclusions demonstrate the significance that employment growth has had on each of these nations.

The essays and commentaries collected in this book provide a variety of methodological, intellectual and practical aspects of the current economic problem of income and wealth disparity. Each contribution aims to answer the thorny questions of why and how standards of living decline, especially during economic expansions, and what the public policy responses should be if they were to arrest this decline and, indeed, attempt to reverse it.

Part I of the book opens with the essay by James N. Morgan and F. Thomas Juster (Chapter 2) which explores the impact that different factors have on the saving behavior of households and, ultimately, in the distribution of wealth. Robert Avery provides a thoughtful commentary which raises interesting methodological and practical questions relating to both the model and data used.

In Chapter 3, Joan R. Rodgers centers her analysis on the so-called 'feminization of poverty,' referring to recent demographic trends on the increasing proportion of female-headed households with absent husbands that are in poverty, and on the important need for policymakers to recognize this shift in family structure when formulating

and implementing public policy. A number of pertinent and provocative policy questions are raised by Rebecca Blank in her commentary
on Chapter 3, derivable from Rodgers's results.

In a comparative analysis, Gordon W. Green, John Coder and Paul
Ryscavage document in Chapter 4, the first Chapter in Part II, the
earnings differentials among prime age men, employed year-round and
full-time, from five industrialized countries – Australia, Canada, West
Germany, Sweden, and the United States – in the early and mid-1980s.
Their study using consistent data drawn from the Luxembourg Income
Study (LIS) database shows some differences in income inequalities
among these countries, especially for the mid-1980s, with the United
States being the most unequal and Sweden the least unequal. Their
results, however, point to the 'internationalization of inequality,' which
they speculate might be due to the mismatch of the supply and demand in labor markets. Howard M. Wachtel's commentary, at the end
of the chapter, raises the question of bias in the authors' results when
one considers the special characteristics in the data for the United States.
These involve abnormally high corporate executive salaries, and
demographics relating to the growth of baby-boomers and women in
the labor force *vis-à-vis* the other countries compared.

The essay by Sourushe Zandvakili in Chapter 5 is also a comparative analysis using the LIS database as in Chapter 4, but differs in that
the measurements of inequality involve households. In addition, em-
ploying the Generalized Entropy measures methodology, Zandvakili
provides estimates for a number of inequality indices which he obtains
from the decomposition of data to such variables as family size, age,
gender, education, and ethnicity of the head of the household. Zandvakili's
results of inequality measures for the twelve industrialized countries
tested indicate that public policy profoundly affects outcomes and that
its effects are not similar in each country. The chapter ends with Alan
Blinder's evaluation of the author's conclusions, and suggestions for
further research in related areas.

In the last chapter of Part II (Chapter 6), Erik Thorbecke demonstrates how a set of well formulated policies can affect the growth and
income distribution patterns of an economy. Using the Indonesian
economy as a case study, he shows how it was possible for an economy
faced with reversing fortunes – from high growth largely due to oil
exports, to growth deceleration and external shocks vulnerability – to
implement a strategy of adjustment which resulted in reducing the overall
incidence of poverty and undernutrition that was expected to occur
during the period of adjustment. Instead, the policies implemented during

the adjustment period reinforced the pre-adjustment, high-growth period employment, education and health care policies which contributed to improving the distribution of income and alleviating poverty.

The essays in Part III of the book take up a number of public policy perspectives, including both macro and microeconomic representations. Edmund S. Phelps, in Chapter 7, extensively pursues the idea of a policy implementation involving wage subsidies to the working poor. His prescription is based on the notion of economic justice and thus, a need for redistribution. In contrast, Thomas Karier, in his commentary on Chapter 7, strongly disagrees with such a policy for both economic and political reasons.

The notion that government action must include a strategy of alleviating income and wealth inequality is the core of Senator Paul S. Sarbanes' essay in Chapter 8. He reviews carefully the effects that the policy initiatives implemented in the decade of the 1980s have had on inequality and poverty, and ends with a plea that much effort needs to be expended if we are to reverse the social damage.

Leonard A. Rapping, in Chapter 9, investigates a host of possible causes for the growing income inequality during the decade of the 1980s. He makes a convincing argument that no relationship exists between the rate of unemployment and inequality as measured by the share of income received by the highest 1 percent of the income distribution ladder (Table 9.1). He concludes by outlining a number of policy responses on both the macro and microeconomic levels.

In Chapter 10, Rebecca Blank assesses the widening gap in wage differentials and its effect on the distribution of income. She reviews the prevailing theories of wage inequality and makes valuable suggestions for further research and policy options that merit serious consideration.

The last chapter of the book (Chapter 11), by Isabel V. Sawhill, is also concerned with the inadequate policy response to a particular segment of the population in the United States which, in addition to suffering endemic poverty, 'is engaged in individually and socially harmful behaviors.' Sawhill explores a number of possibilities in dealing with the problems of the 'underclass' and invokes the success of social programs, i.e., birth control policies, that have been instituted in other countries of the industrialized world.

The essays in this book present theories, findings, and policy recommendations dealing with one or more aspects of the distribution of income and wealth. While many a reader may not agree with all of them, I hope that they help place economic inequality at the top of the nation's agenda.

References

Bishop, J. A., K. V. Chow and J. P. Formby (1991) 'A Stochastic Dominance Analysis of the Effects of Growth and Recessions on the U.S. Income Distribution, 1967–1986,' *Southern Economic Journal*, **57**.

Bishop, J. A., J. P. Formby and W. J. Smith (1991) 'International Comparisons of Income Inequality: Tests for Lorenz Dominance Across Nine Countries,' *Economica*, **58**: 461–77.

Bluestone, B. and B. Harrison (1988) *The Great U-Turn: Corporate Restructuring and the Polarization of America* (New York: Basic Books).

Borjas, G. J. and V. A. Ramey (1992) 'Foreign Competition, Market Power, and Wage Inequality: Theory and Evidence,' paper presented at a conference on 'The Changing Distribution of Income in an Open U.S. Economy,' University of Notre Dame (September).

Gittleman, M. and E. N. Wolff (1993) 'Introduction,' in D. B. Papadimitriou and E. N. Wolff (eds), *Poverty and Prosperity in the USA in the Late Twentieth Century* (London: Macmillan).

Lipsey, Robert E. and H. S. Tice (eds) (1989) *The Measurement of Saving, Investment, and Wealth* (Chicago: University of Chicago Press).

Nelson, C. T. (1992) 'Levels of and Changes in the Distribution of U.S. Income: An Overview of Recent Census Bureau Research,' paper presented at a conference on 'The Changing Distribution of Income in an Open U.S. Economy,' University of Notre Dame (September).

Oliver, M. and T. Shapiro (1990) 'Wealth of a Nation: A Reassessment of Asset Inequality in America Shows at Least One Third of Households are Asset-Poor,' *American Journal of Economics and Sociology*, **49**: 129–51.

Sen, A. (1982) *Choice, Welfare and Measurement* (Cambridge, MA: MIT Press).

Sherraden, M. (1991) *Assets and the Poor* (Armonk, NY: M. E. Sharpe)

Theil, H. (1967) *Economics of Information Theory* (Amsterdam: North-Holland).

US Bureau of the Census (1986). 'Household Wealth and Asset Ownership, 1984', *Current Population Reports*, Household Economic Studies, Series P-70, No. 7 (Washington, DC: US Government Printing Office).

Wolff, E. N. (1987) 'Estimates of Household Wealth Inequality in the U.S., 1962–1983,' *Review of Income and Wealth*, **33**: 231–42.

Wolff, E. N. (1989) 'Trends in Aggregate Household Wealth in the U.S., 1900–1983,' *Review of Income and Wealth*, **35**: 1–29.

Part I

Income and Wealth Distribution in the United States

2 Factors Affecting Household Saving Behavior: An Introductory Analysis

James N. Morgan and F. Thomas Juster*

2.1 BACKGROUND

Saving behaviour has interested economists, but until recently they had only aggregate information from the national accounts. Then the Board of Governors of the Federal Reserve System supported a series of Surveys of Consumer Finances (SCF) from 1947 through 1960, including some reinterviews that allowed estimates of the saving of individual households. One of us analyzed those data, and with Lawrence Klein, George Katona and John Lansing, published some results (Katona *et al.*, 1954). Some attempts were made to use saving data derived from consumer expenditure studies, but the results were somewhat erratic. Indeed, the Surveys of Consumer Finances were ended because of doubts about the quality of the data, largely based on misguided attempts to estimate aggregates. With concern about poverty, we did a study on income and wealth and its intergenerational persistence (Morgan, David, Cohen and Brazer, 1962), though Harrington's book (1962) which had passion instead of precision received much more attention.

Then there were two studies of wealth oversampling the top of the income distribution. One, done by the Federal Reserve, focused on asset detail at various income levels (Projector and Weiss, 1966; Projector, 1968) and used a reinterview in 1964 to get saving data. The second, done by us at the Institute for Social Research of the University of Michigan (Morgan *et al.*, 1962), focused on behavior, and indicated very little effect of marginal tax rates on work effort, and much less use of tax loopholes than often assumed.

More recently there was a study for the President's Commission on Pension Policy that attempted to evaluate pension rights, and a new set of Surveys of Consumer Finances funded largely by the Federal Reserve Board and done by the University of Michigan with a more extensive effort to study pension values. And there are wealth data on the Longitudinal Retirement History Surveys, in the National Longitudinal Surveys, and in the Surveys of Income and Program Participation. But at most, prior data were from two or three waves of interviews at annual intervals.

2.2 INTRODUCTION

For the first time, we have data on household accumulation of net worth over a five year period, long enough for the estimates of saving to be larger than the noise of measurement and conceptual errors. In addition, we have enough information to separate active saving behavior from inadvertent (exogenous) changes resulting from capital gains and losses, inheritances, and people moving in or out of the household.

Of course, there is a price to pay. Over five years, some families disappear and others appear without a simple history. We restrict this analysis to 5124 cases where a family has had the same head all five years. This leaves out women who get married or divorced or widowed during the period, and children or others who leave a family to start a new household. We have reweighted the data to allow for this selection bias, but that is always an imperfect adjustment. In addition, since we are working with preliminary data, the regular weights have not been adjusted since 1987 for panel losses (trivial) and for people marrying into the panel. The remaining possible selection bias is probably much less serious for analysis of saving behaviour than for analysis of saving levels and distributions. Families undergoing change probably save much less.

There is also a major missing component of saving, the increase in equity in pensions, Social Security wealth, and life insurance reserves. Our rough estimate is that they amount to as much as all the saving we do measure. We do know how many private pensions there are, and treat that as an explanatory variable, a substitute that should reduce other saving.

2.3 DATA

The data come from the Panel Study of Income Dynamics, principally the 1984 and 1989 interviews which contain the wealth data, and in

1989 the reports on saving flows, but we use income data from the intervening years as well. An analysis of the quality of the 1984 benchmark wealth data appears in a paper by Curtin, Juster and Morgan (1989). An earlier analysis of the saving data, using categorical regression, appears in a paper presented at a conference in 1989 (Juster and Morgan, 1990).

The data contain very few missing items, but an appreciable number who gave bracket information. We have assigned all the components of saving, using the actual means within brackets, since distributions are not even, and multivariate assignments for those who did not even give a bracket.

We deal with a few extreme cases not by eliminating them, but by truncation. Five year total head-wife income was truncated at $6000 and $2 500 000. Active saving was truncated first at ±$1 000 000 and then as −2 times income and +1 time income. When used as explanatory variables, capital gains and losses and inheritances were truncated at ±$400 000 and annual income trend at +$50 000 and −$30 000. This means that the means of active saving and increase in net worth are not estimates of national aggregates, because of the truncations. It is clear, however, that the vast bulk of the saving is done by those with incomes over $250 000 for the five years. An examination of some extreme cases found one error where the same amount logically belonged in two different places, but the rest were conceptual problems: people moved in with a wealthy mother, reported assets moved in but did not report the mother's assets as current assets, or a very large inheritance was reported, gross not net of estate taxes, or a marriage or divorce led to utter confusion. The most dramatic extreme case was a very old, very wealthy man with vast real estate holdings who was giving property away to his children. It is not hard to imagine his lawyers pointing out that since gifts and estates are combined for final taxes, he would only increase the taxes by waiting while capital gains and incomes accumulated. It seems likely that measurement of income is poor at the top, particularly because of capital gains and losses. We thought of adding some fraction of capital gains to income, but since they seem to reduce active saving anyway, that would only have strengthened that effect.

We experimented with a number of truncations or eliminations, with dramatic effects on mean saving, and even more dramatic effects on its variance, but the main findings were largely unaffected. The paper we presented at the Snowbird Conference (1990) used categorical regression to avoid difficulties with extremes in certain explanatory variables, as well as nonlinearities in their effects. In this chapter, we use dollars, even with some truncations, in order to provide quantitative estimates of effects. We do, however, separate increases from decreases in explanatory variables, on the theory, for example, that most capital losses are realized, but not most capital gains, and that the former are more difficult to adjust.

2.4 VARIABLES AND MODELLING

We omit a few plausible explanatory variables because they proved ineffective: number of equivalent adults representing pressures to consume, working for a government representing stability of income and job security, the fraction of total time parents worked for money representing costs of child care, and the variance of income around a trend line, representing unpredictability of income. Early analysis also ruled out area variables and city size (proxies for economic conditions and cost of living).

But we left in other powerless variables because of their intrinsic interest: race, marital status, sex of head, age, and a life-cycle representation of optimal saving out of income increases depending on age.

We list the explanatory variables we used in somewhat arbitrary categories.

One can think of active behavioral saving as affected first by factors that allow it: income, and trend in income. Since the theory predicts different responses to income increments, we separated total income into the starting point of a trend line of income times five years, and the aggregate increase, which is ten times the annual increment in income, since the first increment lasts for four years, the second for three, etc. We also allow nonlinearity in the income effect in two ways. First, we separate the sample into those whose five year income totalled less that $250 000 and those who had $250 000 or more, because the data showed flat or even decreasing saving below that cutoff and dramatic increases of saving with income above that. Second, we introduced a spline to allow for further nonlinearity, incomes below $70 000 for the low income group and incomes above $500 000 ($100 000/year) for the high income group. (We later switched to income squared for the high income group, while deleting 28 cases of extreme saving or dissaving, which changed the negative effect of income increases to positive, but led to a negative income squared term.)

Then we have indicators of motives to save: self-employment, plans in 1984 to retire early, initial departures from expected levels of net worth, and life-cycle considerations (interaction of income trend with closeness to retirement). The initial asset position can have several not easily distinguishable effects, ranging from distinguishing those who always save a lot (positive relation to subsequent saving) to disequilibrium states (negative relation). The life-cycle theory can relate both to optimal saving given income and current wealth, and to optimal saving out of income increases. The former is difficult to operationalize because we cannot measure pension wealth. We have attempted the simpler test by which the fraction of any income increase that is saved depends on the expected years that increase will continue (till retirement) relative to life expectancy.

Let us explain the last of these, since it is most interesting as well as difficult. Optimal saving for retirement depends on life expectancy, age of expected retirement, and already accumulated wealth and rights. But we do not have good measures of pension rights. Optimal saving out of income increments, however, is simpler. If we assume that these increments are expected to continue to retirement (plausible, if we fit a five year trend line to estimate the increment), then one wants to spread x years of increment over y years of consuming life where x is years till retirement and y is life expectancy. (We need not consider possible additional future increases, since a new calculation would have to guide the fraction of them to save.) Ignoring interest for the moment, then, one can spend x/y of any increment, i.e., should save additionally $(1-x/y)$ of any increment. We could estimate a joint-or-survivor life expectancy using head and wife's ages, but that seems unnecessary. We could assume that couples have a life expectancy equal to when the wife would be 85 or the husband 80, whichever is longer, and that single heads expect to live to 80 for women and 75 for men. And we can use 65 as the expected retirement age. Our estimated annual increment in income times five gives us an estimated increase in annual income (without presuming on future increases). Hence, a predictor variable proxying for ideal saving out of income increases is:

5 times annual trend times (1-(years to 65)/(life expectancy))

For those already 65 or older we can treat years to 65 as equal to one, and for those older than their life expectancy we can set life expectancy to one.

This term becomes more plausible for those not yet retired, but over 45 years of age, just as a bequest motive term becomes more plausible for those over 65.

If we take a constant expectation of work until 65 and 20 years of retirement after that, then we can take account of interest, and use the simple tabulation in Table 2.1.

Table 2.1   Saving expectations

Years until age 65	Fraction of any income increase to save (%)	Fraction ignoring interest (%)
45	14	21
40	17	33
35	20	36
30	24	40
25	29	45
20	36	50
15	44	57
10	58	66
5	75	80

Clearly it seems better to use the pattern that takes account of interest. So we used a variable which is the middle column times the annual increase in income during the period. It had no effect until we restricted it to those 45–64 years old.

(The actual life-cycle variable using 1989 age of head recodes on age as follows:

$<25 = 14$, $<30 = 17$, $<35 = 20$, $<40 = 24$, $<45 = 29$, $<50 = 36$, $<55 = 44$, $<60 = 58$, $<65 = 75$, else $= 80$

and multiplies this times the increase in income.) A test whether this variable did better than the simple annual trend of income would seem a good test of the life-cycle notion.

Then there are factors that affect total increase in net worth, which might be seen as substitutes for active saving: pension coverage, inheritances, capital gains and losses on home or on financial assets, and funds/debts brought in or taken out by movers. We leave these in when we analyze increase in net worth, in which case they are descriptive of what the major components are, rather than explanatory, since they are included in the dependent variable, except for pension coverage.

Finally, we can add some mostly demographic variables, to see whether they have any effect that is not working through the economic forces: race, gender, marital status, age, education, and home ownership. The effects of home ownership in producing capital gains or losses is already taken care of, but it can reflect prior (to 1984) and subsequent (to 1989) capital gains as well. But home ownership can also reflect persistent personality differences that allowed people to become owners (planning, saving family concerns). It will turn out that this proxy effect for persistent interpersonal differences is more powerful, increasing saving, than any depressing of saving because of capital gains.

2.5 FINDINGS

The results are given in two rather full tables (Tables 2.2 and 2.3), where we give the simple correlation of each explanatory variable with two saving measures, then the comparable multivariate beta coefficient, so you can see how much explanatory power remains in the multivariate setting, then the quantitative regression coefficient and its standard error, so you can see how much effect there is in dollars, or dollar per dollar.

Since this is a multistage clustered sample with oversampling of low incomes and minorities, and additional weights to allow for selection bias in taking only families with same head for five year, we indicate by an * as probably significant only where the regression coefficient is at least three times its standard error. For race, even this is probably not sufficient, but race turns out nonsignificant.

2.5.1 Active Saving and Increase in Net Worth – Low to Moderate Incomes

As expected, a larger fraction of income increments than of base (permanent income) was saved. 27 percent versus 10 percent. The slight convexity of income effect was nonsignificant, but perhaps resulted from the fact that at the lowest incomes there are no assets to dissave. The effects on increase in net worth are similar.

The motivational variables are of course the most interesting, and several of them reassuringly reasonable. Higher than expected initial wealth led to dissaving, active and total. Lower than average initial wealth went along with more saving, significantly so for total saving. Our interpretation is that these findings reflect regression toward normalcy. However, our earlier analysis using categorical predictors provided some evidence of a different effect: persistent personality differences, where somewhat lower-than-expected initial wealth identifies low past savers who continue with that behavior.

Table 2.2 Saving for those with five year total income less than $250 000

	Active saving				Incr. in net worth			
	Simple correl.	*Beta coeff.*	*Regr. coeff.*	*Sigma B*	*Simple correl.*	*Beta coeff.*	*Regr. coeff.*	*Sigma B*
Facilitating								
$Base income	0.103	0.151	0.102	0.015	0.222	0.158	0.135	0.015*
$Inc. incr.	0.115	0.176	0.273	0.030*	0.121	0.159	0.313	0.029*
Spline < $70	−0.120	−0.018	−37	35	−0.164	−0.013	−35	34
Motivational								
$Init. wlth high	−0.080	−0.226	−0.182	0.015*	−0.137	−0.202	−0.206	0.015*
$Init. wlth low	0.078	0.046	0.065	0.022	0.077	0.041	0.073	0.022*
84 Ret. early	0.074	0.074	11 266	2 280*	0.113	0.039	7 625	2 259*
Self-employed	0.142	0.155	31 196	2 926*	0.103	0.096	24K	3K*
LCEXP 45−64	0.028	−0.029	−2.36	1.30*	0.098	0.026	2.67	1.29
Substitutes								
Pension cov.	0.052	−0.051	−2 568	838*	0.091	−0.047	−3 033	830*
$Inherited	−0.264	−0.260	−0.645	0.035*	0.157	0.041	0.129	0.035*
$Hse gain	−0.060	−0.036	−0.051	0.031	0.408	0.284	0.508	0.021*
$Hse loss	0.156	0.141	0.588	0.057*	−0.099	−0.049	−0.257	0.057*
$Fin gain	−0.117	−0.021	−0.021	0.016	0.455	0.347	0.460	0.016*
$Fin loss	0.109	0.184	0.241	0.021	−0.372	−0.286	−0.471	0.021*
$Movd in	0.110	0.108	0.387	0.049*	−0.042	0.032	0.147	0.049*
$Movd out	−0.043	−0.026	−0.259	0.133	0.058	0.063	0.773	0.132*

Prior causes

Spouse present	0.101	−0.034	−2 886	1 746	0.162	−0.006	−662	1 730
Nonblack	−0.043	0.004	494	1 714	−0.085	0.009	1 284	1 698
Female head	−0.096	0.003	275	1 758	−0.132	−0.025	−2 804	1 741
Age	−0.042	−0.254	−572	250	0.031	−0.206	−587	248
Age^2	−0.049	0.257	5	2	0.017	0.239	6.36	2.26
Education	0.055	0.007	179	386	0.119	0.022	672	382
Own home	0.100	0.113	9 567	1 428*	0.237	0.102	11 K	1.4K*
Mean			$5 696				$14 923	
R^2 adj.			0.213				0.517	

*Probably significant (three times standard error to allow for design effects).

Table 2.3   Saving for those with incomes of $250 000 or more for the five years

	Active saving				Incr. in net worth			
	Simple correl.	*Beta coeff.*	*Regr. coeff.*	*Sigma B*	*Simple correl.*	*Beta coeff.*	*Regr. coeff.*	*Sigma B*
Facilitating								
$Base income	0.107	−0.365	−0.282	0.067*	0.198	−0.318	−0.440	0.089*
$Inc. incr.	0.077	−0.226	−0.398	0.110*	0.279	−0.179	−0.561	0.147*
Spline >$400K	0.155	0.378	178	46*	0.295	0.287	240	61*
Motivational								
$Init. wlth high	0.097	−0.048	−0.063	0.069	0.088	−0.024	−0.057	0.093
$Init. wlth low	0.094	−0.051	−0.160	0.123	−0.097	−0.035	−0.194	0.165
84 Ret. early	0.027	0.107	43K	16K	0.052	0.065	47K	21K
Self-employed	0.207	0.127	54K	16K	0.327	0.084	63K	21K
LCEXP 45−64	0.153	0.080	3.956	2.480	0.338	0.181	15.98	3.31*
Substitutes								
Pension cov.	−0.053	0.021	2766	4934	−0.045	0.025	6056	6589
$Inherited	−0.018	−0.218	−0.795	0.136*	0.299	0.084	0.547	0.181*
$Hse gain	0.117	0.059	0.134	0.086	0.351	0.201	0.820	0.115*
$Hse loss	0.094	0.106	0.572	0.194	0.003	−0.062	−0.600	0.259
$Fin gain	0.127	0.128	0.169	0.057	0.526	0.415	0.975	0.076*
$Fin loss	0.062	0.073	0.161	0.091	−0.380	−0.282	−1.110	0.121*
$Movd in	0.103	0.107	0.922	0.283*	−0.090	−0.006	−0.099	0.378
$Movd out	−0.313	−0.401	−4.313	0.433	−0.355	−0.239	−4.597	0.578*

Prior causes

Spouse present	−0.021	0.044	28K	23K	−0.008	0.022	25K	30K
Nonblack	−0.054	−0.043	−40K	31K	−0.023	−0.013	−22K	41K
Female head	0.040	−0.072	−133K	67K	0.024	−0.072	−239K	90K
Age	−0.034	0.198	2748	3901	0.002	0.334	8280	5210
Age^2	−0.045	−0.325	−44.6	36.9	−0.012	−0.466	−114	49
Education	0.041	0.048	4905	3523	0.069	0.035	6368	4706
Own home	−0.008	−0.022	−14K	21K	0.036	−0.019	−20K	28K
Mean			$57 379				$131 427	
R^2 adj.			0.205				0.555	

*Probably significant (three times standard error to allow for design effects).

Those, 45 and older, who said in 1984 that they planned to retire before 65 saved significantly more, by $11 265 actively and $7625 total, than others. The self-employed saved $31 196 more actively and $24 000 more in total, reflecting the business demands for liquidity and investment, presumably, as well as the uncertainty.

But when we come to life-cycle theory, our neat test of whether a larger fraction of income increases is saved the closer one is to retirement, fails. The sign is even wrong for active saving.

Other things affecting saving as substitutes had the expected effects with some of the gains being consumed, hence reduced active saving, and more of the losses being replaced by increased active saving. The greater response to losses may well be because more of them are likely to have been realized, and some capital gains may not be realized in the future.

Pension coverage reduced both active saving and increase in net worth, since the wealth increase in pensions is included in neither.

People apparently spent a substantial fraction of what they inherited in the five years, their active saving being reduced by 65 percent of it, and their total saving (increase in net worth) increasing by only 13 percent of it.

Capital gains on the house, which are not included in active saving, reduced active saving insignificantly, and increased net worth significantly. Financial capital losses increased active saving significantly, and of course reduced net worth overall since they were only partially offset by additional active saving.

Financial capital gains and losses were insignificantly offset by reductions in or increases in active saving, and were a significant contributor to total saving.

But where funds were moved in by people joining the family, active saving appeared to increase as well, and the reverse for funds moved out, indicating not merely no offsetting action, but complementary effects. Did leavers disrupt the saving and spending of those remaining, and the addition of new members with wealth encourage additional saving? Only the moved-in effect was significant. The strangest effect was that of net exodus of assets which apparently also reduced active saving, but yet led to increased total saving. Money taken in or out by movers involves very few cases, and conceptual and measurement problems, even with some truncation. We should perhaps have omitted these cases, though their effects on increase in net worth are both sensible and significant. One could invent an interpretation by which people save more to offset funds moved out, but can afford to save more when someone moves in with funds and perhaps earnings as well.

Finally, we come to tests whether certain background variables have direct effects beyond what they influence through the variables we have already looked at. Only one, home ownership, had a significant effect. Remember, home ownership can support two contradictory theories: past and expected future capital gains that would substitute for other saving and depress it, and persistent personality differences by which owners are long-term savers and planners. It is the second of these which apparently wins out, perhaps because the current capital gains on the house during 1984–9 take account of the capital gains side. However, homeowners also save by paying off their mortgages, and such contractual saving may well increase total saving.

We turn now to the much smaller group with annual incomes averaging $50 000 or more.

2.5.2 Active Saving and Increase in Net Worth for those with Five Year Incomes of $250 000 or More

The income effect is more difficult to deal with since the spline implies a substantial curvature, but it would appear that the propensity to save out of income increases is not higher at these income levels than the propensity to save out of base income. It may be suffering from competition with the life-cycle proxy which includes income change for those in ages 45–64. It only becomes positive if we switch from base income to total income for the main income variable.

Of the motivational variables, self-employment still increases active saving, if not total saving, but plans to retire early no longer matter significantly. The life-cycle variable fails again with active saving, but apparently does lead to increase in total saving.

Pension coverage no longer matters, but inheritances are 80 percent consumed and add only 8 percent of their value to increase in net worth at these income levels. The effects of capital gains and losses on active saving are insignificant, but represent significant parts of total saving, of which they are components. As with the lower income group, having assets moved into the family appears to go along with increased active saving. And both active and total saving appeared to be lower when assets had been moved out of the family. Such outmovement may be disruptive, particularly if divorce is involved.

And none of the background variables have any effects that remain once the economic variables have been taken into account.

We add a third table (Table 2.4) on the high income group where

Table 2.4 Saving for those with five year total income $250 000 or more
(Excluding 28 extreme cases formerly only truncated, and using inc. sqd)

	Active saving				Incr. in net worth			
	Simple correl.	Beta coeff.	Regr. coeff.	Sigma B	Simple correl.	Beta coeff.	Regr. coeff.	Sigma B
Facilitating								
$Income	−0.059	0.832	0.479	0.054*	0.321	0.590	0.569	0.063*
$Inc.^{2}	−0.209	−1.037	−0.299	0.025*	0.229	−0.462	−0.244	0.030*
$Inc. incr.	0.106	0.124	0.167	0.061	0.376	0.100	0.246	0.071*
Motivational								
$Init. wlth high	−0.017	−0.104	−0.101	0.049	−0.006	−0.103	−0.182	0.057*
$Init. wlth low	−0.068	−0.028	−0.061	0.082	−0.099	−0.033	−0.132	0.096
84 Ret. early	0.011	0.128	36K	11K	0.011	0.082	42K	13K*
Self-employed	0.130	0.064	19K	11K	0.172	0.052	29K	13K
LFCYEXP 45–64	−0.058	0.039	0.145	0.187	0.215	0.028	0.191	0.218
Substitutes								
Pension cov.	−0.061	−0.043	−4K	3K	−0.100	−0.020	−3K	4K
$Inherited	−0.222	−0.304	−0.963	0.106*	0.150	0.023	0.134	0.124
$Hse gain	−0.041	−0.027	−0.045	0.060	−0.041	0.206	0.632	0.080*
$Hse loss	0.131	0.117	0.584	0.174*	0.131	−0.029	−0.262	0.203
$Fin gain	0.047	0.075	0.073	0.039	0.047	0.459	0.817	0.046*
$Fin loss	0.024	0.032	0.050	0.066	0.024	−0.405	−1.183	0.077*
$Moved in	0.029	0.028	0.225	0.260	0.065	−0.009	−0.128	0.302
$Moved out	−0.065	−0.098	−1.062	0.394	−0.029	−0.002	−0.041	0.4559

Prior causes

Spouse present	−0.008	0.033	15K	15K	−0.024	0.000	−35K	18K
Nonblack	−0.060	−0.035	−21K	20K	−0.021	0.002	3K	24K
Female head	0.010	−0.021	−29K	52K	0.015	−0.015	−37K	60K
Age	−0.039	−0.204	−2K	3K	0.040	−0.156	−3K	3K
Age^2	−0.033	0.121	11.8	25.9	0.052	0.122	22	30
Education	0.004	−0.005	−0.353	2.402	0.076	−0.006	−826	3K
Own home	−0.004	0.039	17K	15K	0.058	0.034	26K	17K
Mean			$45 378			$117 967		
R^2 adj.			0.272			0.706		

*Probably significant (three times standard error to allow for design effects).

we exclude 28 cases of extremely high or low saving, and use income and income squared instead of base income and a spline. Little is changed, except that income increase now has the right sign, and the (competing) life-cycle variable is even weaker.

2.6   WHAT MATTERS?

We can now consider also the interesting question as to how much of saving is exogenous, determined by institutions and events, and how much is response to incentives, and how much is persistent interpersonal differences. We do this by introducing the explanatory variables sequentially and looking at the increment in explained variance (*r* squared).
The results are as in Table 2.5.

Table 2.5   Fractions of variance explained, adjusted for degrees of freedom

	Low–modest income		High income	
	Active saving	Incr. in net worth	Active saving	Incr. in net worth
Facilitators (income, trend)	0.032	0.081	0.023	0.106
+Motivators	0.073	0.135	0.062	0.177
+Substitutes (exogenous)	0.205	0.507	0.189	0.538
+Prior causes? (persistent interpersonal differences?)	0.213	0.517	0.205	0.555

It is clear that motivational forces, even given the advantage of early introduction, account for relatively little of active saving, and even less of increase in net worth. If we consider the fact that Social Security and private pensions are as large as the things we could measure, and are mostly also exogenous, then it is clear that the vast bulk of private saving in the United States is involuntary, or at least, institutional and contractual. Indeed, active saving is influenced more by involuntary (exogenous) saving and dissaving than by other measurable incentives. In fact, active saving includes repayment of mortgages and instalment debt, so even some of that is contractual. While it is dangerous to use small samples to discuss aggregates of skewed variables, the blown-up sample estimates would indicate that the 85 percent of households with five year incomes under $250 000 accounted for 36 percent of the active saving, and 39 percent of the increase in net worth. But they probably accounted for a larger fraction of the increase in Social Security and pension wealth.

2.7 CONCLUSION

While we are still uneasy about extreme cases, and some conceptual and measurement problems, we have found some reassuring confirmation of some theory, particularly the strong effects of income increases, and the partial consumption of inheritances. The effects of plans to retire early and of self-employment indicate some rational behavior exists. Finally, it is interesting that most of the background and demographic variables have their effects not on saving behavior, but on other economic factors like income that in turn affects saving. Blacks, income for income, save as much as anyone else. Finally, it is clear that most private saving is the inadvertent result of exogenous forces, or the constrained result of contractual or legal commitments.

Note

* The authors wish to acknowledge the support of the National Science Foundation, the assistance from the Department of Health and Human Services and other government agencies for the Panel Study of Income Dynamics, and the support of the National Institute of Aging for the 1989 supplement measuring five year flows and 1989 wealth, and for this analysis of the saving data.

References

Curtin, R. T., F. T. Juster and J. N. Morgan (1989) 'Survey Estimates of Wealth: An assessment of Quality,' in R. E. Lipsey and H. S. Tice (eds), *The Measurement of Saving, Investment and Wealth* (Chicago: University of Chicago Press).

Harrington, M. (1962) *The Other America: Poverty in the United States* (New York: Macmillan).

Juster, F. T. and J. N. Morgan (1990) 'Saving Behavior of American Families, 1984–1989,' Second International Conference on the Consumer Interest, (Utah: Snowbird Conference) (August).

Katona, G., L. R. Klein, J. B. Lansing and J. N. Morgan (1954) *Contributions of Survey Methods to Economics* (New York: Columbia University Press).

Morgan, J. N., M. David, W. Cohen and H. Brazer (1962) *Income and Welfare in the United States* (New York: McGraw-Hill).

Projector, D. S. and G. S. Weiss (1966) *Survey of Financial Characteristics of Consumers* (Washington, DC: Board of Governors of the Federal Reserve System) (August).

Projector, D. S. (1968) *Survey of Changes in Families Finances* (Washington, DC: Board of Governors of the Federal Reserve System) (November).

Comment

Robert B. Avery

The authors make the point that they made a number of assumptions in tuning down to measures of savings. They truncate extreme cases, high interval and they also exclude households where the head does not remain the same, which drops out about 20 percent–25 percent of households; in addition there is a skewness to this in that men who divorce will stay in the household and women will not. Thus, this is an issue as to whether or not the person is a member of the original panel, whether (s)he would have been retained anyway. There's also an issue about capital gains and the authors make two different choices as to whether to include capital gains. One, is treating savings as just change in wealth, the other, the flow of funds kind of argument as to what savings should be; whether to differentiate between active savings, capital gains or any other form of savings. Since this dataset is going to be used an awful lot, we ought to ask a question, how close does this concept of savings, or concept of change in wealth correspond to the national income definition of savings, and whether we can draw inferences from one about the other. The answer immediately is in all likelihood, not very close: It may tell us something about the middle class, that is, the behavior of the middle class, or it may tell us a lot about median behavior. It may not tell us very much, however, about mean behavior and national income accounts measure mean behavior.

The authors also use a five year measure of savings for these households rather than annually which is the way we look at national savings rate. What effect does that have? I think, in fact, that makes more difference than one might think. A five year period of time means that these households are stable households, they are receivers of inheritances rather than givers, we are ignoring bequests the mere fact that they survive a five year period of time make them atypical. They had to have been a household five years prior, and that leaves out all young households. There are not any 18 year olds, going from 18 to 23 because they would not have been a household in 1984. These households, when we consider per household savings, tend to contribute a lot of zeros, and the large number of households. What we are doing is putting out and probably overemphasizing middle age stable type households *vis-à-vis* the ones at the extreme, which would be the elderly who die and the young people going through the process of household formation, divorced every three years and then remarried, that sort of household is being left out. Moreover, we tend to look at more stable people and the SCFs show twice as many women after a divorce as men because women keep the house, maintain the same address, and can be found there when they are surveyed. The husband may have a strong interest in not being found and the ratio in this case is of roughly 2:1. The PSID is already pruned out of a lot of those people so even the initial PSID sample is likely to be a stable sample. We observe in the SCF, where many of these problems exist, that 16 percent of the households had a change in marital status, 25 percent had a change in the number of adults. Is that important? In our sample they constituted 31 percent of the total dissaving in the sample. That is a large number, because household change tends to be associated with the dissolution of wealth. It is more expensive to maintain two households and, it might be the case that the aggregate changes in savings rates can be explained by a fact as simple as there are more people getting divorced, or more elderly people choosing to live by themselves in more expensive housing rather than live with their children which they might have done 30 years ago. This is a significant number, which must be considered when national aggregate savings rates are analyzed.

A second issue is the truncation of people at −2 of the income. People could neither save more than their total income nor could they dissave more than twice their total income over a period of time. This is important and in the SCF, where the focus of the survey is on wealth. In there estimates of capital gains – using differences in housing value – were added to income and then was asked the question: How many people ended up saving more than their income? The answer was about 15 percent of households.

Finally there is an issue about real vs. nominal change in wealth, and it is significant. If one looks at the change in real wealth as a form of saving, obviously if wealth was zero in 1984, nominal savings will be the same as real savings. The higher real wealth was in 1984, the lower the ratio of real savings to nominal savings is. Thus, one could get very different results when real savings vs. nominal savings are considered. However, it isn't clear, behaviorally, what households do. Do they indeed save in real terms, or in nominal terms? I doubt whether we know that. But it is possible to get confused in signs and significant variables and draw rather different implications.

3 The Relationship between Poverty and Household Type

Joan R. Rodgers*

3.1 INTRODUCTION

'The feminization of poverty' has received considerable attention, both in the popular press and in the academic literature.[1] It refers to the fact that, over the last few decades, a large, and increasing, proportion of poor families in the United States have been headed by females with no husband present. A second characteristic of the US population, often linked to the feminization of poverty, is the rising proportion of all families headed by females. Columns (1) and (2) of Table 3.1 document the evidence. Almost 52 percent of poor families were female-headed in 1989, compared with 23 percent in 1959. The proportion of all families headed by females rose steadily from 10.0 percent in 1959 to 16.5 percent in 1989.

Discussion of the feminization of poverty draws attention to the relationship between poverty and family type. The fact that, in any given year, the percentage of poor families headed by females far exceeds the percentage of all families headed by females certainly implies that poverty and family type are not independent. But the attention given to the proportion of poor families headed by females is largely misdirected. If there were only 100 poor families in the nation and 90 of them were female-headed, the feminization of poverty, although extreme, would not be an issue because the overall poverty rate would be minuscule. Furthermore, an increase in the feminization of poverty can result from any one of the following (Pressman, 1989, p. 233): (a) an increase in the poverty rate for female-headed families, (b) an increase in the proportion of families headed by females, or (c) a decrease in the poverty rate for households other than families headed by a female. If increased feminization results from an increase in the poverty rate for female-headed families, it is clearly undesirable. If it results from a decrease in the poverty rate for other household types, it is (arguably) desirable.[2] If it is brought about by an increase in the proportion of people living in female-headed families, its desirability is unclear. Thus, the feminization of poverty is not necessarily a bad thing.

Table 3.1   The feminization of poverty in the USA, 1959–89

Year	% of poor families headed by females (1)	% of all families headed by females (2)	% of all persons who are poor (3)	% of persons in female-headed families who are poor (4)	% of persons in other families who are poor (5)	% of unrelated individuals who are poor (6)
1959	23.0	10.0	22.4	49.4	18.2	46.1
1960	23.7	10.1	22.2	48.9	18.0	45.2
1961	23.3	10.0	21.9	48.1	17.6	45.9
1962	25.2	10.1	21.0	50.3	16.4	45.4
1963	26.1	10.3	19.5	47.7	14.9	44.2
1964	25.5	10.5	19.0	44.4	14.7	42.7
1965	28.5	10.3	17.3	46.0	12.8	39.8
1966	29.8	10.6	14.7	39.8	10.3	38.3
1967	31.3	10.7	14.2	38.8	9.6	38.1
1968	34.8	10.8	12.8	38.7	8.3	34.0
1969	36.5	10.8	12.1	38.2	7.4	34.0
1970	37.1	11.5	12.6	38.1	7.7	32.9
1971	39.6	11.6	12.5	38.7	7.5	31.6
1972	42.5	12.2	11.9	38.2	6.8	29.0
1973	45.4	12.4	11.1	37.5	6.0	25.6
1974	47.2	13.0	11.2	36.5	6.2	24.1
1975	44.6	13.3	12.3	37.5	7.2	25.1
1976	47.9	13.6	11.8	37.3	6.4	24.9
1977	49.1	14.4	11.6	36.2	6.2	22.6
1978	50.3	14.6	11.4	35.6	5.9	22.1
1979	48.4	14.6	11.7	34.9	6.3	21.9
1980	47.8	15.1	13.0	36.7	7.4	22.9
1981	47.5	15.4	14.0	38.7	8.1	23.4
1982	45.7	15.4	15.0	40.6	9.1	23.1
1983	46.6	16.0	15.2	40.2	9.3	23.1
1984	48.1	16.2	14.4	38.4	8.5	21.8
1985	48.1	16.1	14.0	37.6	8.2	21.5
1986	51.5	16.2	13.6	38.3	7.4	21.6
1987	52.2	16.4	13.4	38.1	7.2	20.8
1988	53.0	16.5	13.0	37.2	6.9	20.6
1989	51.7	16.5	12.8	35.9	7.0	19.2

Source: *Money Income and Poverty Status in the United States: 1989*. US Dept of Commerce, Bureau of the Census, Current Population Reports, Consumer Income, Series P-60, No. 168 (cols (1) and (2) from Table 21, cols (3) through (6) from Table 19).

The important statistics are the overall poverty rate and the poverty rates for various subpopulations, including female-headed families. The overall poverty rate in the United States in 1989 was 12.8 percent, about as high as it was in the late 1960s and higher than it was during the 1970s (see column (3) of Table 3.1). Since the late 1960s, the poverty rate among people living in female-headed families (see column (4) of Table 3.1) has consistently been almost three times the overall poverty rate, and almost five times the poverty rate among people living in other families (see column (5) of Table 3.1). None of these poverty rates has shown a consistent trend throughout the period 1959–88, although there have been considerable fluctuations during this time period. The poverty rate for female-headed families fell during the 1960s, remained fairly constant during the 1970s, and rose in the early 1980s. The chances of being poor, given that one belonged to a female-headed family, were about the same in the mid- to late 1980s as they were during the period from 1966 to 1976. In contrast, the poverty rate for unrelated individuals has shown a consistent downward trend, from 46.1 percent in 1959 to 19.2 percent in 1989 (see column (6) of Table 3.1).[3] The interesting questions, it seems to me, are: (1) why is the poverty rate for female-headed families so much higher than that of other households, (2) how much impact does the poverty rate for female-headed families have on the overall poverty rate, and (3) why does the United States, which is a highly developed economy, have such a high and nondeclining poverty rate? Clearly, these questions are inter-related.

This chapter investigates the relationship between poverty and family type. It attempts to identify the factors which determine the poverty rates for various family types and, in so doing, tries to isolate the characteristics of 'family type' which are associated with poverty. Intuitively, family type would appear to be important in explaining poverty for reasons such as the following: (i) married-couple families can better take advantage of economies of scale in the purchase of housing and other goods than can families headed by single adults; (ii) married-couple families are less likely than other families to be forced into poverty if one party is laid off or is unable to work because of illness or injury; (iii) to the extent that sexual discrimination exists in the workplace, female-headed families are more likely to be poor than male-headed families. On the other hand, factors unrelated to family type undoubtedly affect the poverty levels of families. It may be that, in general, single adults who head families possess personal characteristics (for example, low levels of human capital) which make it likely that they would be poor even if they lived in married-couple families. If so, society's resources would be better allocated towards modifying those personal characteristics of poor persons (for example, increasing their human capital) rather than encouraging individuals to live in traditional family units.

Section 3.2 of this chapter explores the relationship between the overall poverty rate, the poverty rates for different household types (such as married-couple families, female-headed families and unrelated individuals), and the structure of the population. Section 3.3 describes the model and the data used to analyse the relationship between the type of family in which a person resides and the likelihood of him or her being poor. Sections 3.4 through 3.7 report the results. Some concluding comments are offered in Section 3.8.

3.2 POVERTY RATES AND THE STRUCTURE OF THE POPULATION

The overall poverty rate is a weighted average of the poverty rates for various household types, the weights being the proportions of the population residing in those types of household:

$$Pr\,(poor) = \sum_{j=1}^{J} Pr\,(poor) \mid hh \text{ type } j)\, Pr\,(hh \text{ type } j) \qquad (3.1)$$

where 'Pr' stands for 'probability', 'hh' for 'household', '|' for 'conditional upon', and J is the number of household types.

From equation (3.1) we see that the overall poverty rate is directly related to the poverty rate for each household type, *ceteris paribus*. Furthermore, the rate of change of the overall poverty rate with respect to the poverty rate for a given household type equals the proportion of the population living in that household type. Since a much smaller percentage of people live in female-headed families than in the remainder of the population, a change in the poverty rate for the former has less impact on the overall poverty rate than an equal change in the poverty rate for the latter. The growth in the proportion of the population living in female-headed families, however, means that a given change in the poverty rate for female-headed families is having an increasing impact on the overall poverty rate.

Equation (3.1) also shows that the overall poverty rate is related to the structure of the population. Unlike the poverty rates for all household types, which can rise or fall simultaneously, the proportions of people living in the various household types cannot all rise or all fall. Consequently, the effect of a change in the structure of the population on the overall poverty rate is more complex than the effect of a change in the poverty rate of a given household type. Equation (3.2) shows the effect on the overall poverty rate of a change in the proportion of the population living in female-headed families:

$$\frac{\Delta Pr\,(poor)}{\Delta Pr\,(Fhf)} = Pr\,(poor \mid Fhf) - Pr\,(poor \mid other) + \tag{3.2}$$

$$\frac{\Delta Pr\,(poor \mid Fhf)}{\Delta Pr\,(Fhf)}\,Pr\,(Fhf) + \frac{\Delta Pr\,(poor \mid other)}{\Delta Pr\,(Fhf)}\,Pr\,(other)$$

where '*Fhf*' stands for 'female-headed family' and 'other' stands for 'household other than a female-headed family'.

Consider the simplest case in which the poverty rate for each household type is independent of the proportion of the population living in that household type. In this case the last two terms of equation (3.2) equal zero. Since the poverty rate for female-headed families exceeds the poverty rate for the rest of the population, an increase in the proportion of the population living in female-headed families would increase the overall poverty rate. More generally, in this simple scenario, if the poverty rate for a given household type is larger (smaller) than the poverty rate for the rest of the population then there is a direct (inverse) relationship between the overall poverty rate and the proportion of the population living in that household type.[4]

More realistically, the poverty rate for each household type is affected by the proportion of the population living in that household type.[5] In this more complex case the last two terms in equation (3.2) are nonzero and are likely to have different signs. The implication is that an increase in the proportion of the population living in female-headed families does not necessarily imply an increase in the overall poverty rate, even if the poverty rate for female-headed families exceeds that of the rest of the population. For the overall poverty rate to increase as a result of an increase in the proportion of people living in female-headed families, the rate of increase in the poverty rate for female-headed families must be large enough to outweigh any decrease in the poverty rate for the rest of the population.

The above analysis suggests that policy aimed at reducing the percentage of the population living in female-headed families may well reduce the poverty rate among these families. However, such policy is unlikely to succeed in reducing the overall poverty rate unless it can effect a large enough reduction in the poverty rate for female-headed families to offset any associated increase in the poverty rate

for the rest of the population. For this reason, policy aimed at directly
reducing the poverty rates of the various household types may be
more effective in reducing overall poverty than policy which tries to
influence people's choices concerning the type of household in which
to live.[6] An understanding of the factors which determine the poverty
rates of different types of household will help in designing policy to
reduce these poverty rates and thereby reduce overall poverty.

3.3 POVERTY STATUS AND FAMILY TYPE – A MODEL

In this section, we investigate the relationship between poverty status and
family type. The model used in the analysis has the following (reduced)
form:

$$Y^j = \alpha^j + \sum_{i=1}^{k} \beta_i^j X_i^j + u^j \tag{3.3}$$

where: Y^j is the poverty status of a family of type j;
      X_i^j is the ith control variable for a family of type j;
      α^j is the intercept for families of type j;
      β_i^j is the marginal effect of the ith control variable for fam-
         ilies of type j;
      u^j is a random residual which is assumed to be $N(0, \sigma_j^2)$;
      k is the number of control variables.

If poverty is independent of family type then α^j and β_i^j $(i = 1,2, \ldots k)$
will be the same across family types and, according to model (3.3),
differences in mean poverty levels of different types are due to differences
in the mean levels of the control variables. Conversely, if poverty is
related to family type then at least one of α^j or β_i^j $(i = 1,2, \ldots k)$
will differ across family types.

A simple, but appealing, technique, developed by Blinder (1973),
can be used to decompose the poverty differential between any two
family types, m and f, into three components:

$$\bar{Y}^m - \bar{Y}^f = (a^m - a^f) + \sum_{i=1}^{k} (b_i^m - b_i^f)\, \bar{X}_i^m + \sum_{i=1}^{k} b_i^f\, (\bar{X}_i^m - \bar{X}_i^f) \tag{3.4}$$

     (component 1)   (component 2)   (component 3)

where a and b_i are estimates of α and β_i, respectively. From equation (3.4) we can estimate how much of the average poverty differential between family types m and f is due to:

(a) differences in the average levels of the control variables (component 3),
(b) differences in the marginal effects of the control variables (component 2), and
(c) other unexplained differences (component 1).

Three types of family are considered: married-couple families (with or without children), male-headed families (that is, families headed by a male with no wife present), and female-headed families (that is, families headed by a female with no husband present). The sampling unit is the family, or equivalently the head of the family. The assumption underlying the analysis is that the heads of each type of family constitute a random sample from the population at large. In other words, family type is exogenous. This is a reasonable assumption concerning the sex of family heads, but not necessarily in regard to marital status since individuals have some control over their own marital status. Thus, the potential exists for self-selection bias in the estimated coefficients of equation (3.3). Attempts by the author to correct for self-selection bias gave results which are quite similar to those reported in this chapter.

The dependent variable, our measure of the family's poverty status, is before-tax family income,[7] expressed as a percentage of the poverty line[8] for a family with the same number of adults and the same number of children as the family in question. Government transfers (in cash or in kind) are not included in family income because the objective is to explain poverty which results from market activity (or lack of it); transfer payments counteract the effects of the market.[9] For brevity, the dependent variable will be referred to hereafter as 'relative income'. If relative income is less than 100 then the family is poor. A binary variable, equal to one if the family is poor and zero otherwise, could have been used as the dependent variable but would convey less information about the poverty status of the family than relative income.

The control variables can be divided into two groups: (i) those which describe certain personal characteristics of the members of the family and the location of the family, and (ii) those which measure the size and composition of the family. Each control variable affects either family income, the poverty line, or both.[10]

3.3.1 Characteristics of the Family

HGRADE: number of years of schooling completed by the head of the family.

OGRADE: aggregate number of years of schooling completed by all able-bodied adults in the family, who are 65 years or younger and not in school, other than the head of the family.[11]

HWRKEXP: work experience of the head of the family, computed as the maximum of zero and (*AGE*-GRADE*-5-NYR*), where *AGE** is the minimum of 65 and the family head's age, *GRADE** is the maximum of 10 and *HGRADE* as defined above, and *NYR* is an estimate of the number of years the head of the family was unemployed between 1969 and 1979.

OWRKEXP: aggregate work experience of all able-bodied adults in the family, who are 65 years or younger and not in school, other than the head of the family. Each person's work experience is computed as the maximum of zero and (*AGE*-GRADE*-5-NYR*), where *AGE** is the minimum of 65 and the person's age, *GRADE** is the maximum of 10 and the number of years of schooling completed by the person, and *NYR* is an estimate of the number of years the person was unemployed between 1969 and 1979.

HWKSU79: number of weeks during which the head of the family was unemployed during 1979.

DHDIS1 = 1 if the head of the family has a limited work disability; *DHDIS1* = 0 otherwise.
DHDIS2 = 1 if the head of the family is prevented from working because of a work disability; *DHDIS2* = 0 otherwise.

DHRACE1 = 1 if the head of the family is black; *DHRACE1* = 0 otherwise.
DHRACE2 = 1 if the head of the family is neither black nor white; *DHRACE2* = 0 otherwise.

DAREA1 = 1 if the family is located in an urban fringe area; *DAREA1* = 0 otherwise.
DAREA2 = 1 if the family is located in an urban area which is not

central city nor urban fringe; $DAREA2 = 0$ otherwise.
$DAREA3 = 1$ if the family is located in a rural area; $DAREA3 = 0$ otherwise.

The variables *HGRADE*, *OGRADE*, *HWRKEXP*, *OWRKEXP*, *HWKSU79*, *DHDIS1* and *DHDIS2* are included in the analysis because they measure productivity differences across families, *DHRACE1* and *DHRACE2* capture any racial discrimination in the labor market, while *DAREA1*, *DAREA2* and *DAREA3* take account of geographical differences across labor markets caused by immobility of labor.

3.3.2 Size and Composition of the Family

ADULTS: number of able-bodied adults in the family, 65 years or younger and not in school, including the head of the family and his or her spouse, if present.

INFANTS: number of children, five years or younger, in the family.

DEPEND: number of other dependents in the family, calculated as number of people in the family minus *ADULTS*, minus *INFANTS*.

The variables *ADULTS*, *DEPEND* and *INFANTS* reflect differences in the size and composition of families. These variables may be related to the sex and marital status of the family head. For example, female-headed families are expected to have fewer *ADULTS* but more *IN-FANTS* than other families.

Relative income is expected to be directly related to *HGRADE*, *OGRADE*, *HWRKEXP*, and *OWRKEXP* and inversely related to *HWKSU79*, *DHDIS1*, *DHDIS2*, *DHRACE1*, *DHRACE2*, *ADULTS*, *DE-PEND* and *INFANTS*. The relationship between relative income and *DAREA1* and *DAREA2* is not clear, *a priori*. The coefficient of *DAREA3* is expected to be negative because labor immobility suggests higher incomes for people living in urban rather than rural areas.

The data used to estimate equation (3.3) are the Public Use Microdata Sample (C Sample) for the state of Texas.[12] This is a 1 percent random sample of households from the 1980 United States Census of Population and Housing. For the purpose of this study, vacant households, people living in group quarters or nonfamily households, unrelated individuals living in family households, and families with a head who is over 65 years old and not in the workforce were excluded

from the dataset. This left a sample of 33 608 Texas families of which
28 646 were married-couple families, 981 were male-headed families,
and 3981 were female-headed families. By limiting data to that of a
single state the effect on family income of state specific welfare programs can be ignored.

3.4 POVERTY STATUS AND FAMILY TYPE – RESULTS

Means and standard deviations of the dependent and independent variables, by family type, are presented in Table 3.2. Female-headed families are, on average, the poorest, followed by male-headed families.
On average, heads of married-couple families have higher levels of
education, more work experience, and reside with nondependents who
have more education and more work experience than single heads of
families. These married people were unemployed for fewer weeks during
1979 than heads of other families. They are less likely to be seriously
disabled, are more likely to be white, and less likely to be black.
They are less likely to reside in a central city area, and are more
likely to reside in an urban fringe or rural area. They reside in families with more nondependent adults and at least as many infants as
single adults who head families. Female heads of families have less
education, less work experience and reside with nondependents who
have less education and less work experience than heads of other families.
These single women are more likely to be seriously disabled, are more
likely to be black and less likely to be white, than heads of other
families. They are less likely to live in an urban fringe or rural area,
and are more likely to live in a central city or other urban area. They
live in families with fewer nondependent adults and more dependents
than heads of other families. Single male heads of families have fewer
dependents and are more likely to be neither white nor black than
heads of other family types.
   Regression equations for the three family types are given in Table
3.3. The estimated parameters in all equations have the expected signs.
Ceteris paribus, relative income is directly related to:
(1) the education level of the head of the family,
(2) the aggregate amount of education of other nondependent family
    members,
(3) the amount of work experience of the head of the family, and
(4) the aggregate amount of work experience of other, nondependent
    family members.

Table 3.2 Means and standard deviations of variables, various family types, Texas, 1979

Variable		All families (1)	Married-couple families (2)	Male-headed families (3)	Female-headed families (4)
STINCOME:	mean	366.59	393.66	321.93	182.75
	s.d.	(286.28)	(290.29)	(259.91)	(171.33)
HGRADE:	mean	13.98	14.13	13.28	13.08
	s.d.	(3.97)	(3.97)	(4.36)	(3.79)
OGRADE:	mean	13.33	14.56	7.64	5.89
	s.d.	(8.92)	(8.16)	(9.58)	(9.79)
HWRKEXP:	mean	21.12	21.45	19.43	19.15
	s.d.	(13.53)	(13.60)	(13.66)	(12.76)
OWRKEXP:	mean	12.65	14.21	5.76	3.13
	s.d.	(13.41)	(13.34)	(12.30)	(8.98)
HWKSU79:	mean	1.20	1.07	2.17	1.89
	s.d.	(5.21)	(4.83)	(7.44)	(6.80)
DHDIS1:	mean	0.06	0.06	0.07	0.05
	s.d.	(0.23)	(0.23)	(0.25)	(0.22)
DHDIS2:	mean	0.04	0.03	0.04	0.06
	s.d.	(0.19)	(0.18)	(0.20)	(0.25)
DHRACE1:	mean	0.11	0.08	0.18	0.27
	s.d.	(0.31)	(0.27)	(0.38)	(0.44)
DHRACE2:	mean	0.08	0.07	0.11	0.09
	s.d.	(0.27)	(0.26)	(0.32)	(0.29)
DAREA1:	mean	0.19	0.20	0.16	0.14
	s.d.	(0.39)	(0.40)	(0.37)	(0.35)
DAREA2:	mean	0.15	0.15	0.13	0.15
	s.d.	(0.36)	(0.36)	(0.33)	(0.36)
DAREA3:	mean	0.21	0.22	0.17	0.12
	s.d.	(0.41)	(0.42)	(0.38)	(0.32)
ADULTS:	mean	1.95	2.04	1.60	1.41
	s.d.	(0.70)	(0.64)	(0.80)	(0.79)
DEPEND:	mean	1.08	1.05	0.94	1.37
	s.d.	(1.24)	(1.24)	(1.05)	(1.24)
INFANTS:	mean	0.41	0.42	0.27	0.42
	s.d.	(0.71)	(0.72)	(0.61)	(0.71)
Sample size		33 608	28 646	981	3 981

Source: Public Use Microdata Sample (Sample C), 1980 US Census of Population and Housing.

Table 3.3   Effect of family type on poverty,
various family types, Texas, 1979
Least squares coefficients with *P*-values in parentheses*

Variable	Married-couple families (1)	Male-headed families (2)	Female-headed families (3)
ONE	199.7840	134.9640	99.9872
	(0.0000)	(0.0086)	(0.0000)
HGRADE	21.7220	17.6255	14.5287
	(0.0000)	(0.0000)	(0.0000)
OGRADE	9.5055	5.4390	9.8109
	(0.0000)	(0.0084)	(0.0000)
HWRKEXP	3.4662	3.0155	2.1945
	(0.0000)	(0.0000)	(0.0000)
OWRKEXP	1.7010	1.6357	1.1607
	(0.0000)	(0.0596)	(0.0005)
HWKSU79	−4.4726	−4.2551	−1.9314
	(0.0000)	(0.0000)	(0.0000)
DHDIS1	−63.1803	−48.0936	−58.8240
	(0.0000)	(0.0802)	(0.0000)
DHDIS2	−269.3890	−145.2900	−140.7400
	(0.0000)	(0.0001)	(0.0000)
DHRACE1	−84.0389	−87.5449	−64.2526
	(0.0000)	(0.0000)	(0.0000)
DHRACE2	−27.0378	−40.0936	−21.5937
	(0.0000)	(0.0469)	(0.0013)
DAREA1	28.6713	79.7984	15.1693
	(0.0000)	(0.0004)	(0.0295)
DAREA2	−28.4557	−14.1663	−14.9604
	(0.0000)	(0.4725)	(0.0241)
DAREA3	−43.3475	−3.2488	−28.3900
	(0.0000)	(0.8779)	(0.0000)
ADULTS	−118.8600	−49.9506	−89.5506
	(0.0000)	(0.0523)	(0.0000)
DEPEND	−41.3901	−35.4394	−20.8649
	(0.0000)	(0.0000)	(0.0000)
NINFANTS	−69.7018	−58.0156	−41.8644
	(0.0000)	(0.0000)	(0.0000)
N	28 646	981	3 981
SE-REGN	240.459	225.459	135.750
R^2	0.314	0.259	0.375
ADJ-R^2	0.314	0.248	0.372
F-stat.	874.444	22.491	158.306
(*P*-value)	0.000	0.000	0.000
Wald-stat. (15)	10 644.90	321.43	1 773.08
Breusch–Pagan (15)	7 212.97	151.09	850.51

*P-values are for a 2-tailed test and have been computed using standard errors from White's consistent estimate of the variance–covariance matrix in the presence of heteroscedasticity (see White, 1988).

Ceteris paribus, relative income is inversely related to:

(1) the number of weeks during which the head of the family was unemployed during 1979,
(2) the number of nondependent adults,
(3) the number of children five years or younger, and
(4) the number of other dependents in the family.

Ceteris paribus, each additional nondependent adult, and each additional child of five years or younger, reduce relative income more than each additional dependent who is older than five.

If the head of the family is disabled then, *ceteris paribus*, relative income is lower than for families with an able-bodied head and the greater the disability, the lower is relative income. Families with heads who are black have lower relative incomes than families with heads who are neither black nor white, and the latter have lower relative incomes than families with heads who are white. Geographical differences in relative income are observed, *ceteris paribus*, relative income being largest in urban fringe areas.

In most cases the coefficients are highly significant, the exceptions being families headed by single males, in which case not all geographical locations are significant. Considering the large samples employed, each of the five equations fits the data well as indicated by its coefficient of determination, and its F and Wald statistics, both of which test the hypothesis that all slope coefficients are zero, the Wald statistic being valid in the presence of heteroscedasticity.[13]

The influence on poverty of the three variables which measure family size and composition is of particular interest because when people think of the typical family headed by a single woman they usually have in mind a family with more young children and fewer adults than the typical married-couple family. Table 3.3 shows that an additional infant, five years or younger, an additional dependent over five years, and an additional nondependent adult all reduce relative income· of married-couple families more than that of families headed by a single adult. These rates of change of relative income with respect to each control variable, assume *other things are equal*. In the case of the number of adults, other things are unlikely to be equal. Each nondependent adult will likely contribute some human capital to the family and also some work experience. For example, an additional, nondependent adult, with twelve years of education and ten years of work experience, in a married-couple family would increase relative income by $(-118.86 + 12 \times 9.5055 + 10 \times 1.701) = 12.216$ percentage points. Such an individual would contribute 39.7872 percentage points to relative income of a female-headed family and 31.6744 percentage points to the relative income of a male-headed family.

3.5   POVERTY STATUS DIFFERENTIALS – MALE-HEADED VS. FEMALE-HEADED FAMILIES

Table 3.4 decomposes the relative income differential of 139.18 between male-headed and female-headed families into the three components on the right hand side of equation (3.4) as follows:

Table 3.4   Poverty differential between male-headed families and female-headed families, Texas, 1979

	Average levels of control variables (component 3)	*Marginal effects of control variables (component 2)*	*Total (components 3 and 2)*
Education	20.22	7.71	27.93
Work experience	3.69	18.69	22.38
Unemployment	−0.53	−5.04	−5.57
Disability	2.50	0.53	3.03
Race	5.43	−6.25	−0.82
Location	−0.80	15.06	14.26
Nondependents	−17.01	63.17	46.17
Dependents	14.99	−18.17	−3.18
Subtotal	28.49	75.71	104.20
Unexplained differential (component 1)			34.98
Total differential			139.18

Component 1: If male-headed and female-headed families had the same mean levels of the control variables and the same marginal effects of the control variables then relative income would be 34.98 points higher for male-headed families than for female-headed families. This effect is due to the larger constant term in the equation for males.

Component 2: If male-headed and female-headed families had the same mean levels of the control variables[14] and the same constant terms then relative income would be 75.71 points higher for male-headed families. This differential, which is 54.4 percent of the total, is attributable to the overall 'superiority' of the marginal effects in the relative income equation of male-headed families. Although the marginal effects of unemployment, race and the number of dependents favor female-headed families, the marginal effects of the other variables, particularly work experience, location and number of nondependents favor male-headed families.

Component 3: If male-headed and female-headed families had the same marginal effects of the control variables[15] and the same constant terms then relative income would be 28.49 points higher for male-headed families. That is, a differential of 28.49 (20.5 percent of the total) is attributable to male-headed families' 'superior' mean levels of the control variables. In particular, male-headed families have more education and fewer dependents than female-headed families.

Note that the regression (components 2 and 3) accounts for a differential of 104.20 (74.9 percent of the total differential) in favor of male-headed families. That is, if both family types kept their current levels of the control variables, and kept their current marginal effects of the control variables, but were given the same constant coefficient, male-headed families would have a relative income 104.20 points higher than female-headed families.

3.6 POVERTY STATUS DIFFERENTIALS – MARRIED-COUPLE FAMILIES VS. FEMALE-HEADED FAMILIES

The relative income differential of 210.91 between married-couple families and female-headed families is decomposed into its three component parts in Table 3.5 as follows:

Component 1: If married-couple families and female-headed families had the same mean levels of the control variables and the same marginal effects of the control variables then the relative income differential would be 99.80 points in favor of married-couple families. This effect is due to the much larger constant term in the equation for married-couple families.

Component 2: If married-couple families and female-headed families had the same mean levels of the control variables and the same constant terms then the relative income differential would be 27.06 points in favor of married-couple families. This differential is attributable to

Table 3.5 Poverty differential between married-couple families and
female-headed families, Texas, 1979

	Average levels of control variables (component 3)	Marginal effects of control variables (component 2)	Total (components 3 and 2)
Education	100.44	97.18	197.62
Work experience	17.91	34.95	52.86
Unemployment	1.59	−2.72	−1.13
Disability	3.78	−4.75	−0.98
Race	12.50	−2.01	10.49
Location	−1.98	−2.62	−4.60
Nondependents	−56.95	−59.83	−116.79
Dependents	6.76	−33.14	−26.38
Subtotal	84.06	27.06	111.11
Unexplained differential (component 1)			99.80
Total differential			210.91

the overall 'superiority' of the marginal effects in the relative income
equation of married-couple families. The marginal effects of education and work experience favor married-couple families to such an
extent as to outweigh the marginal effects of the other variables, all
of which favor female-headed families. In particular, the marginal effects of the numbers of nondependents and dependents favor female-
headed families.

Component 3:   If married-couple and female-headed families had the
same marginal effects of the control variables and the same constant
terms then the relative income differential would be 84.06 points in
favor of married-couple families. This differential (39.9 percent of
the total) is attributable mainly to the fact that married-couple families have more education and work experience, and are more likely to
be headed by a white.

   The regression (components 2 and 3) accounts for a differential of
111.11 points (52.7 percent of the total differential) in favor of married-couple families. That is, if both family types were given the same
constant coefficient, but kept their slope coefficients and mean levels
of the control variables then the relative income of married-couple
families would be 111.11 points higher than that of female-headed
families.

3.7 POVERTY STATUS DIFFERENTIALS – MARRIED-COUPLE FAMILIES VS. MALE-HEADED FAMILIES

Table 3.6 decomposes the relative income differential of 71.73 between married-couple families and male-headed families into its three components as follows:

Table 3.6   Poverty differential between married-couples and male-headed families, Texas 1979

	Average levels of control variables (component 3)	*Marginal effects of control variables* (component 2)	*Total* (components 3 and 2)
Education	52.59	117.10	169.69
Work experience	19.89	10.60	30.49
Unemployment	4.68	−0.23	4.45
Disability	1.22	−5.22	4.00
Race	10.05	1.26	11.31
Location	2.42	−21.28	−18.86
Nondependents	−22.28	−140.67	−162.96
Dependents	−12.09	−11.11	−23.20
Subtotal	56.48	−49.57	6.92
Unexplained differential (component 1)			64.82
Total differential			71.73

Component 1: If married-couple families and male-headed families had the same mean levels of the control variables and the same marginal effects of the control variables then relative income would be 64.82 points higher for married-couple families.

Component 2: If married-couple families and male-headed families had the same mean levels of the control variables and the same constant terms then relative income would be 49.57 points higher for male-headed families. This differential is attributable to the overall 'superiority' of the marginal effects in the relative income equation of male-headed families compared with those in the relative income equation for married-couple families. The marginal effects of education and work experience favor married-couple families, but are outweighed by the marginal effects of location, and the numbers of dependents and nondependents which favor male-headed families.

Component 3: If the relative income equations for married-couple families and male-headed families had the same coefficients (constant and slopes) then relative income would be 56.48 points higher for married-couple families. This differential is attributable mainly to married-couple families' higher levels of education and work experience, and the fact that a larger proportion of married-couple families are headed by a white.

The regression (components 2 and 3) accounts for a differential of 6.92 (9.6 percent of the total differential) in favor of married-couple families. That is, if both family types had the same constant coefficient, but kept their current levels of the control variables, and kept their current marginal effects of the control variables, then relative income would be 6.92 points higher for married-couple families than for male-headed families.

3.8 CONCLUSIONS

This chapter has investigated the relationship between poverty and family type, as reflected in the marital status and gender of the head of the family. A number of factors have been identified as important determinants of poverty for all family types: education and work experience of family members, race, disability, and unemployment of the family head, geographical location, size and composition of the family.

Differences among average poverty levels of (i) married-couple families, (ii) families headed by a male with no wife present and (iii) families headed by a female with no husband present can be partially explained by differences in the average levels of these control variables. Female-headed families have 'inferior' levels of the control variables (taken as a group) compared with male-headed families. In turn, the latter have 'inferior' levels of the control variables (as a group) compared with married-couple families. In particular, female-headed families, on average, have less education and work experience, have more dependents, and are more likely to be nonwhite than other family types. They are also more likely than other family types to be headed by someone with a disability, severe enough to prevent her from working. All these factors contribute to the high poverty rate among people living in female-headed families. Married-couple families, on average, have more human capital, and are more likely to be white than male-headed families. However, male-headed families have fewer dependents than other family types, a factor which mitigates poverty among people living in these families.

Some of the differences among the average poverty levels of the three family types can be attributed to differences in the marginal effects of the control variable on poverty. As a group, the marginal effects of control variables favor male-headed over female-headed families, favor married-couple families over female-headed families, but favor male-headed families over married-couple families. In particular, additional units of human capital are more valuable to married-couple families than to families headed by a single adult, and are more valuable to male-headed families than to female-headed families. Each additional family member reduces relative income of married-couple families more than that of other families. However, each additional nondependent adult reduces relative income of male-headed families less than that of female-headed families.

In summary, male-headed families are less poor than female-headed families mainly because the marginal effects of the control variables favor the former over the latter. Married-couple families are less poor than female-headed families mainly because the former have more favorable levels of the control variables. For the same reason married-couple families are less poor than male-headed families. In all three comparisons there is a sizeable unexplained differential favoring married-couple families over families headed by a single adult and favoring male-headed families over female-headed families.

Notes

* I would like to thank Rebecca Blank and Sourushe Zandvakili for their comments on a previous version of this paper. This research was supported by a Summer Excellence Research Award from the University of North Carolina at Greensboro and a Fellowship from the Jerome Levy Economics Institute of Bard College.

1. The term 'feminization of poverty' originated with Pearce (1978). Discussions in the economics literature include those of Moynihan (1986, p. 51), Peterson (1987, 1989), Pressman (1988, 1989), Bassi (1988) and Northrop (1990).

2. Pressman (1988, p. 57) has raised the valid point that as poverty becomes feminized, for whatever reason, the percentage of children living in poverty is likely to increase. As a society, we may find this offensive. It may also lead to increased poverty rates in the next generation.

3. The data in Table 3.1 suggest that a good deal of the feminization of poverty has resulted from the increase in the proportion of the population

residing in female-headed families and the reduction in the poverty rates for unrelated individuals. See Northrop (1990) for further discussion of this point.

4. In this simple scenario, a unit change in the proportion of people living in a given household type will result in a change in the overall poverty rate equal to the difference between the poverty rate for the household type under consideration and the poverty rate for the rest of the population.

5. If people become poor as a result of marriage dissolution, or if poor, married-couple families have a relatively high chance of breaking up (into poor, single-parent families), then a positive correlation is expected between the poverty rate for female-headed families and the proportion of people living in female-headed families (Bane, 1986).

6. Policies intended to influence one's choice of household type include tax breaks for married-couple families, tougher divorce laws, stricter enforcement of alimony payments, and sex education programs which strive to reduce the number of illegitimate births to young women. It may be difficult to influence people's choice of household type. For example, tougher divorce laws are unlikely to preserve failing marriages (Pressman, 1988, p. 60). Furthermore, in some cases it may be undesirable to do so. For example, increased divorce rates are not necessarily indicative of a reduction in social welfare.

7. Family income includes wages and salaries, self-employment income, interest, dividends and net rental income. The paper analyses pre-transfer poverty, so before-tax family income, rather than after-tax family income, is employed and social security and public assistance income are excluded.

8. The poverty lines used were those of the US Department of Commerce, Bureau of the Census (see 1980 Census of Population, Volume 1, Chapter 6, Appendix B), These official poverty thresholds vary according to the size and composition of the family.

9. It would be desirable to include non-cash components of income such as fringe benefits, home produced goods and services, etc., but the necessary data are not available.

10. See Hagenaars (1986, ch. 3) for a review of theories concerning the determinants of family income.

11. The number of years of schooling includes nursery school and kindergarten. Therefore, someone with a high school diploma, but no higher education, is recorded as having 14 years of schooling.

12. These data were collected by the US Department of Commerce, Bureau of the Census, and were made available on magnetic tape by the Inter-university Consortium for Political and Social Research. Neither the Bureau, nor the Consortium, bears any responsibility for the analysis or interpretations presented here.

13. The presence of heteroscedasticity in each equation is detected by a significantly large value of the Breusch–Pagan statistic, which follows a chi-square distribution (see Breusch and Pagan, 1979; and Greene, 1990, pp. 421–2 for a discussion). The Wald statistic is discussed by Greene (1990, pp. 404–5).

14. More precisely, the assumption is that female-headed families have mean levels of the control variables equal to those of male-headed families.
15. More precisely, the assumption is that male-headed families have marginal effects of control variables equal to those of female-headed families.

References

Bane, M. J. (1986)   'Household Composition and Poverty,' Chapter 9 in S. H. Danziger and D. H. Weinberg (eds), *Fighting Poverty* (Cambridge, MA: Harvard University Press).

Bassi, L. J. (1988)   'Poverty Among Women and Children: What Accounts for the Change?,' *American Economic Review*, **78(2)**: 91–5.

Blinder, A. S. (1973)   'Wage Discrimination: Reduced Form and Structural Estimates,' *Journal of Human Resources*, **8(4)**: 436–55.

Breusch, T. and A. Pagan (1979)   'A Simple Test for Heteroscedasticity and Random Coefficient Variation,' *Econometrica*, **47**: 1287–94.

Greene, W. H. (1990)   *Econometric Analysis* (New York: Macmillan).

Hagenaars, A. J. M. (1986)   *The Perception of Poverty* (Amsterdam: North-Holland).

Moynihan, D. P. (1986)   *Family and Nation*, The Godkin Lectures, Harvard University (New York: Harcourt Brace Jovanovich).

Northrop, E. M. (1990)   'The Feminization of Poverty: The Demographic Factor and the Composition of Economic Growth,' *Journal of Economic Issues*, **24(1)**: 145–60.

Pearce, D. (1978)   'The Feminization of Poverty: Women, Work and Welfare,' *Urban and Social Change Review*, **11**: 28–36.

Peterson, J. (1987)   'The Feminization of Poverty,' *Journal of Economic Issues*, **21(1)**: 329–37.

Peterson, J. (1989)   'The Feminization of Poverty – A Reply to Pressman,' *Journal of Economic Issues*, **23(1)**: 238–45.

Pressman, S. (1988)   'The Feminization of Poverty: Causes and Remedies,' *Challenge* (March–April): 57–61.

Pressman, S. (1989)   'Comment on Peterson's "The Feminization of Poverty,"' *Journal of Economic Issues*, **23(1)**: 231–8.

White, H. (1988)   'A Heteroscedasticity Consistent Covariance Matrix and a Direct Test for Heteroscedasticity,' *Econometrica*, **48(4)**: 817–38.

Comment

Rebecca Blank

The question this chapter addresses is 'Why are certain types of households more likely to be poor than others?' It is an interesting question, and this study contributes to our understanding of the answer. In particular, the study shows that a substantial portion (20 percent in Table 3.4 and 40 percent in Table 3.5) of the difference between female-headed families and other families is due to differences in the average human capital and household characteristics of the family, such as education levels, work experience, unemployment, regional location, etc. This is good news from a policy perspective, because it indicates that measures designed to improve such things as labor market readiness and the availability of jobs can decrease poverty among female-headed families.

But Joan Rodgers also finds that some of the difference is due to differences in the coefficients on these characteristics. For example, female-headed families receive lower economic returns on their education and experience. This is less encouraging news, since it almost surely indicates that female household heads work in a very different group of jobs and have a very different set of labor market experiences, as we already know from other evidence. Changing these returns – making the coefficients on the determinants of household income for women look the same as those for men – is not an easy task, and there are few clear policies here, although improving education and job training will probably help.

In addition, Rodgers' regressions also show a substantial 'unexplained differential' in the economic situation of female-headed families and other families. For example, almost half of the difference in income status between female-headed families and married-couple families is unexplained. If this were a model of labor market discrimination, this unexplained component would be labeled 'the effect of discrimination'. But in this context, it is harder to find a label. At best, it indicates that women who head families are struggling with a host of overlapping issues in the labor market, as single parents, and as single household earners, that makes their situation substantially different than that of other families.

While these results are provocative, however, there are some limits to the interpretation of the data in this study. The dependent variable in the analysis is pre-tax pre-transfer household income, divided by the poverty line. This normalization by poverty changes the magnitude of the dependent variable, but has little effect on its interpretation; we are basically investigating the determinants of pre-tax pre-transfer household income, with some adjustment for household size. There are at least three problems with using this as the primary dependent variable in the analysis.

First, the majority of households, even female-headed households, are not poor. Thus, most of the movement in the dependent variable that is being picked up in the regressions is occurring among the non-poor. Thus, it is not clear how generalizable the results are to what is happening only at the bottom of the income distribution. I would find it interesting if this analysis were supplemented by a similar analysis focusing solely on the determinants of poverty, perhaps using a probit model of 'poor/non-poor' as the dependent variable. The coefficients could be decomposed in exactly the same way as is done currently in the chapter, and would show how much of the difference in poverty rates between these groups could be explained by the components of the decomposition. It would be particularly interesting to know if the decomposition of the poverty rate showed similar results as the decomposition of household income seen here.

Second, it is worth noting that pre-tax pre-transfer income, as measured by this study, is not really a true measure of market opportunities for households, as the chapter claims. This variable is defined as total household income minus all government transfers. But labor market behavior, in particular, is causally related to the level and type of government transfers. As many economic studies have demonstrated, other household income sources – particularly labor market income – decline as government transfers rise. While the study uses data from only one state (Texas), that is not enough to get around this problem. Female-headed households have a wider variety of government assistance programs available to them than non-female-headed households in all states in the United States. Thus, their pre-transfer income may be more affected by the presence of government transfers than other households, causing a wider gap between female-headed family income and other family income than 'market opportunities' alone would indicate. Indeed, this may be one reason for the large 'unexplained differential' estimated in the regressions.

Third, the final problem with using a dependent variable composed of pre-transfer household income, divided by the relevant poverty line, is that it is hard to interpret the magnitude of the effects in the decompositions shown in Tables 3.4 through 3.6. What does it mean to say that there is a total 'relative income differential of 139.18 between male-headed and female-headed families', for example? Interpretation of the results would be far easier if these numbers were translated back into a metric that we all understood. For example, one could calculate the income level implied by 139.18 (making some assumptions about which poverty line is on average most appropriate) and report the equivalent estimated income differences. This would make the numbers in the decomposition tables substantially easier to understand. Of course, this should not change the share of the decomposition coming from each component and thus would not change the primary results of the study.

Finally, despite quibbles about the empirical analysis in this chapter, I want to note that I really do agree with one of its main claims: Joan Rodgers concludes that it is not very useful to talk about changing the distribution of the population among different household types; it is far more useful to talk about decreasing poverty among the household types that exist. In other words, our primary policy question should be 'What do we need to do in order to lower poverty rates among female-headed households and is this any different from the policies we should pursue to lower poverty among married-couples?' Focusing instead, as some have suggested, on the question of 'How do we decrease the number of female-headed households' is likely to be a far less useful approach.

If nothing else, this second question is much more difficult to approach in a public policy context. We do not know very much about how to affect household fertility; we do not know very much about how to affect household formation through marriage or divorce rates; and even if we knew how to do these things, it is not clear we want the government involved in doing them. We do, however, know something (perhaps less than we would like, but something) about encouraging human capital formation (education and training) and stimulating the creation of more jobs. Given this, the conclusion of this study is completely on target: we need to attack the poverty problem that exists among households as they are currently formulated.

Part II
International Comparisons

4 International Comparisons of Earnings Inequality for Men in the 1980s

Gordon W. Green, Jr, John Coder and
Paul Ryscavage*

4.1 INTRODUCTION

Growing inequality in the distribution of labor market earnings in the United States has become one of the more popular research topics in labor economics in recent years. Researchers in the early 1980s first observed rising earnings inequality among men (e.g., Henle and Ryscavage, 1980; Plotnick, 1982). Since that time many papers, articles, and books have been written about the increase in earnings inequality during the 1980s and the possible explanations for the development (Levy and Murnane, 1992).

The analytical framework for explaining the greater dispersion in the earnings distribution has typically involved identifying the sources – or groups of workers – responsible for the growing inequality. Initially, an analysis of variance approach was suggested (Dooley and Gottschalk, 1982), but other decomposition techniques have been used. Sources of change in inequality measures are typically decomposed into those generated 'between' and 'within' specific groups of workers. These groups are typically defined on the basis of human capital attributes, such as age, experience, and education.

This new literature, of course, focuses almost exclusively on increasing earnings inequality in the United States over the last twenty years or so, with particular emphasis on its acceleration in the 1980s. In this chapter, trends in earnings inequality during the 1980s for men from five industrialized countries – Canada, Sweden, Australia, West Germany, and the United States – are presented. While our analysis does not involve decomposing changes in inequality, it may prove useful in understanding the changes occurring in the United States. If a pattern of rising inequality is observed in other developed nations, it may be that the same phenomenon causing it there is also at work in the United States (e.g., skill-biased technological changes). Or if there has been no change in earnings inequality in these other nations, the reason for growing inequality in the United States may be due to problems unique to the United States (e.g., import trade imbalances).

Analyses of changes in the inequality of earnings distributions in other countries are rare.[1] Some related evidence, however, was made available by the Organisation for Economic Cooperation and Development (OECD) in their *Employment Outlook for 1987* (OECD, 1987). The OECD examined earnings differentials between non-manual and manual workers in sixteen of its member countries over the last two or three decades. Their analysis revealed that in eight of the sixteen countries studied, the trend in the differentials *since 1980* was upward. These countries were Canada, Denmark, West Germany, Italy, the Netherlands, Norway, the United Kingdom, and the United States. Although the OECD data are only suggestive at best (given comparability problems, the aggregative nature of the data, and so on), they may reflect underlying changes taking place in the earnings and wage distributions of these countries.

This chapter begins with a brief discussion of the various measures of inequality used in the comparison (Section 4.2); Section 4.3 discusses the data from the Luxembourg Income Study (LIS) that was used in the analysis. Section 4.4 presents the results of the comparison and consists of first determining how much inequality existed in each nation's earnings distributions in the mid-1980s and second, whether or not inequality changed in these countries between the early-1980s and mid-1980s. Section 4.5 summarizes the findings and discusses their implications for further research.

4.2 MEASURES OF EARNINGS INEQUALITY

Numerous indices exist for measuring the degree of inequality in an earnings distribution. They range from simple measures like the share of aggregate earnings received by each quintile, the coefficient of variation, and the variance of the natural logarithm of earnings, to more complex measures such as the Gini, Theil, and Atkinson measures, and Generalized Entropy indices. All have different mathematical constructions and can lead to different assessments concerning the degree of inequality (Slottje, 1989). For this reason, multiple measures of inequality are examined in our cross-national comparison of earnings inequality in the interest of robustness.

Four of these measures of inequality deserve discussion since they have particular properties of which some readers may not be aware.[2] The variance of the natural logarithm is a popular measure of inequality, but does not always satisfy the 'principle of transfers.' When income is transferred from a high paid worker to a less highly paid worker, earning inequality should be reduced; however, in some instances this inequality measure can produce the opposite finding. In addition, this measure is particularly sensitive to changes in earnings levels in the lower end of the distribution.

The Gini index, while always satisfying the principle of transfers, is more sensitive to changes in the middle of the earnings distribution rather than the tails. This is because it is derived from the Lorenz curve which expresses the relationship between the cumulated percentage of aggregate earnings and cumulated percentage of earners. An increase or decrease in earnings in the middle of the distribution will have a greater impact on the measure than a similar change at either end, since there are more earners in the middle ranks.

The Theil index also satisfies the principle of transfers, but is also most sensitive to movements within the middle of the distribution. Its primary advantage in analyses of inequality is its property of decomposition: overall inequality can be decomposed into 'between' and 'within' groups comprising the distribution.

Both the Gini and Theil indices, however, have a common disadvantage. If they are derived from distributions with intersecting Lorenz curves, that is, curves showing the relationship between the cumulated percentage of earnings and the cumulated percentage of earners, meaningful comparisons of the indices become problematic (Braun, 1988). This is commonly referred to as Lorenz dominance.

The Atkinson measures were developed to overcome this problem. Basically, the Atkinson measures allow one to shift the 'weight' given to the middle ranks of the distribution to either the lower or upper ends of the distribution. The researcher can specify the degree of sensitivity to transfers within the distribution. In this chapter three different values of ε or the weight, were chosen – 0.5, 0.8, and 1.5. As the value of ε rises, the measure becomes increasingly sensitive to inequality among low earners.

4.3   THE DATA

The data for our comparison have been obtained from the Luxembourg Income Study (LIS), a multinational collection of micro datasets from various countries (Coder, Rainwater, and Smeeding, 1988). All of the data were collected in household surveys or surveys of administrative systems (Sweden) by institutions in countries participating in LIS. Each survey used different questionnaires, collection, and processing techniques, and differences also existed in population universes, variable definitions, and response rates. As far as possible, however, definitions of income sources and family and household characteristics have been placed on a common foundation.

As of mid-1990, the LIS database consisted of micro datasets for fourteen countries.[3] The countries of Canada, Australia, Sweden, West Germany, and the United States were selected for comparison because it is only for these countries that data were available covering two different periods of time in the 1980s. We refer to these periods as the early 1980s and mid-1980s, the former comprising 1979–81 and the latter 1984–7.[4] Table 4.1 shows the specific years used for each country.

Table 4.1   The database used in the study

	Early 1980s	*Mid-1980s*
Canada	1981	1987
Australia	1981	1985
Sweden	1981	1987
West Germany	1981	1984
United States	1979	1986

The universe initially selected for examination was adult men age 25 to 54 who headed households, worked year round, full time, and received no social insurance pension or private pension. This universe was chosen since the objective of the analysis was to focus on, as closely as possible, distributions of labor income which reflected standardized units of labor input (e.g., an hourly wage rate). In other words, by identifying a universe fully committed to the workforce it was possible to minimize the confounding effect of differences in annual hours worked on annual wage and salary earnings.[5]

In defining the universes for analysis, however, a number of potentially troublesome comparability problems were encountered.[6] The most important related to the lower tail of the distributions where sampling and data collection problems tend to be most conspicuous. Since the universe being analyzed was composed of prime-age men, who were household heads and work year round, full time, it would be expected that the lower tail of the earnings distribution would be truncated at a 'minimum wage' level or its equivalent. As shown in Table 4.2a, unreasonably low amounts of earnings for men were observed for Sweden at the 1st percentile of the distribution; in addition, particularly low levels were also observed at the 1st percentile for Canada and Australia. After investigating the data for Sweden in some detail it was found that this problem was caused by self-employed workers (farmers and other entrepreneurs) who had also received small amounts of wage and salary income. This finding was suggestive of a more general problem which applied to the other countries, that is, year-round, full-time 'self-employed' workers with wage and salary income from other jobs.

Other potential problems concerned the upper tail of the distribution where data problems are often concentrated. One of these problems concerns 'top-coding.' In some countries, such as the United States, earnings in excess of certain levels may be top-coded, that is, all amounts higher than the specified limit are reduced to the limit before the data are released to the public. This practice is a means of preserving the confidentiality of survey respondents. However, it does introduce a bias into the data and affects measures of inequality. The presence of top-coding is clearly evident in the data for the United States shown in Table 4.2a where the top-code in 1979 was $50 000 and in 1986, $100 000. In the other countries it is not so evident given the differences between the maximum value of wage and salary earnings reported and the earnings at the 99th percentile.

While no adjustments were made for the problem of top-coding, it was possible to adjust the data for those year-round, full-time self-employed workers with wage and salary income.[7] In each country, they were excluded from the universe of male heads of households, age 25 to 54, who worked year round, full time. The results of this exclusion on the distributions can be seen in Table 4.2b.

The adjusted data in Table 4.2b also provide some preliminary evidence as to how these earnings distributions changed during the 1980s. The mean-to-median ratio for each country rose during the 1980s, indicating that the mean in these distributions were being 'pulled' up by increasingly high earnings values (column (H)). The highest-to-lowest decile ratio increased in all countries except Australia, indicative of greater dispersion in the distributions (column (I)). The 1st percentile-to-median ratio (column (J)) reflects the spread or distance between

Table 4.2a Summary earnings measures for men, heads of households, age 25–54 years, who worked year round, full time in selected countries, early 1980s and mid-1980s, all numbers in currency of specified country

Country/ year	(A) Median	(B) Mean	(C) Lowest decile**	(D) Highest decile**	(E) 1st percentile**	(F) 99th percentile**	(G) Max. value	(H) (B)/(A)	(I) (D)/(C)	(J) (E)/(A) (%)	(K) (F)/(A)
US79*	18 700	20 079	9 750	32 000	3 000	50 000	50 000	107	328	16	267
US86	27 500	30 848	13 000	50 600	5 200	100 000	100 000	112	389	19	364
SW81	81 900	87 185	55 808	126 272	1 807	238 212	700 000	106	226	2	291
SW87	129 800	140 629	86 607	207 963	924	387 609	1 800 000	108	240	1	299
CN81	23 510	24 761	13 501	37 539	4 590	57 835	105 000	105	278	20	246
CN87	31 410	33 398	14 430	52 210	1 765	95 122	260 000	106	362	6	303
AS81	17 490	18 292	10 971	27 213	2 224	42 000	170 000	105	248	13	240
AS85	23 290	24 763	14 088	37 190	1 318	59 352	200 000	106	264	6	255
WG81	36 700	40 071	25 680	58 680	10 000	88 300	200 000	109	229	27	241
WG84	41 200	46 173	28 900	69 300	18 000	107 900	236 000	112	240	44	262

Note: * US = United States, 1979 and 1986; SW = Sweden, 1981 and 1987; CN = Canada, 1981 and 1987; AS = Australia, 1981 and 1985; WG = West Germany, 1981 and 1984.
** Figures for deciles and percentiles are upper limits of the specified group.

the bottom and middle of each distribution. This measure shows that this distance increased dramatically in West Germany and slightly in Australia and Sweden. In Canada and the United States the change in the distance between these two points of the distribution was not very large. The 99th percentile-to-median ratio (column (K)) reflects the gap in the distribution between the median and the top of the distribution. In each country, the distance between these two points increased from the early 1980s to the mid-1980s, with the largest increases occurring in the United States and Canada. Consequently, in each country there was preliminary evidence that distributions of earnings of prime-age men who headed households and were fully committed to the laborforce had become more unequal during the 1980s.

4.4 CROSS-NATIONAL COMPARISONS OF EARNINGS INEQUALITY MEASURES

The results of the comparative analysis of earnings inequality in Canada, Sweden, Australia, West Germany, and the United States are presented in two parts. First, various earnings inequality measures are presented for these countries as of the mid-1980s which address the question as to whose distribution was the most unequal and whose was the most equal. Naturally, differences are expected given the differences in each country's economic structure (e.g., industrial composition, extent of unionization, compensation practises) and other factors that influence the shape of the earnings distribution. Second, we compare these mid-1980s earnings inequality measures to their counterparts as of the early 1980s and address the more interesting question as to whether or not the distributions changed over this period of time. Here, our expectations are less certain, although the preliminary evidence presented above suggests changes have indeed taken place.

4.4.1 Earnings Inequality in the Mid-1980s

Table 4.3 shows the share of aggregate wages and salaries received in each decile by men who were heads of households and worked year round full time in Canada, Sweden, Australia, West Germany, and the United States in the 1984–7 period. The distributions were arrayed (from left to right) on the basis of which country had the *smallest* proportion of aggregate earnings in its lowest decile. In other words, in which country did workers at the bottom of the earnings distribution

Table 4.2b Summary earnings measures for men, heads of households, age 25–54 years, who worked year round, full time in selected countries, after exclusion of the self-employed, early 1980s and mid-1980s, all numbers in currency of specified country

Country/ year	(A) Median	(B) Mean	(C) Lowest decile**	(D) Highest decile**	(E) 1st percentile**	(F) 99th percentile**	(G) Max. value	(H) (B)/(A)	(I) (D)/(C) (%)	(J) (E)/(A) (%)	(K) (F)/(A)
US79*	18 750	20 118	9 800	32 000	3 000	50 000	50 000	107	327	16	267
US86	27 950	31 140	13 000	52 000	4 806	100 000	100 000	111	400	17	358
SW81	84 700	93 149	64 000	131 500	40 300	242 025	700 000	110	205	48	286
SW87	135 900	152 379	103 400	215 400	69 324	399 594	1 800 000	112	208	51	294
CN81	23 610	24 922	13 730	37 640	4 691	58 058	105 000	106	274	20	246
CN87	32 760	35 094	17 485	53 000	5 810	97 985	260 000	107	303	18	299
AS81	17 510	18 429	11 020	27 270	2 709	42 013	170 000	105	247	15	240
AS85	24 000	25 601	15 588	37 672	5 118	59 962	200 000	107	242	21	250
WG81	36 800	40 104	25 730	58 570	10 000	88 300	200 000	109	228	27	239
WG84	41 600	46 508	29 300	69 800	20 800	105 104	236 000	112	238	50	253

Note: * US = United States, 1979 and 1986; SW = Sweden, 1981 and 1987; CN = Canada, 1981 and 1987; AS = Australia, 1981 and 1985; WG = West Germany, 1981 and 1984.
** Figures for deciles and percentiles are upper limits of the specified group.

receive the smallest share of total earnings? As shown in Table 4.3, in the United States the lowest decile of men received only 3.0 percent of all earnings, followed by Canada at 3.4 percent. Australia's and West Germany's lowest deciles, respectively, received the next largest shares, with Sweden's lowest decile, on the other hand, obtaining 5.9 percent.

Table 4.3 Percentage share of aggregate wage and salary income received by men, heads of households, age 25–54 years, working year round, full time by deciles for selected countries, mid-1980s

Decile	US*	Canada	Australia	West Germany	Sweden
Lowest	3.0	3.4	4.4	5.4	5.9
Second	4.9	5.7	6.6	6.7	7.1
Third	6.1	6.8	7.4	7.1	7.6
Fourth	7.2	7.9	8.2	8.3	8.1
Fifth	8.3	8.8	8.9	8.5	8.7
Sixth	9.5	9.9	9.8	9.4	9.2
Seventh	10.7	10.9	10.6	10.3	10.0
Eighth	12.2	12.1	11.7	11.7	11.1
Ninth	14.8	13.8	13.4	13.7	12.9
Highest	23.3	20.7	19.0	18.9	19.4

Note: * United States, 1986; Canada, 1987; Australia, 1985; West Germany, 1984; Sweden, 1987.

Turning to the shares received by the highest deciles in each country produces a somewhat different ranking of countries. Once again the United States would occupy the first position since its highest decile of earners received 23.3 percent of the aggregate followed by Canada whose highest decile received 20.7 percent. Thereafter, the ranking changes. Sweden's 19.4 percent share would now occupy the third position (if the table were rearranged), followed by Australia and West Germany with shares of 19.0 and 18.9 percent, respectively (see Figure 4.1).

Indeed, careful inspection of these distributions reveals that it is difficult to compare the degree of inequality in the distributions of Australia, West Germany, and Sweden. For example, *if* the criterion for judging which distribution was more unequal was based on the shares of earnings received by the lowest and highest deciles, an unambiguous ranking could not be arrived at. In the first instance, Sweden's distribution would be considered the most equal, but in the second it would be West Germany's. Furthermore, the Lorenz curves for these countries can be seen to intersect (see Figure 4.1). Consequently, to

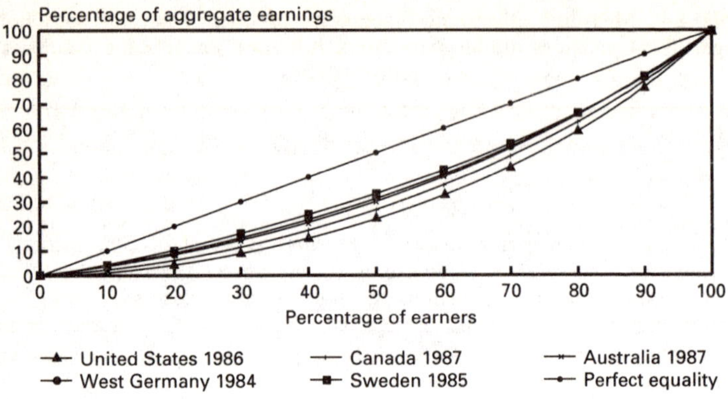

Figure 4.1   Lorenz curves, five nations, mid-1980s, men age 25–54, heads of households, who work year round, full time

completely answer the question as to whose distributions were the most equal and unequal, more sophisticated measures of earnings inequality must be used.

Table 4.4 presents a ranking of the five countries, with respect to earnings inequality, using several earnings inequality measures, specifically, the variance of the logarithm of annual earnings, the Gini and Theil indices, and three Atkinson measures. Table 4.4 indicates that regardless of measure, the United States distribution of earnings showed the highest level of inequality in it in the mid-1980s. The country with the second most unequal distribution among these five countries was Canada. Although these results were anticipated from the share analysis above, these earnings inequality measures quantify how much more unequal the United States and Canadian distributions are from one another, as well as from the other countries.

For Australia, West Germany, and Sweden, the earnings inequality measures provide a somewhat clearer picture of whose distribution was the most unequal and most equal than the share analysis did. All of the measures indicate that Australia's was the most unequal followed by West Germany and then Sweden. The readings from the Gini and Theil indices, of course, should be viewed cautiously since Lorenz dominance was present in these distributions. Each of the Atkinson measures produced the same ranking of countries, although the magnitude of the differences varied between the measure which gives more weight to the low end of the distribution and the measure which weights the upper end more heavily.

Table 4.4   Measures of earnings inequality for men, heads of households, age 25–54 years, working year round, full time for selected countries, mid-1980s

Rank	Ln Y	Gini	Theil	Atkinson (0.5)	Atkinson (0.8)	Atkinson (1.5)
1	0.453(US)*	0.298(US)	0.149(US)	0.074(US)	0.120(US)	0.341(US)
2	0.280(CN)	0.253(CN)	0.116(CN)	0.057(CN)	0.091(CN)	0.185(CN)
3	0.210(AS)	0.212(AS)	0.087(AS)	0.042(AS)	0.067(AS)	0.146(AS)
4	0.133(WG)	0.204(WG)	0.071(WG)	0.034(WG)	0.053(WG)	0.097(WG)
5	0.111(SW)	0.190(SW)	0.071(SW)	0.032(SW)	0.049(SW)	0.082(SW)

*Note:** US = United States, 1986; CN = Canada, 1987; AS = Australia, 1985; WG = West Germany, 1984; SW = Sweden, 1987.

4.4.2   Earnings Inequality – Early 1980s vs. Mid-1980s

Among the many factors that can influence changes in a nation's distribution of earnings are changes in the health of the economy. Although measures of earnings inequality for these countries are compared over somewhat different time periods, the economies of these countries in the early 1980s and mid-1980s were, generally speaking, in similar phases of the business cycle (OECD, 1990). In each country, the mid-1980s represented years of economic growth and recovery from recessions in the early 1980s. Gross domestic products were rising and inflation had moderated relative to the early 1980s. In the early 1980s, on the other hand, economic growth was less robust and inflation more problematic as each country was in or about to enter a period of economic slowdown.

The data presented in Table 4.5 show the percentage share of aggregate wages and salaries by *quintile* for men age 25 to 54 who headed households and worked full time, year round in Canada, Sweden, Australia, West Germany, and the United States in the early 1980s and mid-1980s.[8] In each country there is evidence to varying degrees of a greater concentration of earnings in the upper quintiles of the earnings distributions. For the United States, Canada, and Sweden, the share of earnings received by each of the lowest three quintiles declined while the share for the top quintiles increased. In the United States, for example, the share of aggregate wage and salary earnings received by the top one-fifth of earners increased from 35.0 percent to 38.1 percent, or 3.1 percentage points. Canada had a 2.1 percentage point increase in the share going to the highest earners. The increase in the share going to Sweden's top earners, however, was only 0.7 percentage points.

Table 4.5   Shares (%) of aggregate wage and salary income received by men, heads of households, age 25–54 years, working year round, full time, by quintile for selected countries, early 1980s and mid-1980s

Country/ year	Quintile					
	Total	Lowest	Second	Third	Fourth	Highest
United States						
1986	100.0	7.9	13.3	17.8	22.9	38.1
1979	100.0	8.9	14.6	18.6	22.9	35.0
Canada						
1987	100.0	9.1	14.7	18.7	23.0	34.5
1981	100.0	10.1	15.5	19.0	23.0	32.4
Sweden						
1987	100.0	13.0	15.7	17.9	21.1	32.3
1981	100.0	13.2	16.1	18.1	21.0	31.6
Australia						
1985	100.0	11.0	15.6	18.7	22.3	32.4
1981	100.0	10.8	15.9	19.0	22.7	31.6
West Germany						
1984	100.0	12.2	15.4	17.9	22.0	32.6
1981	100.0	12.0	16.0	18.3	21.8	31.9

In the case of Australia and West Germany, the patterns of change in the distributions were somewhat different than in the other countries. In Australia, the share received by the highest fifth of earners increased *and* the share increased (slightly) for the lowest fifth of earners as well. A similar pattern of change was evident in West Germany, except that the share also rose slightly in the fourth quintile. In other words, in these two countries the middle quintiles received slightly smaller shares of aggregate earnings. It is also important to note that Lorenz curves for the early 1980s and mid-1980s in both Australia and West Germany crossed at the lower end of the distributions.

The above share analysis strongly suggests that earnings of the highest paid men in each of the distribution examined were becoming more concentrated in the 1980s. This development was particularly acute in the United States and Canada. Nevertheless, some change towards greater earnings inequality was detected in Sweden, Australia, and West Germany as well. More sophisticated measures of inequality, however, are required to confirm this finding.

Table 4.6 displays the inequality measures that were previously discussed in connection with the question of which country had the most and least amount of inequality in its distribution. Table 4.6, however, now includes the values of these measures for the early 1980s, and the percentage change in the measures between the early 1980s and mid-1980s. As might be expected from the share analysis, all of the measures indicate a strong increase in inequality in the United States and Canada. The percentage increases in the measures for the United States ranged from 16 percent (the Gini index) to 34 percent (Atkinson, 1.5 ε); for Canada, they ranged from 14 percent (the Gini index) to 38 percent (the Theil index).

All of the inequality measures for Sweden registered increases as well, but they were not as large as for the North American countries. They ranged from as little as 4 percent (Atkinson, 1.5 ε) to 13 percent (the Theil index). Interestingly, the increases in both the variance of the logarithm of annual earnings and the Atkinson measure (1.5 ε) –

Table 4.6 Changes in measures of earnings inequality for men, heads of households, age 25–54 years, working year round, full time for selected countries, early 1980s and mid-1980s

Country/year	Ln Y	Gini	Theil	Atkinson (0.5)	Atkinson (0.8)	Atkinson (1.5)
United States						
1986	0.453	0.298	0.149	0.074	0.120	0.341
1979	0.354	0.258	0.111	0.057	0.094	0.254
% change	28.0	15.5	34.2	29.8	27.7	34.3
Canada						
1987	0.280	0.253	0.116	0.057	0.091	0.185
1981	0.225	0.222	0.084	0.043	0.071	0.148
% change	24.4	14.0	38.1	32.6	28.2	25.0
Sweden						
1987	0.111	0.190	0.071	0.032	0.049	0.082
1981	0.105	0.180	0.063	0.029	0.045	0.079
% change	5.7	5.6	12.7	10.3	8.9	3.8
Australia						
1985	0.210	0.212	0.087	0.042	0.067	0.146
1981	0.234	0.208	0.075	0.040	0.065	0.155
% change	−9.3	1.9	16.0	5.0	3.1	−5.8
West Germany						
1984	0.133	0.204	0.071	0.034	0.053	0.097
1981	0.162	0.195	0.068	0.033	0.054	0.114
% change	−17.9	4.6	4.4	3.0	−1.9	−14.9

two measures sensitive to the low end of the distribution – were on the low side of this range, reflecting the small change that occurred in the share of aggregate earnings received by the lowest quintile.

In Australia four of the six measures increased and in West Germany three measures moved higher. The increases for both were generally smaller than in the other countries (except the Theil measure for Australia). It should be remembered, however, that the span of years comprising the comparisons for these two countries is relatively short. Again, the measures sensitive to the bottom of the distribution – the variance of the logarithm and the Atkinson measure (1.5 ε) – registered declines in inequality, reflecting the share increases at the bottom of the distributions discussed earlier.

4.5   IMPLICATIONS OF RESULTS

The growth of earnings inequality in the United States in recent years has been well documented, and the subject of much concern in both the research and policy communities. One of the concerns has been whether or not the millions of jobs created in the United States during the 1980s were primarily of the 'low paying, low productivity' variety. Another related concern, of course, is how much of the growing earnings inequality was responsible for the growing inequality of incomes among families and households.

The results presented above suggest that the United States was not the only industrialized country during the 1980s to experience an increase in earnings inequality among prime-age men who head families that were fully committed to the laborforce. It was shown that the wage and salary earnings distributions for similar men from Canada and Sweden became more unequal as well. In addition, there was evi-

Table 4.7   Average annual growth rates in total employment for selected countries, early 1980s to mid-1980s

Country	Period	Average annual growth rate (%)
United States	1979–86	1.49
Canada	1981–87	1.28
Australia	1981–85	1.08
Sweden	1981–87	0.43
West Germany	1981–84	–0.77

dence that inequality was growing for these groups of men in Australia and West Germany. These findings may be further evidence of underlying structural changes taking place in the distributions of labor market incomes in many developed countries.

Clearly, the 'job quality' issue as a cause of growing earnings inequality in the United States loses credibility when rates of employment growth in these other countries are compared to the United States experience. Each country had quite different employment experiences during the periods in which inequality was rising, as shown in Table 4.7 (OECD, 1990). In the United States and Canada, the annual average rate of growth was in the 1.3–1.5 percent range and in Australia it was 1.1 percent. In Sweden employment growth was meager, while in West Germany it was declining.

The fact that rising earnings inequality occurred in other industrialized countries with different job creation experiences suggests that rising inequality may be related to more general phenomena occurring across nations. One possibility involves changing technologies. Computer and communication technologies have changed dramatically in recent years and these may have altered the demand for different skill classes of labor. Production processes may have been so altered that companies and factories now require more highly skilled and educated workers, while the demand for less well trained labor associated with older production processes has declined. At the same time as these shifts in demand have taken place, the supply of workers in various skill classes may have changed less rapidly, thereby increasing inequality in the earnings distribution. This, of course, is speculation. Nevertheless, evidence now exists that the phenomenon of growing earnings inequality may have an international dimension.

Appendix

INEQUALITY MEASURES

The mathematical construction of four inequality measures used in this paper are discussed below.

Variance of the Natural Logarithm of Annual Earnings

This is a popular measure of relative earnings dispersion because earnings distributions are approximately lognormal and the lognormal distribution has particular properties conducive for analysis. The measure is written as

$$\text{var ln } Y = \frac{\sum_{i=1}^{n} (\ln y_i - \ln \bar{y})}{n}$$

where $\ln y_i$ is the natural logarithm of person i's annual earnings, $\ln \bar{y}$, is the mean of annual earnings, and n is the number of persons with earnings.

The Gini Index or Coefficient of Income Concentration

The Gini index is also a popular measure of inequality. It can be written as

$$G = 1.0 - \sum_{i=1}^{n} f_i (p_i + p_{i-1})$$

where f_i is the proportion of earners in interval i and p_i is the proportion of total earnings received by earners in interval i and all lower intervals.

Theil's 'Entropy' Index of Inequality

The Theil index can be written as

$$T = (1/n) \sum_{i=1}^{n} (y_i / \bar{y}) \log (y_i / \bar{y})$$

where y_i is the annual earnings of the ith earners, $\bar{y}$ the mean annual earnings, and n the number of earners.

Atkinson's Measures of Inequality

The family of Atkinson measures are constructed as

$$A = 1 - [(1/n) \sum_{i=1}^{n} (y^i/\bar{y})^{1-\varepsilon}]^{\frac{1}{1-\varepsilon}}$$

with the similar notation found in the other measures, except for the ε. As the value of the ε rises, the measure becomes increasingly sensitive to inequality among low earners. Low values of ε produce results similar to the Gini index.

DATA SOURCES

The following is a brief description of the household surveys which were the source of the earnings data. Household sample sizes do not necessarily reflect the size of the original sample in all cases, but rather the number of households comprising the country's micro dataset in the LIS database.

Australia

The Australian data for both 1981 and 1985 were obtained from The Income and Housing Survey. The sample size in 1981 was 15 985 households and in 1985, 7560.

Canada

Earnings data for Canada were obtained from The Survey of Consumer Finances and refer to 1981 and 1987. Sample sizes for the LIS data base were 15 136 and 10 999.

West Germany

Data for West Germany for the year 1981 were taken from the 1981 German Transfer Survey and based on a household sample size of 2727. The German Panel Survey (Wave 2) was the source of the data for 1984 and 5174 households from it comprised the LIS data base.

Sweden

The Swedish Income Distribution Survey in both 1981 and 1987 was the source of the data for Sweden. The LIS database used data from 9625 households in 1981 and 9421 households in 1987.

United States

The data for the United States comes from the Work Experience and Income Supplement to the March Current Population Survey and relate to the years 1979 and 1986. In 1979, the sample consisted of 15 225 households and in 1986, 13 707.

Notes

* The views expressed in this chapter are those of the authors and do not necessarily represent those of the Census Bureau. The chapter was previously published in *The Review of Income and Wealth*, Series 38, no. 1, (March 1992).

1. Cross-national comparisons of 'income' inequality, however, are more common. For example, see O'Higgins, Schmaus, and Stephenson (1989).
2. Their mathematical constructions are given in the Appendix (pp. 72–3).
3. The countries are Luxembourg, Italy, Poland, France, Israel, Netherlands, Norway, Switzerland, the United Kingdom, Canada, Australia, Sweden, West Germany, and the United States.
4. A brief description of the surveys from each country is contained in the Appendix (p. 73).
5. There is, no doubt, variation across countries in the definition of year-round, full-time employment. For example, in the United States the definition was 50 or more weeks of employment at 35 hours or more a week. In Sweden, on the other hand, the definition is 1872 hours of employment or more during the year. In Canada, Australia, and West Germany precise details concerning the definition of year-round, full-time employment was not provided in the dataset, although variables identifying year-round, full-time workers were provided.
6. All of the microdata were weighted using sample weights and all the data presented, therefore, are weighted estimates.
7. Another procedure for reducing 'survey noise' and data collection and processing problems is simply to censor the distributions at the lower and upper ends (e.g., 1st and 99th percentiles). We rejected this procedure on the grounds of its arbitrariness.
8. Quintiles instead of deciles are examined here since the changes in this unit of measurement over time are larger and can be more easily seen.

References

Braun, D. (1988) 'Multiple Measurements of US Income Inequality,' *The Review of Economics and Statistics*, **70(3)** (August): 398–405.

Coder, J., L. Rainwater and T. Smeeding (1988) 'LIS Information Guide,' LIS–CEPS Working Paper, **7**, Walferdange, Luxembourg (rev. November).

Dooley, M. and P. Gottschalk (1982) 'Does a Younger Male Labor Force Mean Greater Earnings Inequality?,' *Monthly Labor Review*, **105(11)** (November): 42–5.

Henle, P. and P. Ryscavage (1980) 'The Distribution of Earned Income Among Men and Women, 1958–1977,' *Monthly Labor Review*, **103(4)** (April): 3–10.

Levy, F. and R. J. Murnane (1992) 'U.S. Earnings Levels and Earnings Inequality: A Review of Recent Trends and Proposed Explanations,' *Journal of Economic Literature*, XXX, **3**.

O'Higgins, M., G. Schmaus and G. Stephenson (1989) 'Income Distribution and Redistribution: A Microdata Analysis for Seven Countries,' *The Review of Income and Wealth*, Series **35(2)** (June): 107–31.

Organisation for Economic Co-operation and Development (1987) *The OECD Employment Outlook* (September) (Paris: OECD).

Organisation for Economic Co-operation and Development (1990) *OECD Economic Outlook* (June) (Paris: OECD).

Plotnick, R. D. (1982) 'Trends in Male Earnings Inequality,' *Southern Economic Journal*, **48(3)** (March): 724–32.

Slottje, D. J. (1989) *The Structure of Earnings and the Measurement of Income Inequality in the U.S.* (Amsterdam: North-Holland).

Comment

Howard M. Wachtel

This chapter makes an important contribution to our descriptive understanding of earnings inequalities in the 1980s. The authors have done a fine job assembling comparative data and presenting their results in an accessible form.

They start by accepting the proposition that earnings inequalities have increased in the United States in the 1980s. They want to see if this phenomenon is confined to the United States or whether it pervades other industrial countries as well. They suggest, but do not develop, three possible explanations for the US data:

(i) Industrial restructuring which has reduced demand for higher paying jobs and increased demand for lower paying jobs.

(ii) Demographic changes in the laborforce – namely more women and younger baby-boomers – who have lower earnings capacities, according to the authors.

(iii) An implied human capital explanation which has increased returns to education and I presume, therefore, means either a more unequal distribution of education in the 1980s or more unequal returns to education.

The results suggest that earnings inequalities have increased in all the industrial countries. The measures used to quantify the change in inequality indicate that the United States has shown the greatest increase in inequality for those measures that weight the middle more heavily. While for those measures that weight the tails more heavily, other countries – even Sweden – show a greater increase in inequality in the 1980s.

In the current debate in Sweden over the future of social democracy, I suspect the Social Democrats could take these results and say: 'We have not done as much redistribution as our critics charge.' Their opponents could counter by saying how ineffective the Social Democrats have been over so many decades. My own suspicion is that there is something in the data that has produced this peculiar result.

In the category of measures that weights the middle more heavily, the familiar Gini coefficient places its money on United States inequality. While the log normal and Atkinson measures, which weight the tails more, place their emphasis on other countries.

It is this result and a more general problem with the data used which invites my first comment. As far as I can see, the data used include both wages and salaries – the salaries of corporate chief executives as well as the blue collar production workers or service employees, depending on the type of enterprise. So Lee Iaccoca's salary in the seven figures are in the same data pool with the janitor who cleans his office.

From other data, we know that United States corporate executive salaries compared to their employees show greater differentiation in the United States than they do in other countries. CEO salaries are simply not as high relative to their employees in other countries as they are in the United States. Taking the year 1980 equal to 100, CEOs' salaries rose to an index of 260 by 1989, while blue collar production workers wages were just under an index number of 150 in 1989. Corporate profits, incidentally were below the 1980s' base until 1987 when they peaked at a rate 10 percent higher than in 1980.

If I read the data definition correctly, therefore, this will explain why the log normal and Atkinson measures should have picked up more disequalization in the United States, but they did not. What is the answer to this riddle?

The answer, I believe, is found in the Appendix to the chapter and reveals an important measurement bias. Owing to issues of confidentiality, the authors tell us that the census 'limits the level of income which is disclosed on data files' – to $50 000 in 1979 and $100 000 in 1986. For other countries, particularly Sweden, there were no outer limits in the data file. The authors chose to 'censor' the data by excluding the lowest and highest 1 percentiles, except for the United States at the top.

I have not worked through all of the biases because I do not quite understand why this decision was made. But it did ring alarm bells and suggest to me that the results may be overly influenced by this decision. If the United States is truncated at the top 1 percent, yet all over $100 000 are coded the same, you miss vast inequalities between the top 1 percent and the top 10 percent of the income distribution. And this is precisely where most of the disequalization of income has occurred in the 1980s.

I do know that the dataset do not pertain to the authors' interpretation. Whenever they move from description to analysis, their reference point is blue collar production workers or service employees. For example, after showing their descriptive results, the authors ascribe growing earnings inequalities to an overabundance of low-paying, low-productivity jobs, or to technological change that has somehow produced this inequality. But this is not what is driving the dataset. The extreme inequality and lack of congruity between high paid salaried executives and ordinary employees is what the data are picking up. And in the 1980s the growth in corporate salaries in the United States was particularly striking. Moreover, I frankly do not understand the theoretical link between these developments – if they are empirically valid – and growing earnings inequality. What we have here is data that are not cleansed sufficiently, in my view, to come to any conclusion in the first instance. And in the second instance, we have empirical results in search of a theory. I would have preferred a more thorough presentation of alternative hypotheses derived from different theories and then a test of the results with a dataset appropriate to the question posed.

It is essential to look at and define precisely this one variable in the analysis. Let this be a warning to others who venture into the earnings distribution thicket – that their results are colored by the insufficient clarity of the data and their interpretations are likewise frequently unrelated to the empirical analysis.

Now let me turn to some other issues mentioned either obliquely or as throw-aways in the chapter. The first of these is the so-called supply-side explanation having to do with baby-boomer demographics or larger numbers of women in the laborforce. First, the point about larger numbers of women in the laborforce should have nothing to do with earnings differentials unless women are paid systematically less than men – which they are. However, this still begs the question – because then one must ask why women are paid systematically less than men. Is it because of lower marginal revenue products or discrimination, or something else? Another analysis is required to sort out this problem. In any event, this a moot point because the chapter deals only with male wage and salary earners.

As to the baby boom issue, the authors are relying on a possible demographic shift explanation that had already run its course by the 1980s. The baby-boomers had caused a distortion in the 1970s, but not in the 1980s. For example, the civilian laborforce grew by 2.8 percent per year in the 1970s. Compared with a rate of growth per year in the 1960s of only 1.7 percent. In the 1980s the yearly rate of growth in the laborforce is back to the pre-boomer rate of 1.7 percent per year. In 1980, 62 percent of the laborforce was in the 25–54-year-old cohort. But it increased in the 1980s to 67 percent in 1985 and 69 percent in 1988. So the metaphor of the baby-boomers moving through the economy like a boa constrictor swallowing a mongoose still holds, only in the 1980s the bulging mongoose moved further toward the tail of the snake. (The European baby boom, incidentally, lagged ours by nearly ten years, so the demographic bulge in their laborforce showed up in the 1980s.)

This leads me to my final point stimulated by this chapter. I am delighted to have international comparisons to look at in terms of the relationship between growth, employment, and equality–inequality. I am afraid, however, that neither Keynesians nor supply-siders would be absolved by the results of this chapter. There seem to be no clear relationships between either degrees of inequality or changes in inequality and economic growth or employment. If a finer statistical analysis could produce an answer, I would be interested in it.

But of considerable importance is what the 1980s provide in terms of an opportunity to assess this problem. In the past decade distributions changed in the industrial countries. Such a development – however one views its impact on modern society – enables us to look at the problem dynamically without being locked into previous comparative international analyses that simply looked at the static cross-section at one point in time. Pooling time series and cross-section data may enable us to learn more about changing distributions and economic outcomes.

The authors have prepared the ground for such analyses and I encourage them and others to pursue it further. But I would urge the authors and others working on this material to be bolder and more adventurous in their pursuit of an answer to this question of why income distributions have disequalized in all the industrial countries in the 1980s when they had remained unchanged from 1948 to 1980.

In the first instance, this result flies in the face of Simon Kuznets' famous proposition that incomes become more equal as economies mature. This suggests going back to his work as the intellectual base line for an analysis of the Luxembourg dataset.

In the second instance, the radical changes in the economic atmosphere of the 1980s cannot be ignored: supply-side and monetarist economic policies, privatization, deregulation, and changes in tax structures. Nor can we ignore the institutional changes in markets that propelled an integrated global financial system to center stage and prompted the growth of 'Rentier Capitalism' in all of the industrial countries, to one degree or another.

All this is confirmation of the importance of this chapter, as seen by the thought trails it has stimulated. There is a rich vein of gold here and worthy of research prospecting.

5 International Comparison of Household Inequalities Based on Microdata With Decompositions

Sourushe Zandvakili*

5.1 INTRODUCTION

There is growing evidence that households are paying more attention to levels of economic well-being beyond their own national boundaries. This is partly due to the increased interdependence of the international community and partly due to the increased mobility of labor across national boundaries as compared with two or three decades ago. Dramatic improvements in communications have also contributed to the process. Consequently, the level of economic well-being of one population relative to those of other nations is of interest from a policy perspective; policy-makers can learn from the policies and practices of other nations. An international comparison of income inequality is a first step towards this goal.

In the past, most researchers have relied upon published, aggregated data for comparative purposes. This approach has several weaknesses. First, aggregation results in a loss of information and limits the methodology that can be employed to measure inequality. Second, the method of aggregation varies across countries, resulting in a lack of comparability of official statistics. These, and other difficulties suggest that comparisons based on published, aggregated data, will be distorted (O'Higgins, Schmaus and Stephenson, 1985). It is only recently that comparable sets of micro data have become available from a number of countries. These data have allowed valid comparisons of economic inequality in several countries, and have enabled a number of interesting policy issues and problems to be addressed.

The measurement and comparison of income inequality in several countries involve a number of problems, including: the appropriate measure of income (disposable income, gross income, non-cash income, etc.); the economic unit whose income is to be measured (the individual, family or household); the weight to be attached to each individual within the economic unit (should total income, income per capita or income per adult equivalent be used?); purchasing power parity across countries; and the choice of inequality index. This chapter emphasizes the usefulness, for the purpose of making international comparisons of income inequality, of the decomposability property of certain inequality measures. Indices with this property can be used to decompose overall inequality into 'between' and 'within' group components according to attributes chosen by the researcher. This will help the researcher identify sources of inequality, which in turn will assist policy-makers in allocating resources to reduce inequality. Furthermore, the success of such allocations can be gauged by comparing decompositions before and after policy has been put into effect.

Policy issues which can be addressed using decomposable inequality indices estimated with comparable sets of microdata include: the role of the welfare state (as it exists in Scandinavian countries) vs. limited social protection (as in the United States and Canada) in controlling inequality; the effect of demography on income distribution; differences in economic systems and economic well-being; and the redistributive effect of taxes and transfers. The need to address these issues is currently pressing since social and economic change is taking eastern and western Europe by storm.

This chapter begins, in Section 5.2, with a brief review of the Generalized Entropy family of measures and their usefulness. Then follows a description of the Luxembourg Income Study (LIS) datasets, which are employed in the empirical study. Overall inequality in each of the twelve countries is computed using indices from the Generalized Entropy family of measures. These overall inequality indices are decomposed according to household size as well as age, gender, education, and ethnicity of the household head in Sections 5.3 through 5.8. Section 5.9 presents the basic conclusions of the analysis.

5.2 THE MEASUREMENT APPROACH

A variety of inequality indices can be found in the income inequality literature. It is natural to expect that, given a set of data, two inequality measures will disagree on the degree of measured inequality. This forces us to evaluate measures of inequality in terms of the properties they satisfy. Although there is no unique rule for the selection process, there appears to be agreement that the inequality measure should satisfy a number of fundamental welfare axioms. The axioms are: (i) symmetry (inequality does not change if agents i and j trade incomes); (ii) homogeneity (proportional changes in the incomes of all agents does not alter inequality; (iii) the population principle (inequality depends on relative density as opposed to absolute density); and (iv) the Pigou–Dalton principle of transfer (a transfer from one agent to another with less income causes inequality to fall). In addition to the above axioms, Theil (1967) advocated an *additive decomposability* property. This property states that overall inequality equals 'between group' inequality plus a weighted average of 'within group' inequality. The more recent axiomatic treatment of inequality measures are demonstrated in Bourguignon (1979), and Shorrocks (1980). Subsequently, the Generalized Entropy family of measures were shown to satisfy all of the above axioms (Cowell and Kuga, 1981).

Let Y_i denote the income of household and $Y^*_i = Y_i / \sum_{j=1}^{n} Y_j$ be the income share of household $i = 1, \ldots, N$. Measures of inequality in the Generalized Entropy family have the form:

$$I_\gamma (Y) = \sum_i [(NY^*_i)^{1+\gamma} - 1] / N\gamma (\gamma + 1) \qquad \gamma \neq 0, \text{ or } -1 \qquad (5.1)$$

$$= \sum_i Y^*_i \log (NY^*_i) \qquad\qquad \gamma = 0 \qquad (5.2)$$

$$= \sum_i N^{-1} \log (1/NY^*_i) \qquad\qquad \gamma = -1 \qquad (5.3)$$

The choice of γ determines the sensitivity of the measure to different portions of the income distribution. For example, I_0 and I_{-1}, which are the well known Theil (1967) information measures, differ in that the former is more sensitive to lower incomes than the latter. This family of measures satisfies the suggestion by Atkinson (1970) and others that every inequality measure must imply a social welfare function (SWF). Thus, our choice of γ demonstrates the 'degree of inequality aversion' given by the underlying SWF. For values of $\gamma < 0$ the Generalized Entropy measure is ordinarily equivalent to the family of measures proposed in Atkinson (1970).

The differences in the nature of decomposability for these measures also sets these measures apart from each other. Let there be G sets (groups) of households, $S_1, \ldots, S_g$, such that there are N_g households in S_g, ($g = 1, \ldots, G$ and $\sum_g N_g = N$). If Y_g is the income share of S_g, then the decomposition of I_0 as shown in Theil (1967) is given by:

$$I_0 (Y) = \sum_{g=1}^{G} Y_g \log \frac{Y_g}{N_g/N} + \sum_{g=1}^{G} Y_g [\log N_g - H_g (Y)] \qquad (5.4)$$

where $H_g (Y)$ is the entropy of group g for all $i \in S_g$. The first term given in (5.4) is 'between group' inequality and the second term is a weighted average of the 'within group' inequalities. This type of decomposition is most useful when the incidence of inequality among the subgroups of the population based on factors such as age, gender, and education is of interest. Theil's I_1 (second measure) is different from I_0 (first measure) in that the 'within group' term is weighted by groups' population shares rather than their income shares. The decomposition of I_{-1} is preferred to that of I_0 in that groups' income shares are sensitive to distributional changes in the latter case whereas the former is based on population shares. This point has been established in Shorrocks (1980).

5.3 OVERALL OBSERVATIONS

For computation purposes, datasets from the Luxembourg Income Study (LIS) are employed. LIS has gathered and organized sets of microdata for several countries with some common standards, definitions, concepts and structures in order to enable comparative analyses. The most important task of LIS has been one of gathering detailed information on income sources. Although other variables have been gathered, in our view, income seems to be the richest variable in the LIS datasets. The datasets vary in size and in the time period to which they pertain (Smeeding, Schmaus and Allegreza, 1985). The countries used in this study are Canada (1981), the United States (1979), Israel (1979), the United Kingdom (1979), France (1979), Australia (1981), Germany (1981), Sweden (1981), Switzerland (1982), the Netherlands (1983), Italy (1986), and Poland (1986). The data sets are intended to be comprehensive with respect to household population. However, the

German dataset excludes families headed by foreign nationals, thus some 8 percent of the population are left out. Also, Israel covers only 90 percent of households, and the rural population is excluded. The dataset for the United Kingdom is unweighted to adjust for the nonresponse within the sample. The dataset for the United States has a top-coding of $50 000. This is particularly important since some measures are more sensitive to the top portion of the distribution than others.

Although data for individuals, families, and households are provided, this study only focuses on the latter. We believe that economic units pool their incomes together, and this behaviour makes the household a better representative of their economic well-being. Furthermore, definitions of what constitutes a family are different from country to country based on different social and cultural norms. It should be noted that the choice of equivalence scale for households generally effects measured inequality. Buhmann, Rainwater, Schmaus and Smeeding (1989) provided a good sensitivity analysis for a range of such scales. The results of their analysis indicate that choice of equivalence scale can sometimes affect inequality and thus rankings of countries. However, for simplicity, in this study we make adjustments for the household size by using Per Capita Household Income (PCHI). We have taken a 30 percent random sample of households from each of the United States, Canada, and Australia; 50 percent random sample from each of France, Sweden, Italy, and Poland. In the case of Israel, the Netherlands, the United Kingdom, Germany and Switzerland the entire LIS dataset was used. Households with nonpositive incomes were excluded because some inequality measures are not defined with nonpositive income values. This could understate our inequality results, especially for Germany where the dataset contains a large number of households with zero and negative income.

There are many studies in the literature which compare overall inequality between nations. The strength of these studies rests upon the method used to measure inequality. Although some have used theoretically sound measures, they have not utilized the decomposability property. In Table 5.1, inequality based on four different choices of γ (-2.0, -1.0, -0.5, and 0.0) and rankings based on these four values are reported. Our choice of γ covers a wide range of measures for sensitivity purposes. It is evident from Table 5.1 that the choice of inequality measure will determine our perception of inequality in each country and among them. For example, the United States has the largest inequality based on $\gamma \leq -1.0$, but its ranking changes to fourth with

$\gamma = -0.5$ and 0.0. Australia ranks anywhere from second to seventh depending on one's choice of γ. The United States, France, Switzerland, Canada, Australia, and Israel report some of the highest inequality. Generally, Sweden, Germany, the United Kingdom, and Poland report the lowest inequality with $\gamma < -2.0$. Further generalizations about rankings are difficult to make. They do not provide detailed information about the breakdown of inequality among the population in a given country, and one needs to look at the decompositions in order to learn about the observed differences, based on characteristics of the population, on the one hand, and differences which are free of such features, on the other.

Table 5.1 Ranking of nations by inequality, Generalized Entropy measures based on per capita household income

Country	$\gamma = -2.0$	$\gamma = -1.0$	$\gamma = -0.5$	$\gamma = 0.0$
United States	1.0040 (1)	0.2483 (1)	0.2191 (4)	0.2121 (4)
Australia	0.5215 (2)	0.2025 (6)	0.1837 (7)	0.1800 (7)
Canada	0.3899 (3)	0.2106 (5)	0.1954 (5)	0.1941 (6)
Switzerland	0.3857 (4)	0.2216 (4)	0.2294 (2)	0.2669 (1)
France	0.3509 (5)	0.2335 (2)	0.2322 (1)	0.2563 (2)
Netherlands	0.3184 (6)	0.1871 (8)	0.1725 (8)	0.1699 (8)
Israel	0.2683 (7)	0.2238 (3)	0.2265 (3)	0.2493 (3)
Sweden	0.2458 (8)	0.1575 (9)	0.1449 (9)	0.1403 (11)
Italy	0.2304 (9)	0.1894 (7)	0.1900 (6)	0.2051 (5)
Germany	0.1832 (10)	0.1408 (11)	0.1376 (11)	0.1407 (10)
United Kingdom	0.1828 (11)	0.1416 (10)	0.1403 (10)	0.1443 (9)
Poland	0.1516 (12)	0.1261 (12)	0.1228 (12)	0.1242 (12)

5.4 LIFE-CYCLE AND INCOME INEQUALITY

The decomposable inequality indices employed in Table 5.1 can provide further information about inequality in a given country and about observed differences in inequality between countries. In this section inequality is decomposed according to age of the household head. Six age categories are employed: under 25, 25–34, 35–44, 45–54, 55–64, and 65 years of age and older. This is done to detect differences between households in different age groups due to the life-cycle patterns, and differences among households in the same age group, which are free from such patterns. Looking at the 'between group' and 'within group' components of inequality in each of the twelve countries given in Table 5.2, it is evident that the between group component is not a

Table 5.2 International comparison of inequalities, Generalized Entropy measures based on per capita household income by age of head of household

Country	Choice of γ	Overall	Between	Within	U25	25–34	35–44	45–54	55–64	65+
USA	−2.0	1.0040	0.0054	0.9990	1.4407	0.5663	2.5813	0.3876	0.5683	0.4379
1979	−1.0	0.2483	0.0055	0.2429	0.2749	0.2516	0.2651	0.2157	0.2442	0.2155
	−0.5	0.2191	0.0055	0.2136	0.2242	0.2249	0.2330	0.1924	0.2115	0.1971
	0.0	0.2121	0.0056	0.2067	0.2064	0.2177	0.2305	0.1848	0.2008	0.1962
Sample size		4468			453	1082	769	667	634	863
Australia	−2.0	0.5215	0.0060	0.5156	1.8126	0.6647	0.3625	0.2534	0.4744	0.1437
1981	−1.0	0.2025	0.0059	0.1967	0.2427	0.2590	0.2211	0.1684	0.1709	0.1096
	−0.5	0.1837	0.0058	0.1780	0.1869	0.2256	0.2084	0.1557	0.1560	0.1117
	0.0	0.1800	0.0057	0.1743	0.1644	0.2139	0.2108	0.1525	0.1545	0.1186
Sample size		4730			464	1067	952	710	703	834
Canada	−2.0	0.3899	0.0027	0.3873	1.3134	0.3286	0.3384	0.3180	0.2587	0.1757
1981	−1.0	0.2106	0.0027	0.2080	0.2838	0.2162	0.2295	0.2080	0.1839	0.1567
	−0.5	0.1954	0.0027	0.1928	0.2267	0.2002	0.2183	0.1941	0.1695	0.1608
	0.0	0.1941	0.0027	0.1916	0.2054	0.1962	0.2221	0.1948	0.1640	0.1733
Sample size		4478			434	1083	803	655	667	836
Switzerland	−2.0	0.3857	0.0077	0.3781	1.0145	0.5667	0.2501	0.4162	0.2530	0.1967
1982	−1.0	0.2216	0.0079	0.2138	0.2092	0.2029	0.2028	0.2376	0.2253	0.2069
	−0.5	0.2294	0.0080	0.2214	0.1563	0.1886	0.2060	0.2533	0.2435	0.2392
	0.0	0.2669	0.0081	0.2590	0.1331	0.1945	0.2219	0.3055	0.2926	0.3150
Sample size		6877			416	1228	1497	1254	1053	1429

France	−2.0	0.3509	0.0055	0.3454	0.2138	0.2478	0.3132	0.4100	0.5677	0.2462
1979	−1.0	0.2335	0.0053	0.2283	0.1276	0.1657	0.2561	0.2582	0.2825	0.1966
	−0.5	0.2322	0.0053	0.2270	0.1141	0.1597	0.2833	0.2466	0.2595	0.2011
	0.0	0.2563	0.0052	0.2512	0.1080	0.1643	0.3790	0.2557	0.2598	0.2186
Sample size		5454			156	1027	967	1236	948	1120
Netherlands	−2.0	0.3184	0.0073	0.3111	0.1617	0.2159	0.2553	0.5801	0.4324	0.1805
1983	−1.0	0.1871	0.0071	0.1801	0.1146	0.1714	0.1940	0.2495	0.1844	0.1310
	−0.5	0.1725	0.0070	0.1655	0.1031	0.1618	0.1930	0.2146	0.1592	0.1273
	0.0	0.1699	0.0070	0.1629	0.0956	0.1574	0.2032	0.2052	0.1512	0.1306
Sample size		4747			209	1146	1045	741	684	922
Israel	−2.0	0.2683	0.0076	0.2607	0.1757	0.2076	0.2265	0.2861	0.2950	0.3311
1979	−1.0	0.2238	0.0074	0.2165	0.1422	0.1754	0.1992	0.2186	0.2199	0.2980
	−0.5	0.2265	0.0073	0.2192	0.1338	0.1754	0.2081	0.2078	0.2107	0.3176
	0.0	0.2493	0.0073	0.2420	0.1293	0.1876	0.2420	0.2080	0.2132	0.3763
Sample size		2271			57	619	462	371	324	438
Sweden	−2.0	0.2458	0.0023	0.2436	0.2769	0.2187	0.2883	0.2760	0.2609	0.0499
1981	−1.0	0.1575	0.0023	0.1553	0.1526	0.1456	0.1835	0.1791	0.1605	0.0471
	−0.5	0.1449	0.0023	0.1426	0.1311	0.1341	0.1713	0.1636	0.1458	0.0472
	0.0	0.1403	0.0023	0.1380	0.1194	0.1296	0.1694	0.1572	0.1389	0.0481
Sample size		4754			214	879	1261	939	961	500
Italy	−2.0	0.2304	0.0011	0.2293	0.2128	0.2236	0.2694	0.2624	0.2301	0.1582
1986	−1.0	0.1894	0.0011	0.1884	0.1748	0.1798	0.2220	0.2074	0.1842	0.1433
	−0.5	0.1900	0.0010	0.1890	0.1692	0.1744	0.2252	0.2077	0.1817	0.1468
	0.0	0.2051	0.0010	0.2041	0.1703	0.1774	0.2494	0.2263	0.1916	0.1594
Sample size		3970			37	484	863	936	791	859

continued on page 88

Table 5.2 continued

Country	Choice of γ	Overall	Between	Within	U25	25–34	35–44	45–54	55–64	65+
Germany	−2.0	0.1832	0.0014	0.1819	0.2241	0.1756	0.1779	0.2065	0.1740	0.1642
1981	−1.0	0.1408	0.0014	0.1395	0.1647	0.1498	0.1419	0.1437	0.1286	0.1276
	−0.5	0.1376	0.0014	0.1363	0.1516	0.1467	0.1415	0.1421	0.1233	0.1237
	0.0	0.1407	0.0014	0.1393	0.1457	0.1487	0.1473	0.1488	0.1244	0.1250
Sample size		2787			102	499	619	565	397	605
UK	−2.0	0.1828	0.0147	0.1682	0.4953	0.2012	0.1933	0.1683	0.1277	0.0904
1979	−1.0	0.1416	0.0140	0.1276	0.1598	0.1723	0.1439	0.1256	0.1108	0.0870
	−0.5	0.1403	0.0137	0.1266	0.1454	0.1691	0.1425	0.1209	0.1083	0.0913
	0.0	0.1443	0.0135	0.1309	0.1415	0.1721	0.1471	0.1213	0.1093	0.0988
Sample size		6878			384	1401	1156	1035	1108	1794
Poland	−2.0	0.1516	0.0079	0.1438	0.1829	0.1723	0.1670	0.1469	0.1203	0.0739
1986	−1.0	0.1261	0.0080	0.1182	0.1328	0.1414	0.1355	0.1205	0.1067	0.0691
	−0.5	0.1228	0.0081	0.1148	0.1252	0.1366	0.1307	0.1161	0.1049	0.0709
	0.00	0.1242	0.0082	0.1161	0.1237	0.1373	0.1315	0.1155	0.1059	0.0758
Sample size		5284			189	1132	1240	993	853	877

major contributor to the overall inequality, except in Poland (6.3 percent), the Netherlands (3.8 percent), and the United Kingdom (9.8 percent). It appears that within each age classification there are other factors that are important as well. This observation is valid regardless of the type of inequality measure employed.

The anticipated life-cycle pattern is observed for countries such as Italy, the Netherlands, Switzerland, Poland, Sweden, Germany, Canada, the United Kingdom, and France. That is, the observed inequality eventually diminishes with age. For some, the pattern starts off with an initial rise in inequality and then, as heads of households are older, inequality tends to drop. Observed income inequality among those who are in the oldest age category (65+) is shown to be rather small, regardless of our choice of inequality measure used. Although, some similarities among most countries, regarding old age benefits are anticipated, our information is inadequate regarding other old age support.

The exceptions to the life-cycle pattern are the United States, Australia ($\gamma = -2$), and Israel. The former two report more inequality among those in the (55–64) age group than among those in the (45–54) age group. An explanation in the case of the United States could be the emergence of pensions and the option of early retirement. As for the latter case, Israel reports higher income inequality with higher age, for all $-\gamma > 0$. The factor that comes to mind as a possible contributor to this pattern is the unique nature of immigration into Israel.

5.5 GENDER AND COMPARATIVE INEQUALITY

In recent decades there have been structural changes in the labor market for women. This has occurred in most western nations. Though most nations have subscribed to particular policies in order to assure equal opportunity, the success of such policies should be evaluated in terms of the economic well-being of households headed by women. This is particularly important due to the rise in the number of such households, particularly single-parent families. In the United States, many households headed by women have dependent children and there is a large concentration of minorities among them. Government policies have brought with them a situation in which two classes of women are created: one class has benefited from these programs and policies, and the other has been left behind. The implication of these structural changes should be of interest to most policy-makers and analysts. The comparison of the observed changes in inequality based on gender across these countries will enable one to see if there is some uniformity regarding the economic progress of female-headed households among these nations.

The data based on PCHI is decomposed according to the gender of the household head for each country, and the measured inequality, based on four choices of γ, is provided in Table 5.3. The 'between group' component of the overall inequality is shown to be rather small in most countries relative to the 'within group' component. This could be given two different meanings. First, in these countries female heads of households have made some economic gains so inequality between males and females should be falling. Secondly, some women may have made economic progress, but others have been left behind. Therefore, inequality among women becomes the dominant factor. In the case of the United States, Australia, France and Canada, the second contention seems to be reasonable since the reported inequality among households headed by women is greater than those headed by men, for all values of γ. Measured inequality in countries such as Germany, Sweden, and the United Kingdom is sensitive to the choice of γ. Thus, the choice of the inequality measure influences our perception of inequality among households headed by men and women. In all other countries, inequality among female heads is smaller than that among male heads of households. The dominance of the 'within group' component for these countries indicates that there are other factors such as education, family size, etc. that need to be investigated as well.

5.6   HOUSEHOLD SIZE AND INCOME INEQUALITY

There has been a lot of discussion in recent literature about the use of equivalence scales for the purpose of inequality measurements. Our approach, using PCHI as opposed to household income is one of many normative scales. However, it is not sufficient to base our judgment on the overall measures, although scale is employed. We recommend the use of the decomposability property in order to learn about the component of inequality that can be attributed to the household size (scale) and to the component which is free of this characteristic. Five household sizes are considered, the last of which is for households of five or more individuals.

As shown in Table 5.4, the 'between group' component of the overall inequality seems to be sizable for most of the twelve countries. The Netherlands, Israel, Germany, Sweden, and Canada report the highest

Table 5.3 International comparison of inequalities, Generalized Entropy measures based on per capita household income by gender of household head

Country	Choice of γ	Overall	Between	Within	Male	Female
USA	−2.0	1.0041	0.0038	1.0005	0.8565	1.2647
1979	−1.0	0.2483	0.0037	0.2447	0.2149	0.3165
	−0.5	0.2191	0.0036	0.2155	0.1955	0.2691
	0.0	0.2121	0.0036	0.2086	0.1925	0.2556
Sample size		4468			3157	1311
Australia	−2.0	0.5216	0.0008	0.5208	0.4212	0.8296
1981	−1.0	0.2025	0.0008	0.2018	0.1903	0.2413
	−0.5	0.1837	0.0008	0.1830	0.1756	0.2098
	0.0	0.1800	0.0007	0.1793	0.1737	0.2005
Sample size		4730			3665	1065
Canada	−2.0	0.3899	0.0005	0.3894	0.2681	0.8065
1981	−1.0	0.2106	0.0005	0.2101	0.1908	0.2821
	−0.5	0.1954	0.0005	0.1949	0.1820	0.2455
	0.0	0.1942	0.0005	0.1937	0.1835	0.2349
Sample size		4478			3534	944
Switzerland	−2.0	0.3858	0.0002	0.3856	0.4000	0.3220
1982	−1.0	0.2216	0.0002	0.2215	0.2256	0.2044
	−0.5	0.2294	0.0002	0.2292	0.2368	0.1985
	0.0	0.2669	0.0002	0.2668	0.2809	0.2103
Sample size		6877			5549	1328
France	−2.0	0.3509	0.0008	0.3501	0.3488	0.3535
1979	−1.0	0.2335	0.0008	0.2327	0.2308	0.2420
	−0.5	0.2322	0.0008	0.2314	0.2251	0.2605
	0.0	0.2563	0.0008	0.2555	0.2360	0.3406
Sample size		5454			4520	934
Netherlands	−2.0	0.3184	0.0047	0.3137	0.3218	0.2578
1983	−1.0	0.1871	0.0048	0.1823	0.1878	0.1615
	−0.5	0.1725	0.0049	0.1676	0.1743	0.1459
	0.0	0.1699	0.0051	0.1648	0.1732	0.1396
Sample size		4747			3762	985
Israel	−2.0	0.2683	0.0001	0.2681	0.2709	0.2475
1979	−1.0	0.2238	0.0001	0.2237	0.2249	0.2153
	−0.5	0.2265	0.0001	0.2264	0.2282	0.2145
	0.0	0.2492	0.0001	0.2491	0.2529	0.2239
Sample size		2271			1988	283

continued on page 92

Table 5.3   continued

Country	Choice of γ	Overall	Between	Within	Male	Female
Sweden	−2.0	0.2459	0.0002	0.2457	0.2422	0.2662
1981	−1.0	0.1575	0.0002	0.1573	0.1600	0.1417
	−0.5	0.1449	0.0002	0.1447	0.1481	0.1255
	0.0	0.1403	0.0002	0.1401	0.1440	0.1188
Sample size		4754			4052	702
Italy	−2.0	0.2304	0.0006	0.2298	0.2345	0.2007
1986	−1.0	0.1894	0.0006	0.1888	0.1939	0.1624
	−0.5	0.1900	0.0007	0.1893	0.1958	0.1576
	0.0	0.2051	0.0007	0.2044	0.2138	0.1601
Sample size		3970			3330	640
Germany	−2.0	0.1832	0.0022	0.1811	0.1792	0.1849
1981	−1.0	0.1408	0.0022	0.1386	0.1384	0.1394
	−0.5	0.1376	0.0022	0.1354	0.1360	0.1336
	0.0	0.1407	0.0023	0.1384	0.1399	0.1341
Sample size		2787			2153	634
UK	−2.0	0.1828	0.0013	0.1815	0.1744	0.2001
1979	−1.0	0.1415	0.0013	0.1403	0.1424	0.1333
	−0.5	0.1403	0.0013	0.1391	0.1406	0.1340
	0.0	0.1443	0.0013	0.1431	0.1438	0.1403
Sample size		6878			5275	1603
Poland	−2.0	0.1516	0.0002	0.1514	0.1578	0.1326
1986	−1.0	0.1262	0.0002	0.1259	0.1304	0.1124
	−0.5	0.1228	0.0002	0.1226	0.1267	0.1100
	0.0	.1241	0.0002	0.1239	0.1278	0.1115
Sample size		5284			3972	1312

'between group' component. For example, for the Netherlands' 'between group' component is 36 percent of the overall inequality with $\gamma = 0$, and 22 percent with $\gamma = -2$, while Canada reports 17 percent and 8 percent respectively. This suggests that for these countries the household size is an important factor that needs to be considered for the analysis of inequality.

It appears that inequality falls as household size increases, and reaches a minimum with a household size of four. This pattern is true for most countries, especially for $\gamma < -2$ (the exceptions are Poland, Italy and France). One possible explanation could be the nature of the tax system and incentive mechanism for tax deductions, and this analysis needs to be undertaken. The second possible explanation is the life-cycle

Table 5.4 International comparison of inequalities, Generalized Entropy measures based on per capita household income by size of household

Country	Choice of γ	Overall	Between	Within	One	Two	Three	Four	Five+
USA	−2.0	1.0040	0.0371	0.9673	1.1186	1.1278	0.3951	1.4922	0.3181
1979	−1.0	0.2484	0.0330	0.2154	0.2764	0.2157	0.1822	0.1609	0.1760
	−0.5	0.2191	0.0314	0.1877	0.2365	0.1863	0.1565	0.1360	0.1563
	0.0	0.2121	0.0301	0.1821	0.2253	0.1760	0.1447	0.1265	0.1479
Sample size		4468			1332	1197	727	652	560
Australia	−2.0	0.5216	0.0332	0.4884	1.0887	0.3860	0.2466	0.2723	0.2360
1981	−1.0	0.2026	0.0307	0.1719	0.2265	0.1717	0.1467	0.1293	0.1372
	−0.5	0.1838	0.0297	0.1540	0.1918	0.1573	0.1328	0.1143	0.1243
	0.0	0.1800	0.0290	0.1511	0.1802	0.1530	0.1275	0.1092	0.1197
Sample size		4730			1360	1223	720	804	623
Canada	−2.0	0.3899	0.0385	0.3514	0.6373	0.4747	0.2091	0.1794	0.1684
1981	−1.0	0.2106	0.0352	0.1754	0.2568	0.1811	0.1433	0.1228	0.1257
	−0.5	0.1955	0.0340	0.1615	0.2259	0.1625	0.1310	0.1134	0.1178
	0.0	0.1941	0.0330	0.1613	0.2176	0.1560	0.1257	0.1095	0.1150
Sample size		4478			1116	1182	743	785	652
Switzerland	−2.0	0.3857	0.0340	0.3518	0.7228	0.2719	0.1633	0.1297	0.1590
1982	−1.0	0.2217	0.0299	0.1918	0.2151	0.2236	0.1379	0.1337	0.1484
	−0.5	0.2294	0.0283	0.2011	0.1964	0.2484	0.1472	0.1471	0.1636
	0.0	0.2669	0.0269	0.2401	0.2015	0.3141	0.1694	0.1724	0.1960
Sample size		6877			2157	2372	844	1023	481
France	−2.0	0.3509	0.0224	0.3285	0.3922	0.4188	0.2914	0.2434	0.2431
1979	−1.0	0.2335	0.0212	0.2123	0.1915	0.2537	0.2037	0.1860	0.2068
	−0.5	0.2322	0.0208	0.2114	0.1833	0.2569	0.1979	0.1868	0.2113
	0.0	0.2563	0.0204	0.2360	0.1907	0.3016	0.2060	0.2007	0.2319
Sample size		5454			1033	1518	1064	1053	786
Netherlands	−2.0	0.3184	0.0703	0.2482	0.1816	0.1393	0.3006	0.1698	0.3413
1983	−1.0	0.1873	0.0645	0.1227	0.1172	0.1058	0.1538	0.1032	0.1760
	−0.5	0.1726	0.0626	0.1100	0.1101	0.1012	0.1359	0.0968	0.1519
	0.0	0.1698	0.0612	0.1087	0.1096	0.1001	0.1300	0.0967	0.1412
Sample size		4747			976	1444	766	1059	502
Israel	−2.0	0.2683	0.0627	0.2055	0.3101	0.3003	0.1350	0.1238	0.1653
1979	−1.0	0.2239	0.0574	0.1665	0.2666	0.2401	0.1135	0.1076	0.1415
	−0.5	0.2266	0.0556	0.1710	0.2684	0.2444	0.1085	0.1058	0.1381
	0.0	0.2492	0.0542	0.1951	0.2875	0.2765	0.1065	0.1078	0.1395
Sample size		2271			246	535	344	505	641
Sweden	−2.0	0.2459	0.0347	0.2112	0.3343	0.2081	0.1806	0.1446	0.1356
1981	−1.0	0.1576	0.0315	0.1261	0.1631	0.1261	0.1158	0.1044	0.1017
	−0.5	0.1450	0.0303	0.1147	0.1400	0.1148	0.1067	0.0971	0.0949
	0.0	0.1402	0.0293	0.1111	0.1285	0.1100	0.1035	0.0937	0.0916
Sample size		4754			955	1761	868	820	350

continued on page 94

Table 5.4   continued

Country	Choice of γ	Overall	Between	Within	One	Two	Three	Four	Five+
Italy	−2.0	0.2304	0.0201	0.2103	0.2021	0.1681	0.1774	0.2053	0.2601
1986	−1.0	0.1895	0.0196	0.1699	0.1695	0.1531	0.1445	0.1856	0.2127
	−0.5	0.1900	0.0195	0.1705	0.1661	0.1576	0.1398	0.1989	0.2176
	0.0	0.2050	0.0194	0.1857	0.1694	0.1721	0.1411	0.2382	0.2473
Sample size		3970			493	945	971	967	594
Germany	−2.0	0.1833	0.0339	0.1494	0.1940	0.1978	0.1136	0.0722	0.1328
1981	−1.0	0.1409	0.0316	0.1093	0.1422	0.1305	0.0889	0.0661	0.0880
	−0.5	0.1376	0.0307	0.1070	0.1352	0.1224	0.0876	0.0660	0.0831
	0.0	0.1406	0.0299	0.1107	0.1349	0.1206	0.0906	0.0674	0.0825
Sample size		2787			693	766	564	507	257
UK	−2.0	0.1828	0.0147	0.1682	0.2553	0.1676	0.1326	0.1237	0.1132
1979	−1.0	0.1416	0.0136	0.1281	0.1647	0.1446	0.1040	0.0876	0.1019
	−0.5	0.1404	0.0131	0.1272	0.1648	0.1403	0.1011	0.0858	0.1010
	0.0	0.1443	0.0127	0.1317	0.1720	0.1401	0.1018	0.0874	0.1029
Sample size		6878			1660	2136	1094	1247	741
Poland	−2.0	0.1516	0.0131	0.1386	0.0960	0.1325	0.1468	0.1235	0.1575
1986	−1.0	0.1262	0.0123	0.1139	0.0968	0.1163	0.1153	0.1055	0.1297
	−0.5	0.1229	0.0120	0.1108	0.1012	0.1150	0.1082	0.1033	0.1260
	0.0	0.1241	0.0117	0.1125	0.1087	0.1173	0.1050	0.1050	0.1276
Sample size		5284			699	1348	1018	1150	1069

phenomenon since the first two categories consist largely of very young and very old households. Although young households do not benefit from accumulated wealth, the return on wealth accruing to older households will likely increase inequality among those smaller households. The third possible explanation could be attributed to human capital accumulation. Those households with a high degree of human capital accumulation tend to have smaller families. Those with low levels of human capital accumulation tend to have larger families and are concentrated in labor markets where wages and salaries are much more similar. If the above contention is true, the decompositions based on education should be rather significant.

5.7   HUMAN CAPITAL CONSIDERATIONS

In this section, we shall investigate the impact of investment in human capital (schooling) upon the level of earnings inequality. Individuals generally invest in human capital to acquire higher future earnings, so the contribution of education to income inequality should be of interest to most policy-makers. The decompositions according to the level of education attained by the head of household could illustrate the magnitude of this contribution, i.e., the direction of inequality as a result of human capital investment.

There are seven countries with common variables for education in the LIS datasets. In Table 5.5, decompositions based on three levels of education for the United States, Poland, Israel, Australia, the Netherlands, Italy, and Germany are provided. The three levels are: (i) less than ten years of education, (ii) between ten and twelve years of education, and (iii) thirteen years or more (including those with college degrees as well as more specialized degrees). Our decompositions reveal that although the 'within group' component is the dominant factor, the 'between group' component is rather conspicuous for the United States, Israel, the Netherlands, Italy, and Germany. Only in Poland and Australia is education's impact negligible. The highest level of contribution to the 'between group' component is reported by Israel (18.3 percent), followed by Italy (12.2 percent), the United States (8.6 percent), and the Netherlands (8.2 percent) respectively.

Looking at the measured inequality for each of the three groups, it is clear that there is no unique pattern. However, it is interesting to note that in the Netherlands and Germany the observed inequality is higher among those households with higher education levels. The opposite is noted in the United States and Poland, where lower measured inequality is reported as we move to higher levels of education, with $\gamma < -2$. It could be that in the Netherlands and Germany, experience, as well as education, is of importance and that the impact of experience is far greater than in other countries. Also, there could be some life-cycle effect with respect to higher job security which brings with it higher earnings for the older generations. Generally, for most countries with higher levels of education, we are observing higher inequality, but this could be attributed to our combining those with more than a high school degree into a single category, which is a limitation of the datasets.

5.8 ETHNICITY AND EARNING OPPORTUNITY

In most nations, it is considered desirable to provide equal opportunity to all households in the labor market. However, the labor market has imperfections which need to be corrected by public policies. One of the basic areas in which public policy has had a role to play is in

Table 5.5   International comparison of inequalities, Generalized Entropy measures based on per capita household income by education of household head

Country	Choice of γ	Overall	Between	Within	LT 10	10–12	13+
USA	−2.0	1.0039	0.0223	0.9820	0.6789	1.0690	1.0040
1979	−1.0	0.2483	0.0216	0.2268	0.2485	0.2226	0.2189
	−0.5	0.2189	0.0214	0.1977	0.2165	0.1960	0.1936
	0.0	0.2122	0.0213	0.1909	0.2083	0.1880	0.1877
Sample size		4468			950	1883	1635
Australia	−2.0	0.5215	0.0055	0.5161	0.3572	1.4605	0.4412
1981	−1.0	0.2025	0.0054	0.1972	0.1852	0.2415	0.1969
	−0.5	0.1837	0.0054	0.1783	0.1723	0.2022	0.1778
	0.0	0.1800	0.0054	0.1747	0.1718	0.1887	0.1732
Sample size		4730			2048	560	2122
Netherlands	−2.0	0.3172	0.0149	0.3024	0.2694	0.3131	0.5897
1983	−1.0	0.1861	0.0153	0.1709	0.1599	0.1808	0.2272
	−0.5	0.1715	0.0156	0.1560	0.1470	0.1640	0.1939
	0.0	0.1688	0.0159	0.1529	0.1436	0.1584	0.1833
Sample size		4579			2713	1617	249
Israel	−2.0	0.2682	0.0426	0.2256	0.2073	0.1919	0.2346
1979	−1.0	0.2238	0.0411	0.1828	0.1808	0.1635	0.2074
	−0.5	0.2264	0.0406	0.1859	0.1802	0.1641	0.2180
	0.0	0.2493	0.0404	0.2089	0.1874	0.1747	0.2512
Sample size		2271			861	752	658
Italy	−2.0	0.2716	0.0223	0.2494	0.2482	0.1994	0.2047
1986	−1.0	0.1933	0.0236	0.1697	0.1662	0.1801	0.1742
	−0.5	0.1904	0.0244	0.1662	0.1594	0.1865	0.1733
	0.0	0.2015	0.0253	0.1761	0.1615	0.2070	0.1812
Sample size		3946			2847	856	243
Germany	−2.0	0.1832	0.0099	0.1734	0.1655	0.1694	0.2222
1981	−1.0	0.1408	0.0103	0.1306	0.1234	0.1351	0.1738
	−0.5	0.1376	0.0105	0.1271	0.1197	0.1314	0.1664
	0.0	0.1407	0.0107	0.1299	0.1212	0.1335	0.1664
Sample size		2787			1902	634	251
Poland	−2.0	0.1516	0.0023	0.1494	0.1482	0.1501	0.1411
1986	−1.0	0.1261	0.0024	0.1238	0.1257	0.1240	0.1131
	−0.5	0.1228	0.0024	0.1204	0.1240	0.1200	0.1078
	0.0	0.1242	0.0025	0.1217	0.1276	0.1205	0.1060
Sample size		5284			2097	2775	412

providing better labor market access to national minorities as well as immigrants. There are many ways that this problem can be addressed, and each country is unique in the nature of its problem. In the United States, this is the problem of white and nonwhite, while in Israel, Switzerland, Australia and Canada, immigration policies affect equality of opportunity. Thus in the latter countries, the decomposition is based on immigrant Group B and nonimmigrant Group A.

The results in Table 5.6 highlight the decompositions. It is evident that the average 'within group' component constitutes a larger proportion of the overall inequality. However, in Switzerland and the United States the 'between group' component is significant. Looking at the 'within group' inequality, it is interesting to note that in Switzerland and Canada, inequality among nonimmigrants is greater than that among immigrants, while in Israel and Australia the contrary holds true. The nature of public policies, immigration policies, as well as the composition of immigrants are areas that need to be analyzed, if one is to have an understanding of the results. For example, Canada's immigration policy is set up as such that skilled and educated individuals have a better chance of being admitted into the country. Consequently, the inequality among the immigrants is smaller. In contrast, Switzerland's immigration policy targets those in the semi-skilled category for jobs that in most cases a Swiss will not take. Inequality among this category of immigrants is small as well. However, in Switzerland we observe an inequality differential between immigrants and nonimmigrants, while in Canada, such a differential is not observed. This provides a partial explanation as to why many emigrants desire to go to Canada, but not to Israel or Australia. In these two countries inequality among immigrants is higher. In the case of Israel the nature of immigration has other important dimensions as well. In Israel, there is homogeneity based on religion, without labor market considerations. Thus, the variance in earnings capacity is substantial. In Australia, the same pattern holds for different reasons. It appears that Australia is competing with Canada and the United States for immigrants, and because of its location it cannot be as selective. Consequently, immigrants with different skill levels are allowed into the country, which will result in higher earnings differentials among them.

Table 5.6 International comparison of inequalities, Generalized Entropy measures based on per capita household income by ethnicity of household head

Country	Choice of γ	Overall	Between	Within	Group A	Group B
USA	−2.0	1.0040	0.0089	0.9953	1.0597	0.7308
1979	−1.0	0.2483	0.0082	0.2401	0.2254	0.3024
	−0.5	0.2191	0.0079	0.2112	0.2008	0.2655
	0.0	0.2121	0.0076	0.2045	0.1958	0.2564
Sample size		4468			3615	853
Australia	−2.0	0.5216	0.0001	0.5216	0.4900	0.6077
1981	−1.0	0.2025	0.0001	0.2025	0.1991	0.2122
	−0.5	0.1837	0.0001	0.1837	0.1817	0.1892
	0.0	0.1800	0.0001	0.1800	0.1785	0.1841
Sample size		4730			3490	1240
Canada	−2.0	0.3899	0.0001	0.3898	0.3989	0.3347
1981	−1.0	0.2106	0.0001	0.2105	0.2134	0.1939
	−0.5	0.1954	0.0001	0.1953	0.1978	0.1814
	0.0	0.1942	0.0001	0.1941	0.1963	0.1817
Sample size		4478			3813	665
Switzerland	−2.0	0.3858	0.0032	0.3825	0.3573	0.4921
1982	−1.0	0.2216	0.0030	0.2186	0.2243	0.1835
	−0.5	0.2294	0.0030	0.2264	0.2339	0.1755
	0.0	0.2669	0.0029	0.2641	0.2743	0.1842
Sample size		6877			5921	956
Israel	−2.0	0.2638	0.0011	0.2627	0.1718	0.2872
1979	−1.0	0.2186	0.0011	0.2175	0.1436	0.2404
	−0.5	0.2195	0.0011	0.2184	0.1406	0.2439
	0.0	0.2380	0.0011	0.2369	0.1441	0.2690
Sample size		2240			529	1711

5.9 CONCLUSIONS

Using the LIS datasets, income inequality among households in each of twelve countries was measured and analyzed. A class of Generalized Entropy measures were employed to demonstrate the robust nature of our results. It has been shown that we need to look beyond the overall inequality within each country to determine the nature and source of inequality. The decomposability property of the Generalized Entropy measures allows for this to be achieved. Decompositions by family size, and by age, gender, education and ethnicity of the household head were conducted, and it was revealed that family size and education were rather influential components of overall inequality. Furthermore, interesting patterns were detected within each group. Although the 'between group' inequality based on age, gender, and ethnicity was shown to be rather small, very important differences and similarities were observed for each group across countries. The usual lifecycle pattern was observed for some countries and not others. The decomposition by gender suggests that the situation of female heads of households varies across countries and that policies to enhance their labor market opportunities have had differential impacts in different countries. It has been shown that inequality does not fall with more education in some of these countries. Without the decompositions, these observations would not have been possible, but further analysis of these patterns requires knowledge of institutional arrangements. We conclude with some words of caution. Our results are accurate only to the extent that the datasets are representative of their respective populations and that the datasets in the LIS are for different years.

Note

* Helpful comments from Alan Blinder, Joan Rodgers and other participants at the conference on 'Aspects of Distribution of Wealth and Income' are appreciated. I would like to thank John Coder of the Luxembourg Income Study Program. Support from The Jerome Levy Economics Institute of Bard College and a Taft Research Grant at the University of Cincinnati is acknowledged.

References

Atkinson, A. B. (1970) 'On the Measurement of Inequality,' *Journal of Economic Theory*, **11**: 244–63.

Bourguignon, F. (1979) 'Decomposable Income Inequality Measures,' *Econometrica*, **47** (2): 901–20.

Buhmann, B., L. Rainwater, G. Schmaus and T. Smeeding (1989) 'Equivalence Scales, Well-Being, Inequality, and Poverty: Sensitivity Estimates Across Ten Countries Using the Luxembourg Income Study (LIS) Database,' *Review of Income and Wealth*, **35**: 115–42.

Cowell, F. A. and K. Kuga (1981) 'Inequality Measurement: An Axiomatic Approach,' *European Economic Review*, **15**: 287–305.

Kakwani, N. (1984) 'The Relative Deprivation Curve and its Applications,' *Journal of Business and Economic Statistics*, **2**: 384–405.

Maasoumi, E. (1987) 'Information Theory,' in J. Eatwell, M. Milgate and P. Newman (eds), *The New Palgrave: A Dictionary of Economics* (London: Macmillan).

O'Higgins, M., G. Schmaus and G. Stephenson (1985) 'Income Distribution and Redistribution: A Microdata Analysis For Seven Countries,' Working Paper, **3**, LIS/CEPS (Walferdange, Luxembourg).

Rosen, S. (1984) 'Comment' on N. Kakwani, 'The Relative Deprivation Curve and its Applications,' *Journal of Business and Economic Statistics,* **2**.

Shorrocks, A. F. (1980) 'The Class of Additively Decomposable Inequality Measures,' *Econometrica,* **48**: 613–25.

Smeeding, T. M., G. Schmaus and S. Allegreza (1985) 'Introduction to LIS,' Working Paper, **1**, LIS/CEPS (Walferdange, Luxembourg).

Theil, H. (1967) *Economics of Information Theory* (Amsterdam: North-Holland).

Comment

Alan S. Blinder

The Luxembourg Income Study (LIS) is a wonderful idea. I say this because the only way to impute meaning to a statement like the 'Gini ratio for US family incomes in 1989 was 0.392' is to compare it with other times or other places. The LIS gives us the opportunity to do the latter, and we should be grateful to Sourushe Zandvakili for doing just that in a wide variety of ways.

Did I say variety? Though the paper is short, a discussant quickly falls victim to information overload because Zandvakili presents four different inequality measures for twelve different countries and looks at the effects of five different characteristics. That's 240 income distributions in all! Clearly, I must be selective. I will begin with a few minor quibbles about the analysis and then discuss some of the findings.

First let me say that the Theil Entropy measures are rather funny objects; they need a bit more interpretation than they get in this Chapter – especially the parameter γ. Setting $\gamma = 0$ gives the usual – and most understandable – Theil entropy measure:

$$\sum_i Y_i \log (NY_i)$$

Sen (1973, p. 36) once wrote that 'the average of the logs of the reciprocals of income shares, weighted by income shares, is not a measure that is exactly overflowing with intuitive sense.' A useful starting point, I would have thought, would be to draw some Lorenz curves. In many cases, they will not cross; so we would not have to worry about mystifying inequality measures to rank distributions. Of course, some Lorenz curves will cross, so the Lorenz criterion alone will not answer all questions about rankings.

A second minor quibble relates to the choice of *per capita* household income as the income concept. I would have thought using an adult-equivalent scale and basing shares on household income *per adult equivalent* makes more sense. The question, of course, is: would making such a change alter the results? Both previous research and Zandvakili's results on household size (see below) suggest that it might.

A third problem is that the rankings of countries look a bit odd. To illustrate, consider the rankings in Table 5.1 for $\gamma = 0$. Of Zandvakili's twelve countries, nine were also studied by Coder, Rainwater and Smeeding (1989), who obtained rather different rankings. Ordered from most to least unequal, the two sets of rankings are:

Zandvakili	*Coder et al.*
Switzerland	USA
Israel	Australia
USA	Netherlands
Canada	Canada
Australia	Switzerland
Netherlands	UK
UK	Israel
Germany	Germany
Sweden	Sweden

Obviously, the two sets of rankings – from the same data source! – do not correspond. Which is correct? Is the Swiss income distribution the most unequal (as Zandvakili's rankings) or near the middle of the pack (as in Coder *et al.*'s)? And what about the high degree of inequality in Israel that Zandvakili finds? I do not know how to reconcile the two sets of figures, but I doubt that differences in the recipient unit (households for Zandvakili, families for Coder *et al.*) can explain the disparities.

Turning now to the results, the most general finding is that the between group component of inequality is always quite small. This is hardly surprising. Every study of income inequality that I know of, and indeed almost every study of individual differences in *anything*, finds this to be true. The reason is simply that unexplained individual idiosyn-cracies are large relative to anything social scientists can explain with available data. The following back-of-the envelope calculation illustrates the point in a way that is perhaps easier to understand than the Theil measures.

Think of a linear regression model for individual incomes:

$$\log y_i = X_i b + u_{i'}$$

where X is vector of explanatory factors, b is a vector of estimated coefficients, and u is an individual-specific residual. It follows immediately that:

$$\mathrm{var}(\log y) = (\mathrm{var}(Xb) + \mathrm{var}(u)).$$

The R^2 of such a regression is the ratio of var (Xb) to var $(\log y)$ and is always below 0.5 in studies of individual incomes (usually way below). Let us suppose that R^2 is 0.5 and that X consists of ten mutually exclusive orthogonal regressors, each of which contributes one-tenth of the explained variance. Then the ratio of the 'between group' variance to the total variance of (log) incomes is not more than 0.05. So, empirically speaking, the 'between group' variance is not likely to be higher than 5 percent of the total variance.

Zandvakili's numbers are based on Theil Entropy measures, not a simple intuitive regression framework like this. So how can we tell whether the 'between group' inequality he finds is 'small' or 'large'? The following example will help us develop a metric. The population consists of two groups with five people in each. Each group has an income distribution that resembles quintile shares in the United States, but group 2 is twice as rich as group 1. Thus the ten incomes are:

Group 1	Group 2
5	10
10	20
15	30
25	50
45	90

Any observer would, I think, agree that 'between group' inequality is quite large in this example – much larger than, say, the black – white or male – female differences in the United States. Theil's Entropy measure (with $\gamma = 0$) for this ten-person distribution is 0.295, which breaks down as follows:

Total inequality	0.295
Between groups	0.057
Within groups	0.238

Thus, 'between group' inequality is 19 percent of total inequality in this example. In what follows, I will focus on this ratio, which I shall simply denote as 'Between/Total'.

If we change the example to make group 2 incomes just 20 percent larger than group 1 incomes, most people would say that 'between group' inequality is modest, though not negligible. In that case, the Theil measure breaks down as follows:

Total inequality	0.243
Between groups	0.005
Within groups	0.238

Thus Between/Total = 2 percent. Keeping in mind that 19 percent connotes a large value for Between/Total while 2 percent connotes a small value facilitates interpretation of Zandvakili's tables.

When we turn to the detailed results, we immediately encounter a difficulty: as γ is varied, 'between group' inequality hardly changes but within group inequality often changes quite a lot. Hence the Between/Total ratio on which I want to focus is very sensitive to the choice of γ. To keep the discussion manageable, and also because I find $\gamma = 0$, easier to understand, I will restrict my remarks to the Theil measure with $\gamma = 0$, focus on the United States, and mention only the things I find of interest!

For age, Zandvakili finds that the Between/Total ratio is just 2.6 percent in the United States – a modest amount. Among the twelve countries, the United Kingdom displays the highest ratio, at 9.4 percent. This is much larger and raises some simple questions like: are British age–income profiles much steeper than US profiles? A look at the data would be enlightening here (and elsewhere in the chapter).

I learned something rather surprising from the results on gender. The Between/Total ratio is just 1.7 percent for the United States and is pretty trivial in all countries. For the United States, 'within group' inequality is higher among female-headed households than among male-headed households. I knew this and – enthnocentrist that I am! – had always assumed it to be true in all countries. Zandvakili's data show clearly that I was wrong. There is no general tendency for female-headed households to have either more or less inequality than male-headed households.

The first large Between/Total ratio we encounter is in Table 5.4, where Zandvakili splits the sample by household size. For the United States, 'between group' inequality is 14 percent of total inequality – which, in view of my numerical example, is quite a lot. It makes me wonder whether the use of data on household income *per capita* (rather than per adult equivalent) is giving rise to spurious inequality. Here is another case in which it would be enlightening to see group-specific means. Furthermore, the Between/Total ratio gets as high as 36 percent for the Netherlands. Knowing what it takes to produce 19 percent in the numerical example, I simply cannot believe that this is true.

'Between group' effects are also fairly large for education: 'Between/ Total is about 10 percent in the United States and as high as 16 percent in Israel. Differences by race, however, are surprisingly small in the United States (where they mean white vs. nonwhites): Between/ Total is just 3.5 percent.

But this is just a highly selective sampling of what is in the chapter. I invite each reader to examine Zandvakili's Tables 5.2–5.6 with his or her own interests (and prejudices) in mind. You will surely learn something.

References

Coder, J., L. Rainwater and T. Smeeding (1989) 'Inequality Among Children and Elderly in Ten Modern Nations: The United States in an International Context,' *American Economic Review*, **79** (**2**) (May): 320–4.
Sen, A. (1973) *On Economic Inequality* (New York: W. W. Norton).

6 Adjustment, Growth and Income Distribution in Indonesia

Erik Thorbecke*

6.1 INTRODUCTION

During the decade of the 1970s and until 1982 the growth performance of the Indonesian economy was very good, with GDP growing at 7.2 percent per annum. Oil exports provided the major engine of growth for the entire economy during that period. In addition, within agriculture, growth was fueled by the boom in paddy production which converted Indonesia from the largest rice importing country in the world to virtual self-sufficiency by the mid-1980s (paddy production increased at an annual rate of 7.1 percent between 1978–80 and 1983/4). The two oil price booms of 1973, and more particularly 1979, fueled a major expansion of the economy which lasted until the crisis. The predominant role of the oil sector is clearly revealed by recalling that earnings from crude oil and petroleum products accounted for two-thirds of all export earnings, one-fourth of total GNP and 70 percent of government domestic revenues in 1982. Oil prices peaked in 1982 and revenues from this sector started to contract, reducing drastically the basis and prospects for economic growth.

Clearly, 1982/3 represented a switching – if not a turning point – from a regime of high growth, largely fueled by oil exports, to a new regime of decelerated growth and stabilization of the economy to reduce its vulnerability to external shocks. During the adjustment period (1983-7) the growth rate of GDP fell to 3.6 percent, i.e., about half of the rate displayed in the preadjustment period. Table 6.1 shows the sectoral growth rates which prevailed in the preadjustment and in the adjustment phases, respectively.

Table 6.2 examines the changing pattern of sectoral production since 1971. Two different times series of sectoral value added, measured at respectively 1973 and 1983 market prices, are used here to reflect the enormous impact of the upward valuation of oil. For four sub-periods

Table 6.1 Growth rates of GDP and sectoral value added during the pre-
and post-1982–3 periods

	Growth rates between *1971–4 (4yr av.)* *and 1981–3 (3yr av.)*	*Growth rates between* *1981–3 (3yr av.)* *and 1987*
Agriculture, forestry & fishery of which	3.75	3.04
Food crops	[4.52]	[2.81]
Mining & quarrying	3.26	−0.88
Manufacturing	12.66	8.49
Electricity, gas & water	14.07	10.43
Construction	12.74	1.50
Wholesale, retail trade & restaurants	7.57	3.55
Transport, storage & communication	11.89	6.08
Finance, insurance, real estate & bus. services	12.33	5.04
Public administration & services	11.72	7.16
Others	2.38	3.66
GDP	7.20	3.63

Source: Thorbecke (1990), Table 1.1.

spanning the period 1971–83 relative sectoral shares are given at constant
1973 prices in row *A* and for four sub-periods spanning the period
1978 to 1987 relative sectoral shares are given at constant 1983 market prices in row *B*. Thus, for two sub-periods (1980 and 1981–3)
comparisons can be made of the effects of the oil price boom on
these relative shares. For example, in 1978–80 the share of mining at
1973 prices amounted to 10.1 percent, whereas at 1983 prices, it
amounted to 26 percent.

Table 6.2 reveals the structural transformation which Indonesia under-
went in the preadjustment period. At 1973 constant prices, the share
of agriculture in GDP declined from 40.7 percent in 1970–4 to 29.8
percent in 1981–3 while that of mining fell from 11.4 to 8 percent. In
contrast, manufacturing increased from 9.6 to 15.4 percent, over the
same timespan, and construction, transport, finance and public administration and services all displayed significant relative gains. This pattern of structural transformation is quite typical of the intersectoral
growth pattern of other countries at a similar stage of development as

Table 6.2   Shares of sectoral value added in GDP 1971-83 at constant 1973 market prices (series *A*) and 1978-87 at constant 1983 market prices (series *B*)

		1971–4 (4yr av.)	1975–7 (3yr av.)	1978–80 (3yr av.)	1981–3 (3yr av.)	1984–6 (3yr av.)
Agriculture, forestry	A	40.70	35.40	31.80	29.80	
& fishery	B			24.70	24.10	23.70
Mining & quarrying	A	11.40	11.60	10.10	8.00	
	B			26.00	20.40	18.00
Manufacturing	A	9.60	11.50	14.20	15.40	
	B			9.80	11.10	13.10
Electricity, gas	A	0.50	0.50	0.70	0.80	
& water	B			0.40	0.60	0.70
Construction	A	3.80	4.90	5.60	6.10	
	B			5.40	6.20	5.60
Wholesale, retail	A	16.80	16.60	16.40	17.30	
trade & restaurants	B			14.60	16.00	15.60
Transport, storage	A	3.80	4.40	5.40	5.80	
& communication	B			4.30	5.00	5.60
Finance, insurance,	A	3.30	4.20	4.80	5.10	
real est. & bus. serv.	B			4.50	5.40	5.70
Public administration	A	6.10	7.50	8.20	8.90	
& services	B			6.00	7.20	8.00
Others	A	4.10	3.40	3.00	2.60	
	B			4.10	4.00	4.00
GDP	A	100.00	100.00	100.00	100.00	
GDP	B			100.00	100.00	100.00

Source: Thorbecke (1990), Table 1.2.

Indonesia. What is, however, remarkable is that the pace of structural transformation appears to have slowed down to a standstill from essentially 1978–80 on, thus already before the onset of the crisis (see Series *B* at 1983 prices in Table 6.2). Except for the continuing fall in the share of mining from 26 percent in 1978–80 to 16.3 percent in 1987 and the continuing upward trend in the relative importance of manufacturing from about 10 to 14 percent over the same period, the shares of the other sectors remained very stable. Particularly noteworthy is that agriculture's share of GDP remained right around 24 percent in the four sub-periods from 1978 to 1987.

It is interesting to compare the evolution in the pattern of sectoral distribution of output to that of the sectoral distribution of employment. In the preadjustment phase the share of agriculture in employment fell from about 64 percent in 1971 to about 55 percent in 1982, while all other sectors gained in relative terms. The rising importance of the public sector is revealed by its share of employment, swelling from 10 percent in 1970 to above 15 percent in 1980. Also noteworthy is the significant increased absorption of labor into the broader trade sector (which overlaps largely with the informal sector) – its share of total employment going from 10.3 percent in 1970 to almost 15 percent in 1985. In general, the sectoral composition of employment appears to have remained quite stable during the early adjustment phase.

The structural transformation in the pattern of employment, particularly on Java, differs significantly from what was observed in two other successful rice economies, Japan and Korea, during similar stages of development, i.e., a much greater part of incremental employment was absorbed into the tertiary sector as compared to the manufacturing sector in Java than in these other two countries.

The most remarkable feature of Indonesia's policy response to the oil crisis is that it was undertaken voluntarily in a timely and balanced fashion. Through basically conservative fiscal and monetary policies, both during periods of expansion and recession, Indonesia has avoided the magnitude of external and internal imbalance that could have undermined the confidence of its creditors and forced it to obtain stabilization and structural adjustment loans under conditions imposed by the IMF and the World Bank. Instead, Indonesia has, *on its own*, adopted a sequence of trade and market liberalizing policies and contractionary budget measures that are very close to what are typically required of countries subject to IMF conditionality. However, in contrast with the great majority of developing countries where stabilization and structural adjustment conditions were the *quid pro quo* imposed from outside by the IMF and World Bank in return for emergency loans, Indonesia, from the outset, was committed to following and implementing its own independent structural adjustment strategy. The government was never placed in a situation where it was 'forced' to implement unpalatable policies and conditions designed by these organisms in a crisis atmosphere.

6.2 MACROECONOMIC DISEQUILIBRIUM AND THE STRUCTURAL ADJUSTMENT PROGRAM

Even though many initial conditions were quite favorable, in the preadjustment phase, in dampening the impact of the oil crisis on income distribution and poverty (such as the high growth rate of GDP, the rice boom and the heavy investment in rural infrastructure), two key features of the Indonesian economy made it potentially vulnerable to shocks originating abroad. First, Indonesia became significantly more dependent on foreign trade between 1970 and 1982; the share of imports to GDP (at current prices) rose from 15.8 percent to 26.3 percent and that of exports increased from 12.8 percent to 22.4 percent. Secondly, at the outset of the crisis, Indonesia suffered from an extreme reliance on non-renewable exports (oil, LNG, timber products and metals and minerals) which constituted roughly three-fourths of the value of total exports. Two other factors account for the direct, although somewhat asymmetrical, link existing between the government budget and oil prices and revenues, mainly (a) the predominant relative importance of the corporate tax on oil as the major source of total government revenues, and (b) the natural tendency on the part of the government to expand public expenditures on the upswing – as oil prices and revenues rise – and conversely, the natural reluctance to reduce planned programs on the downswing.

The origin of the macroeconomic disequilibrium which affected the Indonesian economy starting in 1982/3 is clear and direct. First, the worldwide recession of the early 1980s affected the prices and demand for traditional Indonesian exports (mainly agricultural products) adversely. Secondly, and more dramatically, earnings from oil exports dropped from $10.6 billion in 1981/2 to $7.2 billion in 1982/3. The macroeconomic indicator which probably tracked these shocks best was the ratio of the current account balance to GNP which swung from a positive 4 percent in each of the three years preceding 1981/2 to −3.6 percent that year and −8.4 percent in 1982/3. The slide in oil prices continued steadily until 1988. Indonesia's crude export price reached a peak of $34 per barrel in 1981/2 falling to $25 per barrel in 1985/6 and collapsing in 1986/7, with the average price dropping to below $13 per barrel.

The structural adjustment package which was adopted and implemented can be grouped under four broad categories, i.e., (i) exchange rate management; (ii) fiscal policy; (iii) monetary and financial policies; and, (iv) trade policy and other regulatory reforms. With regard to the first category above, Indonesia resorted to currency devaluations twice during the period under consideration. In March 1983, the Rupiah was devalued by 28 percent and full currency convertibility was established. The second devaluation occurred in 1986 when the Rupiah was again devalued by 31 percent, in direct response to the rapid decline in oil prices. The adoption of full convertibility has resulted in the unusual situation where within an economy that is under pervasive government regulations, there are virtually no controls on the international transfer of domestic capital.

In its fiscal policy the government undertook major changes in the level and pattern of, respectively, government expenditures and revenues. On the expenditure side, the government went through a major budget retrenchment effort the magnitude of which can be judged by comparing the ratio of total realized to planned expenditures during Repelita IV (1984/5 – 1988/9). On average, during this five year period, this ratio amounted to 0.79; in other words, realized expenditures fell in constant terms 21 percent short of planned expenditures (see Panel III of Table 6.3, p. 120). Furthermore, current expenditures on education and health and 'other wages and salaries' were cut relatively much less than subsidies and capital expenditures on investment projects in the various sectors. Several large public investment program were canceled or postponed while smaller labor intensive projects under the regional development INPRES Program were encouraged. In general, the observed budgetary retrenchment was successful in stabilizing the economy while sheltering the more vulnerable socioeconomic group from the unfavorable effects of drastic budget cuts.

On the revenue side, the corporate tax on oil and gas was the predominant source of central government revenues. The share of total domestic revenues generated by this corporate tax fell drastically from about 68 percent, at the outset of the oil crisis, to about 49 percent in the period 1985/6 – 1987/8, and is expected to continue to fall. In response to this rapid absolute and relative decline in the primary source of government receipts, Indonesia undertook important reforms in its tax structure. In 1984, an income tax was introduced based on three relatively low rates and a substantial personal deduction. A value added tax replaced an old sales tax in 1985 and, subsequently, a number of additional taxes were imposed. Overall, the tax reforms are progressive and have been effective in raising nonoil tax revenues from 13 percent of total domestic revenues before the crisis to above 21 percent in 1985/6 – 1987/8.

An important feature of Indonesian public finance is that the government is constitutionally obligated to maintain the equivalent of a balanced budget. This means that any excess of government expenditures over and above domestic revenues has to be financed from abroad and almost totally from project aid. It is this cumulative flow of essentially concessional aid which made Indonesian foreign debt soar from roughly $21 billion in 1983 to $41 billion in 1987.

Throughout the adjustment period the government's monetary policy has been conservative and generally based on maintaining low rates of inflation. In 1983 a major reform of the banking system was undertaken to require banks to follow market principles in attracting deposits and allocating credit. Limits on both deposit rates and lending rates were removed; sectoral credit ceilings were lifted, and subsidized liquidity credits were abandoned. A number of financial measures were adopted to encourage the development of a capital market and strengthening the financial sector by increasing competition.

With regard to trade and other regulatory reforms, Indonesia adopted during the adjustment period a series of measures that have had the effect of significantly liberalizing trade. Tariffs were reduced across the board and the number of tariff categories was significantly cut. The whole import licensing system was revamped and import restrictions were lifted from a wide range of products. Other major regulatory reforms affected the treatment of investment. Prior to 1984, all major investments required government approval. Throughout the adjustment period, Indonesia enacted a continuous stream of measures relaxing restrictions on investment and making the environment for investment more attractive. The results of this deregulation process have been encouraging, 'approved domestic investment' which amounted to Rp 3643 billion in 1982–4 (3 year average) jumped to almost Rp 15 000 billion in 1988. Likewise, 'approved foreign investment' rose from $1795 million to $4435 million over the same period.[1]

6.3 IMPACT OF ADJUSTMENTS ON SOCIOECONOMIC PERFORMANCE

The impact of adjustment policies on performance can be judged from the standpoint of (i) economic growth, the structure of production and efficiency; (ii) external equilibrium, particularly the balance of payments; (iii) fiscal and monetary equilibrium; and (iv) income distribution and poverty alleviation.

As expected the adjustment package occurred simultaneously with a pronounced deceleration of economic growth. Let us recall that the rate of growth of GDP fell by half from 7.2 percent per annum in the pre-adjustment period to 3.6 percent in the adjustment period (1982–7). On the whole, the sectoral composition and structure of production remained extremely stable during the adjustment period. In particular, agriculture's share of GDP has remained constant (at just below one-fourth) which suggests that in addition to a deceleration of aggregate growth, structural adjustment appeared to have slowed down considerably the process of structural transformation which was occurring before the crisis.

The same structural stability can be observed with regard to the sectoral pattern of employment. Here again, the employment share of agriculture remained constant between 1980 and 1985. The most noteworthy change appeared in the relative rise in the employment share of the trade sector from about 13 to 15 percent of the laborforce, reflecting labor absorption into informal activities which is another characteristic feature of the stabilization programme.

There is some evidence that the widespread deregulatory measures initiated by the government have had favorable effects on economic efficiency. A World Bank study[2] indicated that the rate of return on investment which amounted to only about 13 percent per annum in 1982–5 rose to almost 22 percent in 1986–8. This same study revealed also the total factor productivity – which is an even more comprehensive measure of the gains in macroeconomic efficiency – improved during the adjustment phase.

If external equilibrium is defined as a current account deficit just compensated by net capital inflow which can be sustained, and is consistent with the Indonesia's debt servicing capacity, then it can be argued that the country appeared to be approaching this objective. The balance of payments equilibrium was restored through a combination of reduced absorption (compressing aggregate demand through lower growth) and expenditure switching policies. The main measures which appeared to have contributed to the restoration of external equilibrium are the rephasing of large capital projects which had the effect of reducing imports of capital goods, a changing budgetary allocation away from relatively high import intensive sectors to less import dependent sectors; and the two relatively large devaluations which by raising the prices of tradeables relative to domestic goods, led to a shift away from imports towards domestic import substitutes and encouraged exports and, particularly, manufactured exports. A major achievement on the export side was the successful changing commodity composition away from nonrenewable resources exports. The proportion of nonrenewable exports in total exports declined from three-fourths throughout the 1970s and at the outset of the oil crisis to an estimated 46 percent in 1988/9. During the adjustment period Indonesia has reduced significantly its vulnerability to external shocks affecting particularly strongly oil and most of the other nonrenewable exports. It has become recognized that extreme reliance on exhaustible resources is a very precarious foundation upon which to base a development strategy which is sustainable in the long run.

Clearly, in contrast with most other developing countries, the adjustment response in the context of Indonesia was greatly facilitated by its continued access to concessional aid from a variety of sources. Its disbursed and outstanding debt roughly doubled between 1983 and 1987. This represents a very heavy burden on its public finance and its balance of payments as the ratio of debt service payments to total government expenditures rose from about 12 percent in 1983/4 to 23 percent in 1986/7 while the ratio of debt service to exports went up from 17 percent to 41 percent. Such a burden reduces greatly Indonesia's flexibility in its development policy as it relates particularly to the pattern of government current and capital expenditures. Strict fiscal conservatism will be required from now on to avoid a situation which could become unmanageable if the government were to succumb to the existing temptation to rely too heavily on the almost excessive availability of concessional loans from abroad.

In the Indonesian context, fiscal equilibrium constitutes, in some sense, the mirror image of external (balance of payments) equilibrium. Given its constitutional mandate to maintain a balanced budget, the government cannot borrow from the Central Bank to finance the deficit. Any excess of government capital expenditures over and above government savings (i.e., total domestic revenues minus total current expenditures) must be financed, essentially, through project aid or a drawdown of foreign exchange reserves. The trick is to adjust the level and pattern of government expenditures so that it (a) equals total domestic revenues plus what can safely be borrowed from abroad without straining the future debt repayment capacity, on the one hand; and (b) is consistent with external equilibrium, on the other. Financial equilibrium was restored through an increasing share of nonoil revenues following the tax reform combined with the previously mentioned budget retrenchment effort which affected particularly capital expenditures.

Monetary equilibrium entails, first, achieving rates of interest which tend to equate the supply of, and demand for loanable funds (or, in other words, the supply of savings to the demand for investment funds); and, secondly, the maintenance of a relatively stable overall price level. In both of these areas Indonesia has been successful. Since deregulation of the banking system in 1983, interest rates have been market determined. Whereas in the preadjustment phase, real interest rates were either very low or negative real deposit rates varied between 7.5 percent and 9.8 percent over the period 1984–8 while real lending rates fluctuated between 11 and 13.9 percent throughout the same period. The high rates were necessary to prevent capital flight and to expand the banks' deposit base.

To reduce inflation, the monetary authorities curtailed the expansion of reserve money but, more importantly, encouraged households to increase their holdings of money and, particularly, quasi-money (time and savings deposits) by deregulating deposit rates. This phenomenon contributed to a large increase in the financial deepening of the economy. The inflation rate has come down markedly during the adjustment period to approximately 7.5 percent per annum during the adjustment phase.

The most remarkable and surprising achievement in the Indonesian context, is the apparent reduction in the overall incidence of poverty and undernutrition during the adjustment phase. Some of the trends relating to the sectoral composition of employment and the interrelationship among employment, endowment (particularly of land) and income which prevailed during the preadjustment phase continued after 1983. A case can be made that many of these trends which were already underway before the crisis were, in fact, reinforced and accelerated by the adjustment programme. Thus, the persistence of the trend towards land consolidation (smaller number of somewhat larger farms) and increased landlessness could be observed. Micro evidence suggests strongly that off-farm jobs have become increasingly available and have largely – if not more than – offset the absolute decline in job opportunities within agriculture on Java. This would suggest that the observed adjustment process towards more viable and economically sustainable farms which was already under way on Java before the crisis had been accelerated by the structural adjustment program. Furthermore, the pull factors attracting workers to employment opportunities outside of agriculture have become stronger than the factors pushing workers out of agriculture, particularly in the light of stable and/or more likely increasing real wage rates and labor shortages observed in a sample of presumably representative villages.

The best and most comprehensive evidence available regarding the changing poverty and nutritional picture during the adjustment period is contained in two excellent recent studies based on a comparison of the Susenas tapes on household consumption for 50 000 randomly sampled households in 1984 and 1987.[3]

Three different poverty measures – the headcount ratio, the poverty

Figure 6.1   Consumption per person, 1984 and 1987

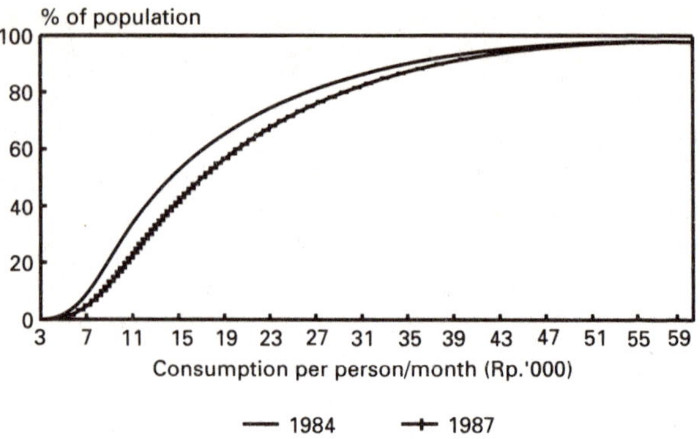

Source: Ravallion and Huppi (1989)

gap and a distributionally sensitive measure – were used to estimate the overall incidence of poverty in 1984 and 1987 and to decompose the changes in poverty between these two years. For all three measures, the incidence of poverty was found to be significantly lower in both urban and rural areas in 1987 as compared to 1984. For example, it was found that the proportion of the population below the lower selected poverty line fell from 1 in 3 in 1984 to slightly over 1 in 5 by 1987. An even more robust test of whether overall poverty declined is the, so-called, first-order dominance test which states that poverty will have unambiguously fallen between two dates if the cumulative distribution of income for the latter date lies nowhere above that for the former date, over the entire interval up to the maximum allowable poverty line. Ravallion and Huppi (1989) give the cumulative distribution of consumption (per person) for the two dates derived from the Susenas surveys and show that the 1984 distribution lies entirely above the 1987 distribution (see Figure 6.1). The same finding applies to the distribution of income per person and almost to the distribution of daily calorie intake per person. These results are highly significant as they indicate that in terms of caloric intake, consumption, and income, every percentile of the distributions was better off in 1987 than in 1984 so that all three of these welfare variables had unambiguously improved in 1987.

An essential finding of the Huppi–Ravallion (1990) study is that very significant changes occurred in the income distributions within groups. More specifically, in the great majority of employment sectors the distributions became significantly more even in 1987 than in 1984. A major complication of this finding is that in the modelling and simulation exercises which were undertaken in this project it would be misleading to assume – as many similar studies have done – that intragroup income distributions remain constant over time around a shifting mean income. This creates a problem for modellers in the sense that in the absence of an endogenous causal mechanism to generate a new income distribution, no solid basis exists for depriving income distribution resulting from different counterfactual policy scenarios.

An analysis of the evolution of government current and capital expenditures on two key social sectors affecting poor households, namely, education and health, suggests that using the first years of the adjustment period the government shielded these two social sectors which must have contributed to the above described process of poverty alleviation at least until 1987. On the other hand, the relatively large retrenchment – particularly in capital expenditures (e.g., construction of schools, hospitals, clinics and dispensaries) after 1985/6 – could well have a possible lagged negative social impact which might only be felt in the present decade. Even though Indonesia appears to have been quite successful in protecting the poor during the adjustment period up to 1987, it is too early to assess in any definitive sense the impact of adjustment policies beyond that year. This is a qualification which should be kept in mind.

6.4 AN INTEGRATED REAL AND FINANCIAL COMPUTABLE GENERAL EQUILIBRIUM MODEL OF INDONESIA

In order to undertake a quantitative evaluation of alternative adjustment policies, a computable general equilibrium model of the Indonesian economy was built. Space limitation precludes reproducing the full model in this chapter.[4] Instead its main features and characteristics are reviewed briefly.

The novelty of this CGE model is that it incorporates and integrates a real and a financial sector, and was purposely designed to explore the impact of adjustment on income distribution, as well as on many other macroeconomic and sectoral variables. In the present context, an exogenous shock (or crisis) brought about an internal and external disequilibrium in the form of a budget and balance of payments deficit, respectively. These disequilibria, in turn triggered a countervailing adjustment policy response on the part of the government.

The adjustment package which was implemented affected the whole socioeconomic system through two quite distinctive major channels. The first channel operates through the real side of the economy and captures the impact of such measures as budgetary retrenchments and changes in relative prices, following a devaluation, on the structure of production and the resulting factorial and income distribution by socioeconomic groups. Ultimately, the consumption patterns of these groups and their standards of living are influenced. Depending on the extent of the supply responsiveness of sectors producing tradeables and a whole set of institutionally determined wage and price rigidities, the full impact of these measures may only be felt in the medium to long run.

The second channel operates through the financial sector. Stabilization measures affect the prices and values of assets held by households, firms and other institutions and thereby the distribution of wealth. For example, capital flight by some agents in anticipation of a devaluation yields windfall gains to these agents if the devaluation is actually implemented. Similarly, the type of financial (credit) liberalization reform which Indonesia undertook led to a large increase in real interest rates affecting savings and shifting the financial portfolios of many institutions towards interest bearing assets. The second channel flows through financial transactions responding to different actual rates of return and expectations, and its impact on the socioeconomic system is felt in the short run.

Thus, this model of the Indonesian economy integrates a general equilibrium macroeconomic model describing the real side of the economy with a more micro-oriented financial model, explaining the behavior of the various institutions relating to changes in their portfolios of asset holdings. Both specifications contain some neoclassical features which are modified and complemented with a number of structural features to conform more closely to the underlying institutional structure and behavior of actors prevailing in Indonesia at the outset of and during the adjustment period.

The real side model consists of eight blocks of equations which determine endogenously prices; production, exports and imports; the labor market; private consumption; incomes; public finance; savings; and the real market equilibrium conditions. In turn, in the financial side model the asset holdings (portfolios) and monetary balance sheets of the various institutions (i.e., households, firms, commercial banks, the central bank, government and rest of the world) are determined endogenously and the financial market equilibrium is derived.

The first step in building a general equilibrium model integrating real and financial transactions is to capture the initial conditions prevailing at the outset of the adjustment period. This requires the specification of a financial SAM in addition to a real SAM.

The real SAM transaction matrix which was adopted as a base for and the classification scheme underlying the model is presented in Table 6.4. It can be seen that it includes the following classification of accounts: (i) *factors:* four labor categories, i.e., agriculture, manual, clerical, and professional (categories 1–4); and five kinds of capital, i.e., housing, rural capital, urban capital, public capital, and foreign capital (categories 5–9); (ii) *institutions:* eight socioeconomic household groups, i.e., agricultural employees (landless), small farmers, medium farmers, large farmers, rural nonagricultural low, rural nonagricultural high, urban low and urban high (10–17); and companies (18); (iii) *production activities-cum-commodities:* 14 different production activities are identified including two typically informal types of activities, i.e., informal trade and transport and informal services (19–32); (iv) *government expenditures:* four types of government current expenditure categories are identified (36–39) and eight types of government capital expenditures by sector of destination (40–47); (v) *other accounts:* total government current, total government capital accounts (48,49), private capital (50), rest of the world (51), and trade and transport margins (33); indirect taxes (34); and subsidies (35).

The financial SAM (not shown here) contains the same classification of households and production activities as in the real SAM. In addition, five other institutions are identified, i.e., firms (companies), commercial banks, the central bank, government, and rest of the world; and six types of assets, i.e., currency, demand deposits, time deposits, foreign deposits, equity, and foreign bonds. The financial SAM and complementary flow of funds table which were constructed as a basis for calibrating the financial sector model are an innovation in CGE modelling. Until now very few financial SAMs had been built, and to our knowledge, no CGE had been based on an integrated set of real and financial SAMs and corresponding flow of funds table.

The following steps were followed in constructing the financial SAM. First, it was assumed that national wealth consists of physical capital in all sectors and land capital, more particularly, in the agricultural sectors. (Human capital and natural resources were not included in fixed physical capital.) We could rely on existing estimates of the value of the sectoral stock of physical capital for 1980, but had to estimate the value of land capital.

Table 6.3   Realized central government expenditures and ratio of realized to planned expenditures, 1979/80 to 1988/89, constant 1980 prices, billion Rupiah

Fiscal years	1979/80	80/81	81/82	82/83
		Repelita III		
I. Total realized (constant 1980 prices)	10 626.32	11 716.10	12 538.47	11 963.25
A. Current expenditures	6 082.56	6 807.98	7 317.16	6 825.00
1. On education & health	781.60	828.73	826.68	763.18
2. Other wages & salaries	2 390.73	2 629.67	2 783.19	2 794.87
3. Other goods & services	1 298.38	1 281.88	1 487.02	1 519.61
4. Interest on debt	501.45	439.00	410.81	566.33
5. Subsidies	1 032.63	1 587.20	1 721.98	1 152.58
a. On food	164.34	281.60	201.80	0.83
b. On chemicals	868.29	1 305.60	1 520.18	1 151.75
6. Others	77.76	41.50	87.48	28.42
B. Capital expenditures	4 543.75	4 908.13	5 221.30	5 138.25
1. Debt amortization	398.68	345.80	427.93	454.08
a. Domestic	48.03	30.80	14.41	16.50
b. Foreign	350.66	315.00	413.51	437.58
2. Transfers to private	613.16	389.00	350.45	234.17
3. Investments	3 531.91	4 173.33	4 442.93	4 450.00
a. Agriculture	425.33	545.22	443.29	359.40
b. Industry & mining	446.43	414.40	628.82	642.14
c. Electric power	366.47	363.76	402.99	533.13
d. Transportation & tourism	517.51	658.32	613.61	616.12
e. Education	402.01	485.30	552.02	494.44
f. Health	157.69	183.99	217.46	182.16
g. Housing & water supply	129.93	161.20	126.22	106.20
h. General public services	255.86	338.19	352.19	318.62
i. Other expenditure programmes	830.67	1 022.93	1 106.32	1 197.78
(implicit deflator)	76.00	100.00	111.00	120.00
II. Total planned (constant 1980 prices)	9 123.55	7 737.24	7 787.77	7 954.68
A. Current expenditures	5 173.77	3 922.00	4 497.19	4 608.34
1. On education & health	671.08	547.29	513.46	507.47
2. Other wages & salaries	2 030.22	2 185.24	1 773.97	1 835.20
3. Other goods & services	1 113.80	1 031.18	949.11	973.38
4. Interest on debt	425.41	360.80	362.98	373.76
5. Subsidies	855.49	850.58	810.20	891.12
a. On food	137.19	138.06	86.87	0.70
b. On chemicals	718.30	712.52	723.33	890.42
6. Others	77.76	41.50	87.48	28.42
B. Capital expenditures	3 949.78	3 267.95	3 290.58	3 346.35
1. Debt amortization	338.23	286.86	288.59	297.37
a. Domestic	48.03	30.80	14.41	16.50
b. Foreign	290.20	256.06	274.18	279.87

83/84	84/85	85/86	86/87	87/88 *Repelita IV*	88/89*	*Yearly average* III	IV
13 463.97	12 667.25	13 917.44	12 715.58	14 432.51	14 767.05	12 061.62	13 699.97
7 070.63	6 946.38	7 795.57	7 674.62	8 167.70	7 989.49	6 820.67	7 714.75
726.83	689.02	784.50	724.45	708.34	692.46	785.41	719.75
2 966.52	2 994.48	3 674.15	3 674.10	3 649.60	3 595.11	2 713.00	3 517.49
1 586.24	1 456.94	1 547.23	1 306.05	1 219.87	1 165.13	1 434.63	1 339.04
855.51	975.16	1 039.02	1 597.34	1 909.47	3 343.37	554.62	1 552.87
920.81	809.35	519.09	288.45	619.94	237.85	1 283.04	494.93
0.00	0.00	0.00	17.08	0.00	0.00	129.72	3.42
920.81	809.15	519.09	271.37	619.94	237.85	1 153.33	491.52
14.71	21.44	231.59	84.22	60.49	55.57	49.97	90.66
6 393.35	5 720.88	6 121.87	5 040.97	6 264.80	6 777.56	5 240.95	5 985.22
690.59	839.54	987.26	1 340.66	2 483.08	3 185.59	463.42	1 767.23
21.91	25.69	12.20	0.00	20.88	20.39	26.33	15.83
668.68	813.86	975.06	1 340.66	2 462.21	3 165.19	437.09	1 751.40
172.06	190.85	134.15	122.79	118.06	106.00	351.77	134.37
5 530.70	4 690.49	5 000.46	3 577.51	3 663.66	3 485.97	4 425.77	4 083.62
365.53	533.43	339.66	207.20	509.81	473.14	427.76	412.65
1 336.13	462.82	611.90	333.71	182.54	161.03	693.58	350.40
409.59	502.54	744.68	470.82	526.34	467.59	415.19	542.39
947.64	787.73	763.72	544.66	672.00	711.88	670.64	698.00
640.45	679.06	727.18	580.64	532.92	462.85	514.84	596.53
173.14	176.52	204.82	159.77	108.36	124.45	182.89	154.78
137.15	123.57	172.40	165.01	214.94	188.65	132.14	172.92
291.69	277.41	266.34	202.44	119.90	111.41	311.31	195.50
1 229.39	1 147.40	1 169.76	903.26	796.85	784.99	1 077.42	960.45
136.00	153.00	164.00	172.16	186.79	196.13	110.06	175.21
7 830.16	13 998.09	15 691.68	17 509.65	19 601.99	21 449.66	8 086.68	17 650.22
4 530.92	7 768.11	8 650.36	9 696.75	10 796.07	12 049.43	4 546.44	9 792.15
422.70	780.00	837.05	898.28	963.99	1 034.50	532.40	902.77
1 866.75	2 973.41	3 313.94	3 820.59	4 309.57	4 778.82	1 938.28	3 839.27
971.06	1 507.64	1 705.91	1 935.45	2 171.27	2 368.33	1 007.70	1 937.72
366.21	1 334.14	1 604.92	1 695.94	1 845.64	2 219.46	377.63	1 740.02
889.50	1 150.60	949.11	1 261.85	1 444.53	1 593.78	859.38	1 279.97
0.00	0.00	0.00	0.00	0.00	0.00	72.56	0.00
889.50	1 150.60	949.11	1 261.85	1 444.53	1 593.78	786.81	1 279.97
14.71	22.33	239.42	84.64	61.07	54.55	49.97	92.40
3 299.24	6 229.98	7 041.32	7 812.90	8 805.91	9 400.23	3 430.78	7 858.07
291.16	839.54	813.35	894.54	1 100.08	1 188.14	300.24	967.13
21.91	26.76	12.61	0.00	21.08	20.02	26.33	16.09
269.25	812.78	800.74	894.54	1 079.01	1 168.13	273.91	951.04

continued on page 122

Table 6.3   continued

Fiscal years	1979/80	80/81	81/82	82/83
		Repelita III		
2. Transfers to private	90.79	63.80	64.25	65.27
3. Investments	3 520.76	2 917.29	2 937.75	2 984.70
a. Agriculture	354.94	292.01	294.06	298.76
b. Industry & mining	514.17	346.16	348.59	354.16
c. Electric power	368.69	248.31	250.05	254.05
d. Transportation & tourism	568.59	513.79	517.39	525.66
e. Education	395.35	343.66	346.07	351.60
f. Health	147.70	124.51	125.38	127.39
g. Housing and water supply	86.62	81.22	81.79	83.10
h. General public services	291.78	212.51	214.00	217.42
i. Other expenditure programmes	792.92	755.12	760.41	772.57
(implicit deflator)	76.00	100.00	111.00	120.00
III. Total realized/planned (constant 1980 prices)	1.16	1.51	1.61	1.50
A. Current expenditures	1.18	1.74	1.63	1.48
1. On education & health	1.16	1.51	1.61	1.50
2. Other wages & salaries	1.18	1.20	1.57	1.52
3. Other goods and services	1.17	1.24	1.57	1.56
4. Interest on debt	1.18	1.22	1.13	1.52
5. Subsidies	1.21	1.87	2.13	1.29
a. On food	1.20	2.04	2.32	1.19
b. On chemicals	1.21	1.83	2.10	1.29
6. Others	1.00	1.00	1.00	1.00
B. Capital expenditures	1.15	1.50	1.59	1.54
1. Debt amortization	1.18	1.21	1.48	1.53
a. Domestic	1.00	1.00	1.00	1.00
b. Foreign	1.21	1.23	1.51	1.56
2. Transfers to private	6.75	6.10	5.45	3.59
3. Investments	1.00	1.43	1.51	1.49
a. Agriculture	1.20	1.87	1.51	1.20
b. Industry & mining	0.87	1.20	1.80	1.81
c. Electric power	0.99	1.46	1.61	2.10
d. Transportation & tourism	0.91	1.28	1.19	1.17
e. Education	1.02	1.41	1.60	1.41
f. Health	1.07	1.48	1.73	1.43
g. Housing & water supply	1.50	1.98	1.54	1.28
h. General public services	0.88	1.59	1.65	1.47
i. Other expenditure programmes	1.05	1.35	1.45	1.55

83/84	84/85	85/86	86/87	87/88	88/89*	Yearly average	
				Repelita IV		III	IV
64.38	154.48	173.86	193.13	215.12	229.25	69.70	193.17
2 943.70	5 235.96	6 054.12	6 725.22	7 490.71	7 982.84	3 060.84	6 697.77
294.65	412.04	517.00	574.31	639.68	681.70	306.88	564.95
349.30	531.87	587.87	652.26	726.51	774.24	382.48	654.41
250.56	589.16	863.04	958.71	1 067.84	1 137.99	274.33	923.35
518.44	799.93	855.77	950.64	1 058.84	1 128.40	528.77	958.72
346.77	863.02	1 006.90	1 118.52	1 245.84	1 327.65	356.69	1 112.39
125.64	234.44	311.82	346.39	385.82	411.16	130.12	337.93
81.95	248.64	255.59	283.92	316.24	337.01	82.94	288.28
214.43	289.89	310.86	345.32	384.62	409.89	230.03	348.12
761.96	1 266.98	1 345.95	1 495.15	1 665.34	1 774.75	768.60	1 509.63
136.00	146.88	158.63	171.32	185.03	199.83	107.61	175.16

83/84	84/85	85/86	86/87	87/88	88/89*	Yearly average	
1.72	0.90	0.89	0.73	0.74	0.69	1.50	0.79
1.56	0.89	0.90	0.79	0.76	0.66	1.52	0.80
1.72	0.88	0.94	0.81	0.73	0.67	1.50	0.81
1.59	1.01	1.11	0.96	0.85	0.75	1.41	0.94
1.63	0.97	0.91	0.67	0.56	0.49	1.43	0.72
2.34	0.73	0.65	0.94	1.03	1.01	1.48	0.87
1.04	0.70	0.55	0.23	0.43	0.15	1.51	0.41
1.00	1.00	1.00	1.00	1.00	1.00	1.00	1.00
1.04	0.70	0.55	0.22	0.43	0.15	1.49	0.41
1.00	0.96	0.97	1.00	0.99	1.02	1.00	0.99
1.94	0.92	0.87	0.65	0.71	0.72	1.54	0.77
2.37	1.00	1.21	1.50	2.26	2.68	1.55	1.73
1.00	0.96	0.97	1.00	1.00	1.00	1.00	1.00
2.48	1.00	1.22	1.50	2.28	2.71	1.60	1.74
2.67	1.24	0.77	0.64	0.55	0.46	4.91	0.73
1.88	0.90	0.83	0.53	0.49	0.44	1.46	0.64
1.24	1.29	0.66	0.36	0.80	0.69	1.40	0.76
3.83	0.87	1.04	0.51	0.25	0.21	1.90	0.58
1.63	0.85	0.86	0.49	0.49	0.41	1.56	0.62
1.83	0.98	0.89	0.58	0.63	0.63	1.28	0.75
1.85	0.79	0.72	0.52	0.35	0.35	1.46	0.56
1.38	0.75	0.66	0.46	0.30	0.30	1.42	0.49
1.67	0.50	0.67	0.58	0.56	0.56	1.60	0.60
1.36	0.96	0.86	0.59	0.27	0.27	1.39	0.60
1.61	0.91	0.87	0.60	0.44	0.44	1.40	0.66

* Realized expenditures in 1988/89 were assumed to be equal to the expenditures budgeted at the beginning of that fiscal year.

Source: Thorbecke (1990), Table 2.5.

The second step entailed allocating the total capital stock to five capital categories (housing, rural capital, urban capital, public capital, and foreign capital). By assuming that the rates of return on capital are the same across different categories, it was possible to allocate the total capital stock in each of the 14 sectors into the five different types of capital by capitalizing the known returns (i.e., value added streams) received by the latter which can be read from the 1980 real SAM in Table 6.4.

The third step consisted of allocating these five types of capital to the eight household groups plus government and rest of the world according to ownership. Companies are owned by households, government or foreigners. Hence, they do not own wealth themselves; the value of the total stock of capital in each of their production sectors is distributed exclusively to the above three institutions. Public capital was considered to be owned by government, and foreign capital by foreigners (rest of the world). The remaining three capital types (housing, rural and urban capital) were divided among the household groups by assuming that the rate of return to capital is independent of who owns it (e.g., the rate of return to land held by a small farmer is equal to that of land held by a large farmer). Again, using information from the real SAM relating to the returns received by the various household groups, the corresponding capital stocks held by each household group could be computed from these three types of capital. The final step was to estimate, respectively, the financial asset holdings of households and companies, borrowing by firms from the central bank and from commercial banks, and the financial transactions among institutions. The balance sheets of the institutions are explicitly contained in the financial SAM.

One critical issue linking the financial SAM to the real SAM is that the former is expressed in terms of stocks whereas the latter is expressed in (annual) flows. In any given year, households and other institutions *adjust*, their portfolios of assets in response to changes in real and financial variables. Therefore to provide the necessary bridge between the real SAM and the financial SAM the flow of funds for 1980 had to be computed. The procedure which was followed to obtain the latter was to build a financial SAM for 1979, in addition to 1980, so that the corresponding flow of funds table could be derived residually. Since the 1980 wealth of a given institution (say household group) is equal to its preceding year's wealth (corrected for changes in valuation) plus current (1980) savings, the flow of funds table provides information on how the institutions allocated the increased (or possibly decreased) wealth among the various assets.

Table 6.4 Transaction Matrix of SAM in 1980–51 sectors, billion Rupiah

	Agric 1	Manual 2	Cler 3	Prof 4	Housing 5	RurCap 6	UrbCap 7
1 Agric	0.00	0.00	0.00	0.00	0.00	0.00	0.00
2 Manual	0.00	0.00	0.00	0.00	0.00	0.00	0.00
3 Cler	0.00	0.00	0.00	0.00	0.00	0.00	0.00
4 Prof	0.00	0.00	0.00	0.00	0.00	0.00	0.00
5 Housing	0.00	0.00	0.00	0.00	0.00	0.00	0.00
6 RurCap	0.00	0.00	0.00	0.00	0.00	0.00	0.00
7 UrbCap	0.00	0.00	0.00	0.00	0.00	0.00	0.00
8 PubCap	0.00	0.00	0.00	0.00	0.00	0.00	0.00
9 ForCap	0.00	0.00	0.00	0.00	0.00	0.00	0.00
10 AgEmploye	1 092.77	111.58	122.74	40.17	47.74	115.33	0.00
11 SmFarm	2 662.46	251.07	299.79	52.20	100.64	717.70	0.00
12 MedFarm	710.27	52.73	65.13	17.54	46.13	1 495.01	0.00
13 LgeFarm	705.77	34.30	49.70	19.73	82.02	3 516.32	0.00
14 RurLow	202.28	1 861.59	1 472.05	90.69	84.47	628.75	0.00
15 RurHigh	71.85	158.40	569.76	885.54	45.58	811.67	0.00
16 UrbLow	20.87	1 773.95	2 063.50	154.29	269.79	23.72	570.60
17 UrbHigh	8.58	205.36	1 436.57	1 271.65	267.58	35.69	1 054.31
18 Companies	0.00	0.00	0.00	0.00	0.00	0.00	3 590.37
19 FoodCrops	0.00	0.00	0.00	0.00	0.00	0.00	0.00
20 OtherAg	0.00	0.00	0.00	0.00	0.00	0.00	0.00
21 Mining	0.00	0.00	0.00	0.00	0.00	0.00	0.00
22 FoodProc	0.00	0.00	0.00	0.00	0.00	0.00	0.00
23 Textiles	0.00	0.00	0.00	0.00	0.00	0.00	0.00
24 Manufact	0.00	0.00	0.00	0.00	0.00	0.00	0.00
25 Utilities	0.00	0.00	0.00	0.00	0.00	0.00	0.00
26 PrivConst	0.00	0.00	0.00	0.00	0.00	0.00	0.00
27 PubAg	0.00	0.00	0.00	0.00	0.00	0.00	0.00
28 PubWorks	0.00	0.00	0.00	0.00	0.00	0.00	0.00
29 IntTrdTrn	0.00	0.00	0.00	0.00	0.00	0.00	0.00
30 FinBusServ	0.00	0.00	0.00	0.00	0.00	0.00	0.00
31 IntServ	0.00	0.00	0.00	0.00	0.00	0.00	0.00
32 EduHealth	0.00	0.00	0.00	0.00	0.00	0.00	0.00
33 TrdTrnMrg	0.00	0.00	0.00	0.00	0.00	0.00	0.00
34 IndTaxes	0.00	0.00	0.00	0.00	0.00	0.00	0.00
35 Subsidies	0.00	0.00	0.00	0.00	0.00	0.00	0.00
36 GCEdHealth	0.00	0.00	0.00	0.00	0.00	0.00	0.00
37 GCWageSal	0.00	0.00	0.00	0.00	0.00	0.00	0.00
38 GCGdsSrv	0.00	0.00	0.00	0.00	0.00	0.00	0.00
39 GCTransf	0.00	0.00	0.00	0.00	0.00	0.00	0.00
40 GlAgri	0.00	0.00	0.00	0.00	0.00	0.00	0.00
41 GlIndMine	0.00	0.00	0.00	0.00	0.00	0.00	0.00
42 GlEnergy	0.00	0.00	0.00	0.00	0.00	0.00	0.00
43 GlTranTur	0.00	0.00	0.00	0.00	0.00	0.00	0.00
44 GlEdHlth	0.00	0.00	0.00	0.00	0.00	0.00	0.00
45 GlHseWat	0.00	0.00	0.00	0.00	0.00	0.00	0.00
46 GlGenServ	0.00	0.00	0.00	0.00	0.00	0.00	0.00
47 GlOther	0.00	0.00	0.00	0.00	0.00	0.00	0.00
48 GovtCur	0.00	0.00	0.00	0.00	0.00	0.00	0.00
49 GovtCap	0.00	0.00	0.00	0.00	0.00	0.00	0.00
50 PrivCap	0.00	0.00	0.00	0.00	0.00	0.00	0.00
51 ROW	0.00	Manual	Cler	0.00	0.00	0.00	350.55
Total	5 474.85	4 448.98	6 079.24	2 531.81	943.95	7 344.19	5 565.83

continued on page 126

Table 6.4   continued

PubCap 8	ForCap 9	AgEmploy 10	SmFarm 11	MedFarm 12	LgeFarm 13	RurLow 14	RurHigh 15
0.00	0.00	0.00	0.00	0.00	0.00	0.00	0.00
0.00	0.00	0.00	0.00	0.00	0.00	0.00	0.00
0.00	0.00	0.00	0.00	0.00	0.00	0.00	0.00
0.00	0.00	0.00	0.00	0.00	0.00	0.00	0.00
0.00	0.00	0.00	0.00	0.00	0.00	0.00	0.00
0.00	0.00	0.00	0.00	0.00	0.00	0.00	0.00
0.00	0.00	0.00	0.00	0.00	0.00	0.00	0.00
0.00	0.00	0.00	0.00	0.00	0.00	0.00	0.00
0.00	0.00	0.00	0.00	0.00	0.00	0.00	0.00
0.00	0.00	4.23	4.11	0.97	2.90	2.84	1.65
0.00	0.00	3.87	24.81	2.22	8.66	7.53	3.81
0.00	0.00	0.90	2.01	1.58	2.88	3.63	2.59
0.00	0.00	2.79	9.70	2.30	7.16	6.75	3.79
0.00	0.00	3.04	10.06	2.37	7.11	13.21	4.04
0.00	0.00	0.81	2.28	0.95	2.70	21.02	2.99
0.00	0.00	4.92	15.50	3.64	10.43	10.68	6.43
0.00	0.00	2.77	7.70	3.92	11.29	5.24	5.59
6 061.80	7 894.68	0.00	0.00	0.00	0.00	0.00	0.00
0.00	0.00	475.68	1 087.72	542.94	727.01	713.99	349.07
0.00	0.00	285.23	683.09	299.02	486.55	493.50	313.35
0.00	0.00	5.48	14.03	7.29	9.46	9.13	4.78
0.00	0.00	579.89	1 224.38	556.67	886.40	1 097.51	655.05
0.00	0.00	32.16	150.10	83.48	169.00	159.34	116.14
0.00	0.00	32.43	200.64	179.54	387.93	416.47	304.61
0.00	0.00	1.26	3.23	3.36	11.04	16.24	20.08
0.00	0.00	0.00	0.00	0.00	0.00	0.00	0.00
0.00	0.00	0.00	0.00	0.00	0.00	0.00	0.00
0.00	0.00	0.00	0.00	0.00	0.00	0.00	0.00
0.00	0.00	14.63	67.44	47.58	105.89	150.52	123.53
0.00	0.00	29.02	141.50	95.41	252.15	249.69	151.31
0.00	0.00	14.01	122.69	143.05	295.38	345.85	223.44
0.00	0.00	0.67	215.37	94.04	167.93	173.08	132.73
0.00	0.00	0.00	0.00	0.00	0.00	0.00	0.00
0.00	0.00	0.00	0.00	0.00	0.00	0.00	0.00
0.00	0.00	0.00	0.00	0.00	0.00	0.00	0.00
0.00	0.00	0.00	0.00	0.00	0.00	0.00	0.00
0.00	0.00	0.00	0.00	0.00	0.00	0.00	0.00
0.00	0.00	0.00	0.00	0.00	0.00	0.00	0.00
0.00	0.00	0.00	0.00	0.00	0.00	0.00	0.00
0.00	0.00	0.00	0.00	0.00	0.00	0.00	0.00
0.00	0.00	0.00	0.00	0.00	0.00	0.00	0.00
0.00	0.00	0.00	0.00	0.00	0.00	0.00	0.00
0.00	0.00	0.00	0.00	0.00	0.00	0.00	0.00
0.00	0.00	0.00	0.00	0.00	0.00	0.00	0.00
0.00	0.00	0.00	0.00	0.00	0.00	0.00	0.00
0.00	0.00	0.00	0.00	0.00	0.00	0.00	0.00
0.00	0.00	34.57	67.72	55.24	103.71	60.62	74.97
0.00	0.00	0.00	0.00	0.00	0.00	0.00	0.00
0.00	0.00	47.61	138.39	304.48	829.11	464.35	319.76
17.14	2 025.44	0.00	0.00	0.00	0.00	0.00	0.00
6 078.94	9 920.12	1 575.97	4 192.47	2 430.05	4 484.69	4 421.19	2 819.71

UrbLow 16	UrbHigh 17	Companies 18	FoodCrops 19	OtherAg 20	Mining 21	FoodProc 22	Textiles 23
0.00	0.00	0.00	3 827.92	1 528.16	0.00	0.00	0.00
0.00	0.00	0.00	16.22	292.16	192.12	394.73	218.21
0.00	0.00	0.00	7.88	58.08	93.68	47.99	16.58
0.00	0.00	0.00	5.73	15.49	48.75	6.80	9.83
0.00	0.00	0.00	0.00	0.00	0.00	0.00	0.00
0.00	0.00	0.00	2 197.68	3 065.38	132.39	423.79	92.45
0.00	0.00	0.00	3.25	608.89	19.30	321.61	148.07
0.00	0.00	0.00	0.03	293.09	3 033.49	169.82	24.47
0.00	0.00	0.00	0.05	207.59	8 898.93	101.69	52.38
3.83	4.35	0.00	0.00	0.00	0.00	0.00	0.00
12.90	14.10	0.00	0.00	0.00	0.00	0.00	0.00
1.82	2.45	0.00	0.00	0.00	0.00	0.00	0.00
8.52	9.45	0.00	0.00	0.00	0.00	0.00	0.00
9.39	10.64	0.00	0.00	0.00	0.00	0.00	0.00
6.62	4.31	222.16	0.00	0.00	0.00	0.00	0.00
20.41	17.73	0.00	0.00	0.00	0.00	0.00	0.00
42.30	52.46	1 132.38	0.00	0.00	0.00	0.00	0.00
0.00	0.00	268.35	0.00	0.00	0.00	0.00	0.00
461.82	235.07	0.00	1 272.82	19.16	0.00	2 727.17	1.45
499.44	508.14	0.00	35.84	1 820.90	1.87	1 211.72	172.94
7.36	7.20	0.00	0.00	4.95	418.76	10.19	0.10
937.09	860.76	0.00	0.00	111.29	0.01	406.39	1.50
124.03	205.81	0.00	4.10	15.08	27.44	16.82	692.09
584.13	626.88	0.00	287.16	348.74	457.47	198.24	244.79
39.11	50.66	0.00	0.00	8.74	0.75	13.52	8.33
0.00	0.00	0.00	4.58	7.37	7.86	4.94	1.64
0.00	0.00	0.00	5.80	26.96	0.00	0.00	0.00
0.00	0.00	0.00	0.00	13.28	58.67	0.68	0.78
366.48	469.70	0.00	1.41	11.64	40.91	10.00	2.16
486.12	495.25	0.00	38.05	96.06	424.03	52.40	11.96
665.29	791.61	0.00	2.30	95.18	158.41	17.50	3.60
11.57	10.17	0.00	0.04	3.37	8.60	1.69	0.40
0.00	0.00	0.00	1 017.62	2 509.44	310.54	968.12	279.05
0.00	0.00	0.00	54.69	80.60	19.66	398.52	43.07
0.00	0.00	0.00	0.00	0.00	0.00	0.00	0.00
0.00	0.00	0.00	0.00	0.00	0.00	0.00	0.00
0.00	0.00	0.00	0.00	0.00	0.00	0.00	0.00
0.00	0.00	0.00	0.00	0.00	0.00	0.00	0.00
0.00	0.00	0.00	0.00	0.00	0.00	0.00	0.00
0.00	0.00	0.00	0.00	0.00	0.00	0.00	0.00
0.00	0.00	0.00	0.00	0.00	0.00	0.00	0.00
0.00	0.00	0.00	0.00	0.00	0.00	0.00	0.00
0.00	0.00	0.00	0.00	0.00	0.00	0.00	0.00
0.00	0.00	0.00	0.00	0.00	0.00	0.00	0.00
0.00	0.00	0.00	0.00	0.00	0.00	0.00	0.00
0.00	0.00	0.00	0.00	0.00	0.00	0.00	0.00
0.00	0.00	0.00	0.00	0.00	0.00	0.00	0.00
145.42	167.73	7 808.16	0.00	0.00	0.00	0.00	0.00
0.00	0.00	0.00	0.00	0.00	0.00	0.00	0.00
600.94	1 040.55	8 314.24	0.00	0.00	0.00	0.00	0.00
0.00	0.00	145.03	142.58	193.32	695.99	655.51	115.05
5 034.59	5 585.02	17 890.32	8 925.75	11 434.92	15 049.63	8 159.84	2 140.90

continued on page 128

Table 6.4   continued

Manufact 24	Utilities 25	PrivConst 26	PubAg 27	PubWorks 28	IntTrdTrn 29	FinBusServ 30	IntServ 31
0.00	0.00	0.00	118.78	0.00	0.00	0.00	0.00
526.02	42.93	763.27	14.51	404.68	886.00	57.62	490.15
112.71	20.96	30.10	2.49	21.02	3 442.38	305.32	660.05
106.10	22.29	30.49	1.42	20.64	75.39	69.52	39.53
0.00	0.00	0.00	0.00	0.00	0.00	943.95	0.00
147.99	0.82	141.82	11.50	20.11	753.67	116.03	211.53
703.90	16.71	498.15	8.47	190.32	2 087.61	497.81	368.23
938.85	114.72	0.00	67.72	85.15	830.41	462.03	32.06
308.00	11.32	0.00	0.00	16.03	286.06	29.17	8.90
0.00	0.00	0.00	0.00	0.00	0.00	0.00	0.00
0.00	0.00	0.00	0.00	0.00	0.00	0.00	0.00
0.00	0.00	0.00	0.00	0.00	0.00	0.00	0.00
0.00	0.00	0.00	0.00	0.00	0.00	0.00	0.00
0.00	0.00	0.00	0.00	0.00	0.00	0.00	0.00
0.00	0.00	0.00	0.00	0.00	0.00	0.00	0.00
0.00	0.00	0.00	0.00	0.00	0.00	0.00	0.00
0.00	0.00	0.00	0.00	0.00	0.00	0.00	0.00
0.00	0.00	0.00	0.00	0.00	0.00	0.00	0.00
0.00	0.00	0.00	0.00	0.00	0.00	0.00	0.00
2.29	0.00	18.95	0.00	0.00	0.31	2.53	106.92
106.70	0.00	904.87	18.66	81.95	8.90	1.01	466.53
1 763.36	3.93	245.92	67.79	232.38	1.20	0.00	0.00
23.65	0.00	0.00	0.00	0.00	8.84	3.24	442.78
48.42	0.62	3.38	0.20	0.31	24.13	5.80	73.48
3 428.33	177.78	2 039.60	209.94	957.61	733.62	75.39	677.90
54.52	73.23	4.47	0.37	1.23	52.09	28.55	99.80
11.41	0.24	8.09	0.84	3.85	68.27	162.88	29.32
0.00	0.00	0.00	0.00	0.00	0.00	0.00	0.00
5.91	15.73	0.00	0.00	0.00	30.18	1.05	1.27
28.42	3.41	4.81	1.67	5.98	440.53	48.35	27.70
82.58	6.97	50.30	11.63	40.48	360.10	190.62	104.61
57.97	10.84	11.42	5.39	14.22	564.10	58.03	49.38
4.20	0.13	2.52	0.00	1.41	19.25	9.86	4.50
3 459.21	9.14	0.00	0.00	0.00	0.00	0.00	54.97
615.20	0.85	90.82	13.86	31.07	241.72	88.75	113.51
0.00	0.00	0.00	0.00	0.00	0.00	0.00	0.00
0.00	0.00	0.00	0.00	0.00	0.00	0.00	0.00
0.00	0.00	0.00	0.00	0.00	0.00	0.00	0.00
0.00	0.00	0.00	0.00	0.00	0.00	0.00	0.00
0.00	0.00	0.00	0.00	0.00	0.00	0.00	0.00
0.00	0.00	0.00	0.00	0.00	0.00	0.00	0.00
0.00	0.00	0.00	0.00	0.00	0.00	0.00	0.00
0.00	0.00	0.00	0.00	0.00	0.00	0.00	0.00
0.00	0.00	0.00	0.00	0.00	0.00	0.00	0.00
0.00	0.00	0.00	0.00	0.00	0.00	0.00	0.00
0.00	0.00	0.00	0.00	0.00	0.00	0.00	0.00
0.00	0.00	0.00	0.00	0.00	0.00	0.00	0.00
0.00	0.00	0.00	0.00	0.00	0.00	0.00	0.00
0.00	0.00	0.00	0.00	0.00	0.00	0.00	0.00
7 032.59	0.00	0.00	0.00	0.00	174.23	389.85	486.51
19 584.33	532.62	4 848.98	555.24	2 128.44	11 088.99	3 547.36	4 549.63

EduHealth 32	TrdTrnMrg 33	IndTaxes 34	Subsidies 35	GCEdHlth 36	GCWageSal 37	GCGdsSrv 38	GCTransf 39
0.00	0.00	0.00	0.00	0.00	0.00	0.00	0.00
36.07	0.00	0.00	0.00	0.00	114.21	0.00	0.00
166.02	0.00	0.00	0.00	0.00	1 093.98	0.00	0.00
943.35	0.00	0.00	0.00	0.00	1 136.50	0.00	0.00
0.00	0.00	0.00	0.00	0.00	0.00	0.00	0.00
29.03	0.00	0.00	0.00	0.00	0.00	0.00	0.00
93.49	0.00	0.00	0.00	0.00	0.00	0.00	0.00
27.10	0.00	0.00	0.00	0.00	0.00	0.00	0.00
0.00	0.00	0.00	0.00	0.00	0.00	0.00	0.00
0.00	0.00	0.00	0.00	0.00	0.00	0.00	11.90
0.00	0.00	0.00	0.00	0.00	0.00	0.00	2.84
0.00	0.00	0.00	0.00	0.00	0.00	0.00	1.02
0.00	0.00	0.00	0.00	0.00	0.00	0.00	1.43
0.00	0.00	0.00	0.00	0.00	0.00	0.00	2.58
0.00	0.00	0.00	0.00	0.00	0.00	0.00	2.03
0.00	0.00	0.00	0.00	0.00	0.00	0.00	47.82
0.00	0.00	0.00	0.00	0.00	0.00	0.00	11.51
0.00	0.00	0.00	0.00	0.00	0.00	0.00	0.00
26.01	0.00	0.00	0.00	0.00	0.00	0.00	0.00
39.43	0.00	0.00	0.00	0.00	0.00	17.07	0.00
0.00	0.00	0.00	0.00	0.00	0.00	0.00	0.00
28.53	0.00	0.00	186.96	0.00	0.00	3.52	0.00
22.68	0.00	0.00	0.00	0.00	0.00	48.46	0.00
267.56	0.00	0.00	1 205.20	0.00	0.00	444.18	0.00
16.88	0.00	0.00	0.00	0.00	0.00	25.16	0.00
28.16	0.00	0.00	0.00	0.00	0.00	156.22	0.00
0.00	0.00	0.00	0.00	0.00	0.00	7.00	0.00
10.06	0.00	0.00	0.00	0.00	0.00	12.58	0.00
9.68	8 608.09	0.00	0.00	0.00	0.00	148.67	0.00
17.56	0.00	0.00	0.00	0.00	0.00	128.81	0.00
15.40	0.00	0.00	0.00	0.00	0.00	770.45	0.00
0.84	0.00	0.00	0.00	917.47	0.00	0.00	0.00
0.00	0.00	0.00	0.00	0.00	0.00	0.00	0.00
2.08	0.00	0.00	0.00	0.00	0.00	0.00	0.00
0.00	0.00	0.00	0.00	0.00	0.00	0.00	0.00
0.00	0.00	0.00	0.00	0.00	0.00	0.00	0.00
0.00	0.00	0.00	0.00	0.00	0.00	0.00	0.00
0.00	0.00	0.00	0.00	0.00	0.00	0.00	0.00
0.00	0.00	0.00	0.00	0.00	0.00	0.00	0.00
0.00	0.00	0.00	0.00	0.00	0.00	0.00	0.00
0.00	0.00	0.00	0.00	0.00	0.00	0.00	0.00
0.00	0.00	0.00	0.00	0.00	0.00	0.00	0.00
0.00	0.00	0.00	0.00	0.00	0.00	0.00	0.00
0.00	0.00	0.00	0.00	0.00	0.00	0.00	0.00
0.00	0.00	0.00	0.00	0.00	0.00	0.00	0.00
0.00	0.00	0.00	0.00	0.00	0.00	0.00	0.00
0.00	0.00	0.00	0.00	0.00	0.00	0.00	0.00
0.00	0.00	1 794.40	0.00	0.00	0.00	0.00	0.00
0.00	0.00	0.00	0.00	0.00	0.00	0.00	0.00
EduHealth 32	TrdTrnMrg 33	IndTaxes 34	Subsidies 35	GCEdHlth 36	GCWageSal 37	GCGdsSrv 38	GCTransf 39
0.00	0.00	0.00	0.00	0.00	0.00	0.00	0.00
1 779.93	8 608.09	1 794.40	1 392.16	917.47	2 344.69	1 762.10	81.13

continued on page 130

Table 6.4   continued

GlAgri 40	GlIndMine 41	GlEnergy 42	GlTranTur 43	GlEdHlth 44	GlHseWat 45	GlGenServ 46	GlOther 47
0.00	0.00	0.00	0.00	0.00	0.00	0.00	0.00
0.00	0.00	0.00	0.00	0.00	0.00	0.00	0.00
0.00	0.00	0.00	0.00	0.00	0.00	0.00	0.00
0.00	0.00	0.00	0.00	0.00	0.00	0.00	0.00
0.00	0.00	0.00	0.00	0.00	0.00	0.00	0.00
0.00	0.00	0.00	0.00	0.00	0.00	0.00	0.00
0.00	0.00	0.00	0.00	0.00	0.00	0.00	0.00
0.00	0.00	0.00	0.00	0.00	0.00	0.00	0.00
0.00	0.00	0.00	0.00	0.00	0.00	0.00	0.00
0.00	0.00	0.00	0.00	0.00	0.00	0.00	0.00
0.00	0.00	0.00	0.00	0.00	0.00	0.00	0.00
0.00	0.00	0.00	0.00	0.00	0.00	0.00	0.00
0.00	0.00	0.00	0.00	0.00	0.00	0.00	0.00
0.00	0.00	0.00	0.00	0.00	0.00	0.00	0.00
0.00	0.00	0.00	0.00	0.00	0.00	0.00	0.00
0.00	0.00	0.00	0.00	0.00	0.00	0.00	0.00
0.00	0.00	0.00	0.00	0.00	0.00	0.00	0.00
0.00	0.00	0.00	0.00	0.00	0.00	0.00	0.00
0.00	0.00	0.00	0.00	0.00	0.00	0.00	0.00
0.00	0.00	0.00	0.00	0.00	0.00	0.00	0.00
0.00	39.81	0.00	0.00	155.17	0.00	0.00	60.40
0.00	0.00	0.00	0.00	0.00	0.00	0.00	0.00
0.00	224.45	0.00	0.00	487.59	69.77	302.93	182.88
515.49	0.00	0.00	0.00	0.00	0.00	0.00	0.00
0.00	153.96	361.85	627.58	0.00	84.07	16.72	734.12
0.00	0.00	0.00	0.00	0.00	0.00	0.00	0.00
0.00	0.00	0.00	0.00	0.00	0.00	0.00	0.00
0.00	0.00	0.00	0.00	0.00	0.00	0.00	0.00
0.00	0.00	0.00	0.00	0.00	0.00	0.00	0.00
0.00	0.00	0.00	0.00	0.00	0.00	0.00	0.00
0.00	0.00	0.00	0.00	0.00	0.00	0.00	0.00
0.00	0.00	0.00	0.00	0.00	0.00	0.00	0.00
0.00	0.00	0.00	0.00	0.00	0.00	0.00	0.00
0.00	0.00	0.00	0.00	0.00	0.00	0.00	0.00
0.00	0.00	0.00	0.00	0.00	0.00	0.00	0.00
0.00	0.00	0.00	0.00	0.00	0.00	0.00	0.00
0.00	0.00	0.00	0.00	0.00	0.00	0.00	0.00
0.00	0.00	0.00	0.00	0.00	0.00	0.00	0.00
0.00	0.00	0.00	0.00	0.00	0.00	0.00	0.00
0.00	0.00	0.00	0.00	0.00	0.00	0.00	0.00
0.00	0.00	0.00	0.00	0.00	0.00	0.00	0.00
0.00	0.00	0.00	0.00	0.00	0.00	0.00	0.00
0.00	0.00	0.00	0.00	0.00	0.00	0.00	0.00
0.00	0.00	0.00	0.00	0.00	0.00	0.00	0.00
0.00	0.00	0.00	0.00	0.00	0.00	0.00	0.00
0.00	0.00	0.00	0.00	0.00	0.00	0.00	0.00
515.49	418.02	361.85	627.85	642.76	153.84	319.65	977.40

GovtCur 48	GovtCap 49	PrivCap 50	ROW 51	TOTAL
0.00	0.00	0.00	0.00	5 474.86
0.00	0.00	0.00	0.00	4 448.90
0.00	0.00	0.00	0.00	6 079.24
0.00	0.00	0.00	0.00	2 531.83
0.00	0.00	0.00	0.00	943.95
0.00	0.00	0.00	0.00	7 344.19
0.00	0.00	0.00	0.00	5 565.81
0.00	0.00	0.00	0.00	6 078.94
0.00	0.00	0.00	0.00	9 920.12
0.00	0.00	0.00	8.87	1 575.98
0.00	0.00	0.00	27.86	4 192.46
0.00	0.00	0.00	24.35	2 430.05
0.00	0.00	0.00	24.96	4 484.69
0.00	0.00	0.00	19.04	4 421.31
0.00	0.00	0.00	11.04	2 819.71
0.00	0.00	0.00	20.31	5 034.59
0.00	0.00	0.00	30.12	5 585.02
0.00	0.00	0.00	75.08	17 890.28
0.00	0.00	118.83	36.00	8 925.74
0.00	0.00	213.06	2 765.22	11 434.99
0.00	0.00	903.30	11 333.01	15 049.62
0.00	0.00	26.20	119.17	8 159.83
0.00	0.00	30.06	89.68	2 140.81
0.00	0.00	3 500.70	1 324.34	19 584.36
0.00	0.00	0.00	0.00	532.62
0.00	0.00	3 085.69	0.00	4 848.98
0.00	0.00	0.00	0.00	555.25
0.00	0.00	0.00	0.00	2 128.45
0.00	0.00	0.00	349.78	11 088.98
0.00	0.00	0.00	30.75	3 547.36
0.00	0.00	0.00	114.14	4 549.65
0.00	0.00	0.00	0.07	1 779.91
0.00	0.00	0.00	0.00	8 608.09
0.00	0.00	0.00	0.00	1 794.40
1 392.16	0.00	0.00	0.00	1 392.16
917.47	0.00	0.00	0.00	917.47
2 344.69	0.00	0.00	0.00	2 344.69
1 762.11	0.00	0.00	0.00	1 762.11
81.13	0.00	0.00	0.00	81.13
0.00	515.49	0.00	0.00	515.49
0.00	418.02	0.00	0.00	418.02
0.00	361.85	0.00	0.00	361.85
0.00	627.56	0.00	0.00	627.56
0.00	642.76	0.00	0.00	642.76
0.00	153.84	0.00	0.00	153.84
0.00	319.65	0.00	0.00	319.65
0.00	977.40	0.00	0.00	977.40
0.00	0.00	0.00	22.32	10 334.86
3 386.48	0.00	0.00	1 401.35	4 787.83
0.00	468.38	0.00	0.00	12 527.81
450.82	302.88	4 649.97	0.00	17 827.46
10 334.86	4 787.83	12 527.81	17 827.46	

The complete model consists of 86 distinct equations which when disaggregated by sector, types of institution and factor yield a total of over 600 equations. Space limitation precludes presenting or discussing the full set of equations underlying the CGE model. Rather only some of the key behavioral and technical relations are scrutinized here.

Production activities are disaggregated into 14 categories and each activity is assumed to produce only one corresponding commodity. (These 14 production activities appear in both the real and financial SAMs.) Domestic output of each activity is a CES production function of a composite labor input and the stock of capital assumed fixed in the short run. In the medium to long run the capital stock can vary and sectoral productivity is also influenced by past cumulative government investment. For example, government investment in agricultural infrastructure, that is irrigation or rural roads, increases agricultural productivity through the shift parameter in the production functions.

The labor market specification is as follows. Each production sector's demand for the four labor skills is derived from the first-order conditions for firms' profit maximization. Thus, sectoral labor demand will depend on its product price, wages and the prices of intermediate inputs. Next, a composite labor demand function for each sector is postulated as a Cobb–Douglas function of the four labor skills. This is the composite labor input which appears as an argument in the sectoral domestic output functions.

A characteristic feature of Indonesian labor markets is that sectoral wage rates are strongly influenced by the inflation rate, the price of the sectoral output, and the growth rate of labor productivity, respectively. These wage equations were statistically estimated over a 12 year period and used to derive sectoral wage rates endogenously. When the model is run in a comparative static fashion, in the short run, a lower elasticity of wage response to inflation is used than when the model is run to simulate medium and long run effects. This means that it is assumed that the real wage rate is more sticky in the short run than in the medium to long run. A key implication which underlies the form of the wage equations is that labor market segmentation exists in Indonesia with wages being strongly sector-specific. Again, this reflects the institutional conditions prevailing in Indonesia, where one observes significant wage differentials across sectors for the same general skill categories. (Of course, to some extent, the limited disaggregation of labor into only four skill categories contributes to the above phenomenon.)

The average wage rates for each skill category are arrived at on the basis of the sectoral wage rates and the wage shares of each type of labor in each sector. Finally, labor supply of each skill type is assumed to be fixed in the short run, but can vary in the long run. It is also assumed that some labor slack prevails (in the form of unemployment or underemployment) in the base year. The labor market equation states that labor supply of each labor skill equals the sum of total labor demand, in addition to possible unemployment. In turn, total labor demand consists of demand by the government, which is exogenously determined, and total private demand which is determined through the endogenously derived wage rates. Consequently, any excess of labor supply over demand can lead to unemployment or underemployment.

Household consumption is derived in two stages. First, household aggregate consumption for each socioeconomic group is assumed to be a function of that group's permanent income and transitory income. Of the several formulations of consumption functions which were considered such as the life-cycle model, the rational expectations model and the error correction model, the above specification best fitted the Indonesia case. One key implication of the above chosen specification for consumption is that the corresponding household savings functions also become directly related to households' incomes. In the econometric tests which were run to explain household savings, interest rates on various financial assets did not come out to be significant as explanatory variables. Since interest rates in Indonesia were controlled by the government rather than market determined, at least until the financial reform of 1983, it would not be appropriate to conclude that under the new financial regime savings do not respond to interest rates. In fact, evidence would seem to suggest that the recent very substantial increase in household savings deposits might have been influenced by the significantly higher real interest rates after the reform.

After having determined aggregate consumption of each household group, *per capita* demand for each consumption good is derived through a two-level utility maximizing specification. For the upper level aggregation (food, manufacturing, electricity, services, paper) a restricted form of the almost ideal demand system (AIDS) is postulated and for the lower (more disaggregated) level, a conventional LES specification is chosen.

The treatment of private investment is crucial in a CGE. In principle, investment by firms is thought to depend on the present discounted value (PDV) of the future income stream generated by the investment. The problem in testing and deriving empirically such a function is that it is difficult to specify clearly (in measurable terms) the variables used as arguments in this function since the PDV is an expected value. The key issue is to identify an appropriate and measurable proxy variable for an expected variable (PDV) which may not be measurable *per se*. Ultimately the formulation (reduced form) which yielded the most significant statistical results is an investment function which states that private investment depends only on the previous period output, current output, and the lending rate.

Since many policy instruments which were part and parcel of the adjustment package were financial and monetary, or had important financial and monetary repercussions, a financial sector model which could be integrated with the real side model had to be designed to capture the combined effects of these measures. Another reason for including a financial sector is that some of the neo-Keynesian features specific to the Indonesian economy which were incorporated in the real side model – such as the prevalence of price rigidities in some markets – cannot be adequately captured by a purely neoclassical (real) model. In the latter model changes in the aggregate price level is the numeraire which cannot be endogenously derived (relative prices are not affected by change in the aggregate price level). In the Indonesian context wages and the exchange rates were relatively sticky compared to other prices. Still another reason for relying on a financial model is that both savings and investment are endogenously determined in the present CGE. The effects of changes in such financial variables as interest rates and the removal of credit rationing (following the financial liberalization reform) on both investment and savings, and through them on the medium and long run growth path of the economy, can be substantial and can only be captured through the explicit modelling of the financial sector.

The financial sector model which was designed is mainly based on Tobin's specification (1969) which included bank deposits and loans. However, the specification of assets and rates of return is modified in order to conform to the institutional characteristics of Indonesian financial markets and also to add commercial banks as an additional institution. The portfolio selection process is illustrated here for households. Asset demand of other agents can be explained in a similar way as for households, if it is not set exogenously.

Households' total wealth at the end of a period is equal to current savings in addition to beginning period wealth adjusted for asset revaluation. It should be noted that both equity and assets denominated in foreign currency are revalued on the basis of rates of change in the price of equity and the exchange rate, respectively. Households are assumed to reallocate their portfolios of assets at the end of each period depending on their nominal incomes and changes in (a) the ratio of the real interest rates to assets (b) the exchange rate, and (c) the aggregate price level.

The portfolio selection process which is adopted in the model for the different socioeconomic household groups and firms is a hierarchical decision-making process. The first step consists of the determination of household money demand. Since foreign exchange transactions are free in Indonesia and the foreign exchange system is a managed floating system, the expected inflation rate affects household money demand in various ways. When the domestic inflation rate is greater than the world inflation rate, the domestic currency is expected to be depreciated. If the exchange rate is overvalued under a managed floating system, official foreign exchange reserves will tend to be depleted leaving the public to expect a devaluation. This discrepancy between the actual and equilibrium exchange rates induces a shift by households of asset holdings for money to inflation-protected assets or financial assets denominated in foreign currency. In the Indonesian case there are two important assets which are denominated in foreign currency (mainly in US dollars). One is foreign currency deposits in domestic banks which is classified as quasi-money. This asset differs from domestic time deposits since it protects depositors from capital loss in case of a devaluation. The second foreign asset consists of household overseas deposits which are tantamount to capital flight. The econometric results confirm that the inflation rate was very significant as an explanatory variable of money demand.

The second step in the hierarchical decision-making process consists of allocating remaining wealth after money demand has been satisfied among interest-bearing assets. It is assumed that, at each successive step, households decide between two types of relatively substitutable assets. Thus, interest-bearing assets are, first, divided between equities and 'other financial assets' according to a proportion which is endogenously determined in the model as a function of the ratio of the rate of return to equity to the average rate of return to 'other financial assets'. Once this proportion is determined it yields the share of interest-bearing assets allocated to 'other financial assets', with a complementary share allocated to equities.

Similarly the next hierarchical step entails allocating 'other financial assets' between 'time deposits in Rupiah' and 'financial assets denominated in foreign currency'. These shares are again endogenously derived.

The final step consists of households deciding between 'time deposits in foreign currency' and 'foreign bonds' according to a share which is also endogenously derived.

Obviously, the budget constraint for asset allocation is always met under this hierarchical process. Though the specification seems *ad hoc*, it is convenient to work with and is capable of capturing the effects of changes in various interest rates on household financial portfolios.

An important implicit identity which can be derived from the system of equations in the model is the previously mentioned balanced budget objective which government is committed to fulfil. In the Indonesian context, where government borrowing from abroad is not a binding constraint, any excess of a government investment over and above savings on current account was financed through net public borrowing from abroad. Hence, the endogenously determined balancing variable which ensured that total government expenditures equaled total government revenues was net foreign borrowing.

6.5   POLICY SIMULATION

The model, as designed, can be run in two distinct ways to simulate, respectively, short run and long run effects. In the short run, the sectoral capital stocks are assumed fixed and investment during the period only affects the economy from the demand side by generating a demand for primary and intermediate inputs during the construction phase, but not by adding to capacity. Furthermore, public investment is not considered to affect sectoral productivity. The more limited output effects in the short run dampen, among other things, labor demand and the resulting income distribution. The behavioral response of agents is also considered more inelastic in the short than in the long run. For example, the elasticity of real wage rate response to inflation in the sectoral wage equations is assumed lower in the short run. This implies a greater degree of nominal wage rigidity in the short run than in the long run (the degree of wage indexation is greater in the long run). In brief, to simulate short run conditions, the model is run as a one period comparative static model. Although, the length of the short run period is left somewhat undefined, it can be taken to reflect changes occurring within a two year timespan.

In contrast, when the model is run to simulate medium to long run effects, the timespan which it is supposed to track is the full adjustment period itself, i.e., 1983–8. Sectoral capital stocks are augmented by private and public investment flows during the whole period and cumulative government investment affects productivity. Exogenous variables are updated and agents respond somewhat differently in the long run.

The model does not replicate the observed values of the endogenous variables, year by year, between 1983 and 1988 and therefore cannot be used to check possible annual fluctuations around trends. Instead when the model is applied to simulate long run effects, it can be interpreted as a two period model, where the first period reflects the initial conditions and values of variables at the beginning of the adjustment period and the second period reflects the conditions and values of variables at the end of the adjustment period which in this study was taken as 1988.[5] Hence, the results generated endogenously by the model should be interpreted as annual rates of change over the five year adjustment period. This means, of course, that the exogenous variables (including policy variables) constituting the base run and the various counterfactual policy scenarios have to be expressed, likewise, as annual rates of change between 1983 and 1988.

The following alternative policy scenarios were chosen for simulation purposes.

Experiment 0: Base Run

All exogenous variables including exogenous policy variables under the control of the government are taken as observed during the adjustment period (1983–8).[6] The base run is the reference run reflecting the adjustment package actually implemented by the government against which all the counterfactual policy scenarios are confronted.

Experiment 1: Equiproportional Budget Retrenchment

It is assumed that the government reduced its expenditures on each and every category (except for interest payment on the foreign debt and subsidies) by 20 percent compared to the base run. All other exogenous variables take their actual (observed) values during 1983–8 as in the base run.

Experiment 2: Increased Government Investment and Reduced Government Current Expenditures

While total government expenditures are assumed equal to their actual level during the adjustment period as in the base run, the composition of expenditures is changed. Government current expenditures are cut by 20 percent and government investment is increased by 27 percent (thus maintaining total public expenditures as in the base run). Two variances of this experiment were run: *Experiment 2-1* allocated public investment by sector proportionately to the base run allocation; while *Experiment 2-2* raised the allocation of investment to agriculture by 50 percent and to other sectors by 23 percent (resulting in an overall rise in public investment of 27 percent). All other exogenous variables take the same values as in the base run.

Experiment 3:   Reduction in Government Investment and Increase in Government Current Expenditures

Total government expenditures are kept equal to their actual (observed) level as in the base run and in *Experiment 2*. A 16 percent increase in government current expenditures was postulated and a 20 percent cut in government investment. All other exogenous variables remain as in the base run.

Experiment 4:   Accelerated Devaluation

This counterfactual scenario assumes that the foreign exchange rate would have been depreciated by 20 percent more than actually occurred during the adjustment period. All other exogenous variables remain as in the base run.

Experiment 5:   Monetary Contraction and Expansion

Even though the annual rate of growth of money supply during the adjustment period was modest (8.4 percent), *Experiment 5-1* simulates further monetary contraction with money supply decreasing by 15 percent as compared to the base run. Alternatively, *Experiment 5-2* simulates a monetary expansion where money supply increases by an additional 15 percent as compared to the base run. All other exogenous variables remain as in the base run.

The logic behind *Experiments 2* and *3* was to test the tradeoff over time between a pattern of government expenditures emphasizing public investment projects vs. an alternative pattern favoring government current expenditures (and, in particular, government consumption and a larger wage bill for civil servants). The objective was to compare the short run vs. long run consequences of these two alternative patterns of public expenditures on the socioeconomic system and more specifically on income distribution. A larger share of total government expenditures allocated to public investment entails a lower stream of aggregate consumption in the short run in favor of larger streams of incomes and consumption in the long run. Alternatively, maintaining high levels of government current expenditures shelters household incomes in the short run, but results in lower growth rates and a contraction of incomes and consumption in the long run.

The results of these policy experiments were summarized and consolidated in Tables 6.5 and 6.6. These tables show the impact in the short run and long run, respectively, of the five counterfactual policy scenarios (*Experiments 1–5*) on key endogenous indicators, including the income distribution by socioeconomic groups. For each counterfactual scenario, the results on key indicators is expressed as index numbers relative to the base run to facilitate comparisons among them in Panel I. In addition, in Panel II, the average annual values of some key variables over the adjustment period (1985–8) are given.[7]

The first comparison is between the base run and *Experiment 1*. Not surprisingly, a drastic budget retrenchment (by 20 percent compared to the base run) would have been highly deflationary and GDP growth would have come to a standstill (in the short run, GDP annual growth would have been 2.5 percent below the base run and in the long run 4.1 percent below it).[8] Likewise, all socioeconomic groups would have been worse off income-wise than in the base run and more so in the long than in the short run. The two urban groups and the two nonagricultural rural groups would have suffered relatively the most. The rate of inflation would have fallen by 2.9 percent in the short run and by 6.7 percent in the long run relative to the base run. Because of the large cut in government expenditures, the government would have reduced its net foreign borrowing by about half.

The next useful comparison is among *Experiments 2, 3* and the base run. *Experiment 2* simulates a situation where the government emphasizes public investment relative to government current expenditures whereas *Experiment 3* simulates an even larger share of total government expenditures allocated to current expenditures than in the base run and, conversely, a significantly lower share going to public investment. Hence, a comparison of these two counterfactual scenarios with the base run reveals the short run vs. long run consequences during the adjustment period of sheltering public consumption and the wage bill of civil servants at the expense of reduction in public investment and vice versa. In the short run, *Experiment 2* (emphasizing investment)

Table 6.5   Short run simulation results, index numbers, billion Rupiah, million $

	BASERUN	EXP1 Publ. exps cut	EXP2-1 Gov. inv. up gov. cons. cut	EXP2-2 Gov. inv. up gov. cons. cut ag. inv. up	EXP3 Gov. inv. cut gov. cons. up	EXP4 Accel. Deval.	EXP5-1 Monetary contraction	EXP5-2 Monetary expansion
GDPFC(Real)	100.00	97.49	99.16	99.24	101.09	100.87	99.60	100.54
AGEMPLOYE(Real)	100.00	99.04	99.47	100.04	100.58	97.66	100.95	98.79
SMFARM(Real)	100.00	99.35	99.76	100.27	100.27	98.38	100.76	99.02
MEDFARM(Real)	100.00	99.21	99.60	99.80	100.35	101.18	100.01	99.92
LARGEFARM(Real)	100.00	99.11	99.54	99.62	100.39	102.17	99.70	100.19
RURALLOW(Real)	100.00	95.80	99.38	99.19	101.14	97.88	99.21	100.66
RURALHIGH(Real)	100.00	93.60	94.71	94.75	105.48	99.64	100.01	99.93
URBANLOW(Real)	100.00	94.56	98.51	98.32	102.01	97.54	98.94	101.04
URBANHIGH(Real)	100.00	93.30	95.85	95.87	104.56	99.38	99.13	101.09
GFBOR($)	4 266.56	2 478.79	4 500.46	4 529.62	4 128.58	3 858.25	4 256.80	4 255.89
GOVSAV(Real)	6 026.90	6 952.09	7 064.94	7 075.68	5 007.19	6 284.52	5 958.19	6 125.70
FBOR($)	2 155.44	3 084.88	2 153.68	2 125.29	2 132.48	1 679.61	1 022.05	3 461.62
CUR.BOP($)	6 422.00	5 563.67	6 654.13	73.93	6 261.06	5 537.87	5 278.85	7 717.51
EXPORT($)	19 235.00	19 474.94	19 129.71	19 129.19	19 323.60	19 699.46	19 626.02	18 795.36
IMPORT($)	22 037.00	21 472.32	22 144.32	22 145.61	21 977.69	21 639.66	21 348.50	22 809.34
PRIV.INV(Real)	9 074.60	9 454.94	9 001.39	8 994.17	9 171.58	8 671.92	7 713.31	10 491.02
GOVT.INV(Real)	9 905.20	8 871.93	115.25	10 949.95	8 871.93	9 905.20	9 905.20	9 905.20
GOVT.FOR.DEBT($)	25 920.56	24 132.79	26 154.46	26 183.62	25 782.58	25 512.25	25 910.80	25 909.89
PINDEX	100.00	95.85	100.99	100.98	99.30	112.99	95.46	105.69

Table 6.6 Per capita income share of each household groups

	BASERUN	EXP1	EXP2-1	EXP2-2	EXP3	EXP4	EXP5-1	EXP5-2
AGEMPLOYE	5.29	5.45	5.37	5.40	5.20	5.19	5.36	5.20
SMFARM	5.44	5.62	5.54	5.57	5.34	5.38	5.51	5.37
MEDFARM	11.94	12.32	12.13	12.15	11.71	12.13	11.98	11.88
LARGEFARM	17.66	18.21	17.95	17.95	17.34	18.13	17.68	17.65
RURALLOW	9.67	9.64	9.81	9.79	9.56	9.51	9.64	9.70
RURALHIGH	11.71	11.40	11.32	11.31	12.07	11.72	11.75	11.65
URBANLOW	15.24	14.99	15.33	15.29	15.21	14.94	15.14	15.34
URBANHIGH	23.05	22.37	22.55	22.54	23.57	23.01	22.94	23.21
SUM	100.00	100.00	100.00	100.00	100.00	100.00	100.00	100.00

Notes:

Experiment 1   20 percent cut in government current expenditures.

Experiment 2–1   20 percent cut in government current expenditures and 27 percent increase in government investment.

Experiment 2–2   20 percent cut in government current expenditures and 50 percent increase in agricultural government investment and 23 percent increase in other government investment.

Experiment 3   20 percent cut in government investment and 16 percent increase in government current expenditures.

Experiment 4   20 percent devaluation of foreign exchange rate.

Experiment 5-1   15 percent point decrease of money supply.

Experiment 5-2   15 percent point increase of money supply.

The exchange rate (Rupiah/$) is set at 1039 in the base run.

Source: Thorbecke (1990), Table 4.6.

results in a lower growth rate of GDP relative to the base run of respectively 0.84 percent and 0.76 percent in the two variants (*Experiments 2-1* and *2-2*). The incomes of the 'rural high' and 'urban high' groups are significantly reduced by between 5.3 percent and 4.2 percent, annually, depending on which variant is considered. Since both of these groups include the bulk of the civil servants, they are directly affected by the 20 percent cut in the wage bill. Other socioeconomic groups are only marginally touched; indeed agricultural employees and small farmers even benefit very slightly under *Experiment 2-2* from the additional employment opportunities and incomes generated during the construction phase of public investment projects in agriculture.

In contrast in the short run under *Experiment 3* (emphasizing government current expenditures), the growth rate of GDP would have been about 1.1 percent higher than in the base run. All socioeconomic groups' incomes are higher than in the base run with the 'rural high' and 'urban high' households enjoying substantial improvement in their real incomes of the order of 5.48 percent and 4.56 percent per annum, respectively, above the base run.

In the long run, a strategy of concentrating on public investment projects pays off in terms of higher GDP growth (0.94 percent and 1.08 percent above the base run, respectively, in *Experiment 2-1* and *2-2*). There are relative gainers and relative losers among household categories. Agricultural employees, small and medium farmers benefit as do, to a lesser degree, the rural and urban poor (the first two groups above benefit, of course, most under variant 2-2 which concentrates on public investment in agriculture). On the other hand, the relative losers consist of the 'rural high' and 'urban high' groups and, to a very limited extent, the large farmers.

Conversely, a pattern of government expenditures emphasizing current expenditures at the expense of capital expenditures (*Experiment 3*) leads to a slowdown of GDP growth (1.18 percent per annum below the base run), while contributing to inflation (1.71 percent per annum above the base run) and entailing larger foreign borrowing. The only groups which are better off in this counterfactual exercise are the urban high and rural high (mainly through the wage bill received by the civil servants) and the large farmers.

Experiment 4 simulates accelerated devaluation relative to the actual (observed) depreciation of the Rupiah which is part and parcel of the base run adjustment package. As expected this scenario encourages exports and discourages imports (by, respectively, 2.2 percent per annum and −3.3 percent in the long run). The strengthening of the balance of payments induces a fall in government foreign borrowing needs. At the same time, the rise in import prices induced by the accelerated devaluation is very inflationary (leading to an increase in the rate of inflation relative to the base run of 12.99 per cent per annum in the short run and 14.2 percent per annum in the long run). These inflationary pressures, in turn, encourage capital flight, as can be seen from the marked increase in private deposits denominated in foreign currency (*FBOR* in Tables 6.5 and 6.6).

Interestingly, real GDP growth is marginally higher than in the base run in this experiment by 0.19 percent per annum largely because of the favorable balance of payments repercussions. The distributional consequences are mixed: large farmers and medium farmers (who produce much of the export crops) benefit from the increase in the prices of tradeables following the devaluation and see their real incomes go up by respectively 1.7 and 0.94 percent per annum more than in the base run. All other household categories are unfavorably affected, and particularly the non-agricultural rural and urban groups.

The final experiment reported in Tables 6.5 and 6.6, simulates a monetary contraction and a monetary expansion.[9] Monetary contraction (*Experiment 5-1*) is very deflationary, the price level falls by about 4.5 percent per annum in the short run and by 3.4 percent per annum in the long run below that prevailing during the base run. GDP growth is practically not affected in the short run, but is reduced by over 1 percent per annum in the long run compared to the base run. The current account of the balance of payments (CUR BOP in Table 6.6) improves by a substantial 1143 billion Rupiah, mainly because of the slowdown in import demand. The distributional consequences are generally quite neutral.

A counterfactual policy of monetary expansion (*Experiment 5-2*) would have boosted slightly real GDP growth in the short run (by 1.29 percent per annum) and marginally in the long run (by 0.54 percent per annum). Again its distributional impact appears quite neutral. The main disadvantages of this strategy are (a) the inflation that it would generate (the price level rising by 4.4 percent per annum more in the short run than in the base run and by 5.69 percent per annum more in the long run); (b) the dramatic worsening in the current account of the balance of payments by almost $1.3 billion a year compared with the base run; and (c) the appearance of a net flow of private borrowing abroad instead of the traditional flow of net private lending abroad (see *FBOR* in Tables 6.5 and 6.6).

One noteworthy piece of information provided by Table 6.5 is the average total Indonesian foreign debt (*GOVT. FOR. DEBT*) obtained in each of the experiments. It is expressed as the average total foreign debt existing at the midpoint of, respectively, the short run period (i.e., the amount after one year of a two year period – say end 1983) – and the long run (i.e., the amount of the debt which would have prevailed at the end of 1985 (the midpoint of the six year period 1983–8).

What a comparison of alternative experiments suggests is that a strategy of emphasizing public investment projects (*Experiment 2*) yields the largest level of indebtedness, but the differences are small – except for *Experiment 1*. Interestingly, *Experiment 2* would have entailed only a marginal increase in indebtedness compared to the base run scenario.

At this stage, it should be recalled that the various experiments which were simulated all consist of the same base run set of policies except for one which is allowed to vary. Thus, for example, in the case of the fiscal experiments (*Experiments 1-3*) only the pattern of government expenditures was altered while all other policy measures (i.e., the exchange rate and money supply) were kept as in the base run. In *Experiment 4*, all policies remained as in the base run except for a simulated accelerated devaluation and, finally, *Experiment 5* only alters the money supply. A question which suggests itself is whether, starting from the actual base run package, formulating counterfactual scenarios consisting of *different combinations* of policies and simulating their joint effects would provide some additional insights. With this goal in mind a new set of experiments was designed using different combinations of mixed policies. In general, the results of the effects of joint policy measures tend to be more additive than multiplicative. On the whole, a comparative evaluation of the mixed policies counterfactual scenarios confirms the conclusions reached on the basis of the previous set of experiments. It does not appear that important additional insights are gained from the mixed policy experiments as compared to varying one policy instrument at a time within the base run set of instruments.

6.6   CONCLUSIONS

In comparing the outcomes of the various counterfactual scenarios with the adjustment package adopted by the government (the base run) the major conclusion which is reached is that the latter appears, not so surprisingly, most consistent with the multiple objectives of the government under both sets of experiments. In particular, it sheltered the incomes of the civil servants in both the short run and in the long run relative to each and every alternative counterfactual experiment simulated above except *Experiment 3* which called for an even greater level of government current expenditures than in the base run scenario. The problem with *Experiment 3* is that it would have entailed a conflict with GDP growth in the long run and required the government to borrow significantly more from abroad. In the interests of growth and fiscal stability (two important objectives of the government), the base run yielded an outcome preferable to the expenditure pattern contained in *Experiment 3*.

Experiment 2 (emphasizing public investment) is potentially attractive in the long run in terms of higher GDP growth, lower inflation and higher incomes for most agricultural household groups, but these advantages have to be weighed against significantly lower standards of living (particularly in the short run) for the urban and rural high groups. Given the political power of civil servants, this cost could not be borne by the government. Public investment benefits those socioeconomic groups whole employment opportunities depend, at least partially, on construction and public works projects, i.e., rural low, urban low, agricultural employees and small farmers. These groups provide the bulk of the unskilled and manual labor required in the construction phase of investment projects and later enjoy the fruits of increased productivity.

The other two counterfactual *Experiments* (4 and 5) would have yielded outcomes clearly inferior to those resulting from the base run. In the case of an accelerated devaluation, the cost in terms of a much higher inflation rate and lower standards of living for most socio-economic groups would not have been sufficient to compensate for the improvement in the balance of payments. The size of the actual devaluation (reflected in the base run) appeared sufficient to constrain capital flight within a tolerable level while providing the necessary price incentives to encourage the production of tradeables. In particular, because of the greater relative importance of agricultural exports, compared to manufactured exports, at the outset of the adjustment period, and the larger proportion of output consisting of tradeables goods in the rural areas than in the urban areas, it seems that devaluation *per se* benefited the rural households more than the urban households. Finally, the monetary contraction scenario would have been so deflationary as to be quite unpalatable; conversely, monetary expansion would have threatened external equilibrium and fueled inflationary pressures with very little income or equity gains compared to the base run.

In conclusion, it is clear that the adjustment strategy which was, in fact, adopted and implemented contributed to the restoration of internal and external equilibrium. Even though it entailed an unavoidable slowdown in economic growth during the adjustment period, this strategy reinforced some of the desirable distributional trends which were underway in the preadjustment period and allowed them to continue after the oil crisis. The vulnerability of the Indonesian economy to external shocks has been reduced as judged by the higher share of renewable resources (e.g., manufacturing goods) exports in total exports and the declining relative importance of oil revenues in total government revenues.

At the same time, it should be underlined that the adjustment process is a continuing one. Some of the recent cuts in current and capital expenditures may have a delayed negative impact on the observed trend towards poverty alleviation. Even though the adjustment experience of Indonesia between 1983 and 1988 appears to have been a successful one, it is still too early to pass any definitive judgment.

Notes

* This chapter is based on and draws extensively on a recent volume by the author: E. Thorbecke, *Adjustment, Growth and Income Distribution in Indonesia* (1990). The information and statistical data presented in this chapter, unless specifically mentioned, originate in the above volume which is available from the author. A variant of this chapter was prepared for a special issue of *World Development* devoted to the modeling of the impact of structural adjustment on income distribution.

1. See World Bank, *Indonesia's Strategy for Growth and Structural Change* (3 May 1989), Statistical Tables 10.3 and 10.1.
2. World Bank (1989), pp. 18–9.
3. See Ravallion and Huppi (1989) and Huppi and Ravallion (1990).
4. This complete model is presented and discussed in Thorbecke (1990); see in particular, Chapter 4 and Table 4.5.
5. In a sense the adjustment process is a continuous process. By choosing 1988 as the end year of the adjustment period, it is not implied that the full impact of all adjustment measures had by that time permeated throughout the socioeconomic system. However, it can be argued that a five year period is long enough to capture at least the major changes. Furthermore, 1988 was the last year for which reliable data were available.
6. In particular, the following observed average annual rates of change be-

tween 1983 and 1988 of the corresponding key variables were plugged in the model: export price of oil (which in the classification scheme of the model corresponds to mining products), in US dollars, minus 13.1 percent exchange rate (Rupiah/US dollar), 19.86 percent; government real investment in agriculture, 2.6 percent; government real investment in non-agricultural sectors, −5.8 percent; interest payments to rest of the world, 16.3 percent; other government real current expenditures, −3.2 percent; and, finally, money stock, 8.4 percent.

7. It should be noted that for the short run, these values are expressed as two year averages while in the long run simulation they are expressed as annual averages over six year (1983–8). To make the comparison more meaningful the actual observed values are reported under the base run expressed in Rupiah at 1983 prices or in US dollars using the average *real* exchange rate during 1983–8. The set of values in Panel 2 for the various counterfactual experiments (*Experiments 1–5*) was obtained by subtracting the differences between the original base run values and experiment values from the corresponding actual values given under the base run experiment.

8. Since actual GDP growth during the adjustment period was about 3.6 percent per annum, it means that stagnation would have resulted during the adjustment period.

9. A few additional simulations were run, i.e., (a) a central bank policy of using money supply as an instrument to achieve a target real deposit rate necessary to stem capital flight; and (b) the impact of the fixed interest rates (credit rationing) system in place in Indonesia before the financial reform of 1983.

References

Huppi, M. and M. Ravallion (1990)   'Indonesia's Sectoral Structure of Poverty in the 1980s' (Washington, DC: World Bank) (mimeo).

Ravallion, M. and M. Huppi (1989)   'Poverty and Undernutrition in Indonesia during the 1980s' (Washington, DC: World Bank) (mimeo).

Thorbecke, E. (1989)   'Indonesia's Strategy for Growth and Structural Change,' *World Development Report* (May).

Thorbecke, E. (1990)   *Adjustment, Growth and Income Distribution in Indonesia* (Paris: OECD Development Center).

Tobin, J. (1969)   'A General Equilibrium Approach to Monetary Theory,' *Journal of Money, Credit, and Banking*, **1** (February): 15–29.

Part III

Policy Perspectives

7 Economic Justice to the Working Poor Through a Wage Subsidy

Edmund S. Phelps

In this chapter an attempt is made to analyze the status of the working poor in the United States and the ways by which, acting collectively through the government, we can improve the terms at which the working poor participate in the cooperative enterprise we call the economy. Motivating these concerns are some old ideas of equity, or economic justice.

The assumption, which once would have passed without much dissent, that the working poor merit public assistance because, being poor, they deserve our sympathy, falls mostly on deaf ears. The low wage worker in the United States has no monopoly on suffering and, not uncommonly, has a more comfortable life – though perhaps not a more self-fulfilling life – than the laborforce participant in quite a few countries we could name. The position taken in this chapter is, rather, that the working poor are owed better rewards than now received, as a matter of economic justice. If the cost has to come out of the budget for our national defense, so that the chance of our survival is diminished, or out of the budget of those who need the money more, such as the physically or mentally impaired and sick or elderly persons requiring special care, that is a real pity; but justice is prior.

What, then, is economic justice?

The concept of economic justice is the idea of just desserts. It is justice in the rewards from contributing to the economy: collaboration in production, engaging in trade, and sharing the burden of collective goods. There is, generally, the possibility of mutual gains for the participants in the economy as a result of these exchanges, and justice is achieved by appropriate arrangements with regard to the 'production and distribution' of these gains among the participants. Where there is no contribution to the economy, to the production of gains, economic justice does not apply. For the purposes of this chapter, we may think of economic justice as justice in the governmental and institutional arrangements determining the profile of wage rates.

There is more than one standard, or conception, of justice that can be implemented where the problem of doing economic justice arises. One can borrow, as some do, the standard used in the nineteenth century utilitarianism of Bentham and Mill: the sum of utilities – in the present context, the utilities, or satisfaction levels, of the contributors to the economy. There is also the Rawlsian standard: the reward of those contributors receiving the least reward for their contribution. The utilitarian standard is prone to problematic and paradoxical implications while, in the judgment of quite a few, the Rawlsian standard accords with certain, widely (though not universally) accepted and intuitively appealing, principles of equity. In discussing some principles of equity, I take a Rawlsian standpoint. But the conclusions of this chapter do not require that preference; a devout utilitarian could concur.

One widely accepted principle of justice is that of equal rights, independently of the relative numbers of people in each category. Intellectually or physically disadvantaged persons who are, nevertheless, able to contribute to the economy, do not deserve less merely because their abilities do not command a high scarcity premium. Free markets, however, pay according to scarcity. Hence, justice is not, generally, produced by the voluntary and bilateral relationships among the economy's participants; in real life societies it never is. Justice requires the mediation of government, at one level of government or another, aimed at pulling up the rewards of the least rewarded, who suffer from the plethora of their abilities – more precisely, those abilities of theirs having a commercial value. (The Rawlsian standard, applied all the way, would have the government pull up the lowest wage to the greatest extent feasible.) In market economies, increased justice toward the working poor can be sought by intervention in the labor market, via public subsidies and, possibly, public expenditures (which can operate as latent subsidies) favoring the employment of low wage labor; or by intervention in the capital market, via subsidies favoring investments in the working poor (such as their training), or by interference with the market via controls. When the low-productivity participants are subsidized or benefited, indirectly, through a suitable choice of public expenditures, the activities of high-productivity participants must be taxed sooner or later to pay for those subsidies or expenditures.

The payment, by participants, of taxes, for that purpose, should not be imagined so large that a participant might be made worse off than he would be without the coparticipation of the others in the economy (the subsidies and the subsidizers) – so that he would curse having found himself shoulder to shoulder with the others, instead of in a system where he and everyone else is born onto his own little sovereign slice of the land. On any conception of justice, having the further principle that all should gain from their cooperation in the economy or, at least, none should lose; those prospering more would have to give back, through taxes, to those prospering less, a fraction of their before tax gain that is not to exceed 100 percent. (It could be, though, that the advantaged, as a group, will do less well after redistribution than they would have done had the disadvantaged not grown up alongside them or had they exercised a constitutional right to expel the disadvantaged from the economy. The impermissibility of excluding anyone is another of the basic principles.)

Another principle of justice, certainly in any liberal conception of justice, is the Pareto principle that a social change that makes one or more persons better off, without making the others worse off, is a social gain, not an injustice. In this view, the economic arrangements of a just society are equalitarian only up to a point; some arrangements tolerate and even promote inequality, but have the redeeming virtue that, in doing so, they provide a gain to everyone, at least if not carried too far, and hence, are not unjust. If the society's current arrangements ensured equality, even if they achieved the highest feasible level of equality, these sharing arrangements enforcing equality would be so wasteful – so stifling of people's incentives to work – as to leave all participants worse off than they could be if they were given incentives having inequality side-effects; so the equalitarian arrangement would be jettisoned in favor of some arrangement better for everyone though unequal (but not unjust for that). So, inequality is not *prima facie* unjust, only excessive inequality (and deficient inequality) is unjust. There is no way of telling whether economic justice is being done to various strata of workers and other participants in the economy simply by looking at income distribution and wage rate distribution data to see how unequal they are. We have to look at data describing what the society is doing for the various groups, and then make a judgment as to whether the society is overdoing it in the sense of causing everyone to be worse off, as a result.

Neither is there any obvious connection between the general living standard of a country, as measured by average income, and the degree of economic injustice produced. People who are very comfortable, even affluent, can be rewarded unjustly little for their contribution. There may be something to the idea that when people's income expectations are disappointed they become more sensitive to the injustices they had previously let pass in view of the opportunity costs of their time and energy. If the usual technical progress over decades would produce a doubling of everyone's rewards and opportunity costs, assuming no one responded to it by doing different things, the 'substitution effect' of that progress would, by itself, operate to divert attention from injustice; but, the 'income effect' of that progress could operate to increase the attention people gave to that injustice by precisely enough as to leave no net increase in the importance placed on it. (Possibly, the money people would be willing to pay to end injustice, as they see it, would be the same proportion of income as it was before.)

How much justice is done to the working poor in this country at this stage in its social development? Not much, so far as I can see. There seems to be little in the way of a subsidy from the rest of the economy to the workers at the bottom of the heap, which is the focus of Rawlsians. The expensive subsidies we read about are, mostly, for the middle class – the subsidies to university education of their children, the subsidies (in the form of tax deductibility) to their mortgages for home owning, FHA loan guarantees to keep their single-family home costs down, and, to end the partial listing with the largest of them all, huge farm subsidies. The major subsidy to low paid earners is the actuarial, or statistical, deficit that the social security programs tend to run over the life of such workers. It is not altogether clear how large that deficit is, though, since the disadvantaged workers have a higher mortality rate than the other workers and, therefore, fail to reach the retirement years at a higher rate. (On the other hand, there may be differential payments of disability claims to the disadvantaged, and, perhaps, this factor goes some distance toward cancelling the previous factor.) It may be true that between 1970, say, and 1990 there has been an increase in the size of the overall welfare budget of the public sector – federal, state and local government. But, most of this welfare expenditure is for child raising and to permit single-parent families to remain intact. Even the so-called earned income credit does nothing for the low-wage earner *qua* earner. It is not a recognition that there would be an injustice in his or her remuneration were it not for the income supplement offered in the form of tax adjustment. The earned income credit does not, I believe, raise the rewards of any worker not bringing up children or having other dependents; and it would not be effective if, perchance, the worker had won a lottery or had some other source of unearned income taking him or her out of the poverty zone.

Of course, it may be true that the working poor benefit, disproportionately, from these family-oriented benefit programs, if only because there is a means test or the tax benefit is phased out as higher income brackets. So, one could say that, statistically, the working poor are being subsidized in this indirect way. Similarly, if the working poor were disproportionately left-handed and there were a tax benefit for left-handedness, one could say that the government was improving the lot of the working poor on the average. But, if we look at matters from the standpoint of Rawls' criterion, the reward or life prospects of the least rewarded workers then, since we do not advance the position of those in the rear of the race by giving a helping hand arbitrarily to some (though some of those helped would have been in the rear), we do not succeed in reducing the Rawlsian measure of the injustice – only in reducing the number who are the full victims of it.

The other observation that cries out to be made here is that, in the past two decades, the distance that subsidies have left to go to achieve economic justice seems to have widened – not because the subsidies themselves have been shrinking, thus marching the wrong way, but because the degree of inequality in before-tax-and-subsidy wage rates has widened. Such a widening increases the amount of the subsidy/tax required to achieve economic justice, even though it does not aspire to go all the way to equality, as that would hurt everyone. (If perchance productivity shifts in the past twenty years had caused all differences among workers to become economically irrelevant, so that all wage rates were equal, there could then be economic justice with no subsidy/tax at all; what has happened, since 1970, is the reverse, with the before-intervention wage rate of the least skilled workers falling relatively to that of the median worker.) So, the same subsidy level as a ratio to the mean wage rate as two decades ago leaves us with a larger job undone than was the case before. (With perfect justice all the time, there would have been some widening of the inequality between after-tax-and-subsidy wage rates; but the actual wage inequality, besides being higher to begin with, has widened more than it would have with justice before and after. That is, the after-tax-and-subsidy wage of the working poor, as a percentage of the after-tax-and-subsidy wage of the mean worker – one minus the percentage *wage gap* – fell by more than it would have under the cushion of a just subsidy/tax system.)

It seems reasonable to believe that this trend of the past couple of decades is interrelated to what might be the major development in American life over the same period – the rise of an underclass in American cities. As everyone knows, an alternative economy of fire-arms and drugs has been constructed in the depressed neighborhoods of the underclass that has developed over the past fifteen years or so. I suppose that the increase in the degree, or burden, of injustice just noted – the rise of the percentage wage gap by more than would have occurred in a regime of economic justice – accounts to *some* degree for the rise of this underclass. Some of the rise would have been unavoidable, but the rise of the percentage wage gap would have been cushioned, and the consequent rise of the underclass mod-erated, were there economic justice in the subsidies and taxes affect-ing economic justice – and this even if justice was already in place in 1970, so that the one-time gain of shifting to justice was not available to help out further. It may be true that other factors were at work as well, of course. Another hypothesis is that the underclass growth is a response not only to the disaffection with participation in the legitimate sector of the economy but is also a result of a reduc-tion in the penalties for participation in the illegitimate, underworld sector. Even if that is true, it still leaves plenty of room for the previous hypothesis to share the explanation.

I would add here the reflection that if and insofar as the class of bottom earners has become relatively more numerous, achieving lesser injustice in the sense of an increase in the reward received at the bottom will as a consequence be more of an uphill struggle and, in that sense, less improvement can be expected – though more will share such improvement as is achieved.

What is to be done? There are, as suggested above, three broad types of instruments that governments use to benefit groups within the population and which can be (and have been) used to better the treatment of the working poor: public expenditures of the right type, public controls of some kind, and public subsidies of certain kinds.

Keynesian economics convinced the public, by the 1950s, that high public expenditure was the preferred and, perhaps, the only reliable way to high employment. No doubt many economists and laymen also believed, as a sort of corollary, that a large public sector was also a source of high real wages. Let the government stand ready as an employer of last resort to make sure that real wages do not fall to the level to which they would be driven if people had to go out and sell apples to make a living. When, after two decades of neo-Keynesian revisionism – the 'neoclassical synthesis' – the public was finally persuaded that this was not so, the result was the taxpayer revolt of the 1980s. Ironically, however, there are some non-Keynesian reasons to think the Keynesians were half-right to begin with: that the right type of public expenditure does lift the equilibrium path of employment.

Today it is a standard neo-classical exercise to sift out some grains of truth in the old Keynesian dogma. Insofar as the government contrives to step up spending on comparatively labor intensive goods, such as street sweeping and national park monitoring, there surely is a positive real wage effect; and in some models there would also result as a side-effect an increase of the employment rate as well. By tilting the extra public expenditure more toward the least skilled, and hence, the lowest earners, the government can assure that the wages pulled up are disproportionately those at the bottom end of the distribution.

The objection to such a method of driving up wages at the bottom of the distribution is that, in the absence of some suitable mechanism for doing it, the additional public expenditure would not be apt to have a very high value; the cost effectiveness of this approach might be awfully low. It is not so much that the marginal utility of an additional dollar of expenditure in the public sector, even if optimally directed, would not be as high as the corresponding marginal utility of a dollar of expenditure in the private sector; the situation may well be the reverse precisely because there is so much inefficiency in the allocation of public resources. (Consider an extra dollar of gun control.) The question is whether the appropriate average of the marginal utilities of the various goods provided by the public sector would be up to the level of the corresponding average marginal utility in the private sector. On the pork-barrel theory of overtaxation and overexpenditure on vested interest groups, perfected by the Scandinavians, we must take the *actual* marginal utility of public expenditure (when the extra dollar of expenditure is divided up as it would actually be) to be a good deal lower than that of private expenditure. So, public expenditure, as an instrument for higher real wages at the bottom of the distribution, would require increasing an expenditure level that is already too high for economic efficiency. To put it simply, the legislators have already bloated the public sector with army bases and shipyards and the like, with a view to pulling up the lowest wages and thus, buying votes at a low price; doing still more of that kind of thing would be quite expensive in terms of the inefficiency added, so one wants to find another instrument not already in heavy use.

We come, then, to controls. The most familiar and conspicuous way to raise wages at the bottom end is the minimum wage law making it illegal for businesses to pay less than the statutory minimum wage. There is a criticism of this method that must be taken seriously. Economists are quick to point out that, in the absence of significant monopsony power by an important number of firms in the labor market, the result of raising the minimum wage is to reduce the quantity of labor demanded. (The operation of labor unions may modify that result a little, as they could compel firms to follow a no-layoff policy; but, it is not obvious that the unions would find that optimal to do, and it is quite implausible to suppose they would force firms to hire replacements of low-wage workers with the attrition of the existing work-force. In any case, the unions are not so large in the United States as to invalidate the main proposition just offered.) This effect of the minimum wage, and of each increase of the minimum wage, a contraction in the quantity of labor demanded, has welfare consequences rather similar, in one respect, to the effect of a tax on employment (or low paid employment, as here). A divergence results between the marginal social productivity of labor and the marginal opportunity cost of labor – what is required as compensation per unit of extra work – and thus a departure from the first-order conditions for first-best economic efficiency; since there are also income taxes and sales taxes present already, it is actually a widening of the departure from the first-order condition. But this observation is hardly decisive, since it was clear, from the outset, that society must accept a departure from the conditions for the first-best optimum that would be obtainable with lump-sum taxes and transfers set by an omniscient planner, if society is to achieve a redistribution less tilted away from the low paid worker, given that those lump-sum measures are not safely used in the world of imperfectly informed government agencies.

The more serious objection to the employment-reducing effect of the minimum wage is that some people will find themselves involuntarily unemployed, since the market will not clear. If in fact the labor market is not necessarily one that would have cleared anyway – its equilibrium may, very well, be a job-rationing equilibrium – the result is that more workers will find themselves involuntarily unemployed as the result of the minimum wage. This involuntary joblessness strikes, precisely, those whom the law is ostensibly aiming to help, those workers who are least advantaged; they are the ones priced out of the market by the minimum wage.

Even if we were to suppose that the consequence of this increased involuntary unemployment rate was the certainty or, at least, a strong likelihood that some workers would be deprived of a job for their whole lives, it would not be morally clear that a social decision to enact such a minimum wage would be unjust. Throughout history, every society, it seems, has mandated various collective actions despite the certainty that some individuals would actually be harmed, thereby, justifying the action on the ground that all would face the expectation of a gain – of expected benefits exceeding expected burdens. If in a referendum all the working poor would vote for a (higher) minimum wage in spite of the risks of lifelong unemployment, a liberal case against this method of proceeding can still be mounted: although the point is not developed here, it could be argued that, as an empirical matter, the additional unemployment brought by the minimum wage is unnecessarily wasteful; this method of achieving the estimated increase of expected lifetime earnings by the working poor is more costly than need be – the lifelong unemployed would cost the treasury so much as they became wards of the state and the reduced employment and income would deprive the state of so much tax revenue that it would be cheaper simply to subsidize the payment of higher wages to the working poor. The case against using the minimum wage as the instrument is strengthened if it can be shown to be plausible that the increase in expected wage income of the working poor, resulting from a higher minimum wage, would ultimately become seriously eroded by a consequent decline of employment opportunities as factor substitution finally takes its toll.

Economists have typically entertained a presumption in favor of subsidies to improve the terms obtained by the working poor. But, there has been astoundingly little systematic analysis of the concrete forms that subsidization might take. What to subsidize, and how to design that subsidy? With those questions provisionally answered, we can then begin to estimate the cost of achieving a given improvement in the position of the working poor by the subsidy route.

Discussions by many economists and laymen have frequently been addressed to the subsidization of the education and training of the working poor. I have two difficulties with that approach. The first is that, as its proponents themselves clearly imply, the benefits from the increased education envisioned would accrue to future generations of the working poor. The middle-aged and older persons among the working poor and, indeed, the entire stock of working poor already in the laborforce, but not beyond the years of education, would not benefit. The education approach does not speak to the desire for economic justice here and now. The second difficulty with the education approach is its assumption either that the best feasible allocation of resources, from the point of view of the working poor, must depart from the neo-classical principle that social welfare is best served by efficiency in production and efficiency in the allocation of capital expenditure over investment *or* that the working poor are underinvesting in their education in relation to their earnings possibilities. The more usual approach in economics would be to attach the rewards of the working poor directly, pulling up their wage rates, thereby, and leave it to the judgment of the poor to decide whether to respond to their improved potential with increased investment of their own financing in their education and training.

But, of course, the matter of education and poverty is a very big subject. The criticism that existing public education has failed to instill, in the working poor, the optimum level of skills because of inefficiencies in the delivery system, is undoubtedly well-founded. Perhaps, there is aggregate underinvestment in education in the United States. (It would be interesting to know whether in such American cities as New York and Los Angeles the amount spent on primary and secondary education per student is comparable to that in London, Liverpool, Paris, Marseilles, Tokyo and Osaka. I would guess that teachers' and administrators' salaries in US dollars were about the same in 1990.) But, one cannot help suspecting that, in addition, the school children in the inner cities are inefficient at learning in school because of the distractions and disturbances of family and social life they suffer as a result of the poverty of their communities and the absence of attractive earnings possibilities, other than criminal activities that are risky or degrading.

The most direct public subsidy to pull up the rewards of the working poor is a payment that subsidizes the employment of the working poor. A firm that has low paid workers in its employ would then benefit both from the productivity of those workers, as before, and from the subsidy payment which each of those employees would entitle the firm to receive. Hence, the after-subsidy marginal revenue productivity of low wage labor would be increased at the firm. If we were to take the amount of such labor supplied to be a constant, perfectly inelastic with respect to the wage rate received by the worker, the firms would be induced by the increased marginal revenue productivity to bid the market wage rate to a higher level; if we take the amount of low wage labor supplied to exhibit some elasticity, but a finite elasticity, the result will be some increase of the wage rate and some increase in the level of employment of the working poor. For purposes of the calculations below, I will take the labor supplied to be a constant at all wage levels.

How might such a wage-subsidy scheme be designed? It is an interesting question, as it raises the not unfamiliar problem of incentives to evade the intent of the subsidy law through false reports on the books; much as the income tax creates incentives to earn unreported income. The design task of the government is to achieve the desired effect of the subsidy program at a cost that is tolerably close to the minimum possible, making some allowance for additional bookkeeping costs at firms and additional monitoring costs of the government.

First, the hypothetical data. For illustrative purposes, let us take $7 an hour as the level to which we wish to drive the wage of the bottom group. For simplicity, I will assume that a minimum wage law survives and that it forbids firms from paying less than $7 an hour. If the government provides a subsidy of $4 an hour, then no worker will be hired (under full compliance) whose marginal revenue productivity, excluding the subsidy, is less than $3 an hour. So the relevant population of workers here is those with a productivity of $3 an hour or higher. Having in mind that the employment of such workers in the United States currently is around 120 million, and putting together odd bits of information on the distribution of the laborforce by wage, I will suppose there to be about 5 million workers in the 3–4 dollar an hour category, another 5 million in the 4–5 dollar an hour category, and so forth – a more or less flat distribution at the low end of the scale.

It is instructive to begin with an example of a design that could not fly. We can imagine a subsidy scheme in which the government stands ready to make up the difference between $7 an hour and the amount the firm pays out of its pocket to those of its employees receiving less than $7; that is, an employee costing the firm $3 an hour would cause the government to contribute $4 an hour, an employee whom the firm pays $4 out of its own pocket would produce a subsidy payment of $3, an employee that costs the firm $5 would occasion a $2 subsidy, and so forth. Then these low paid workers would all find their wage rates jumping to $7. *If* it were true that firms would not cheat in response to the temptations created by such a scheme, its cost would be minimal: a $4 subsidy per hour times 5 million workers times 2000 hours, hence $40 billion per year, for workers in the bottom wage interval; plus $3 per hour times 5 million workers times 2000 hours, hence $30 billion per year, for workers in the next wage interval, and so forth. This series $40, $30, $20, and $10 billion adds up to a bill of $100 billion per year. Not much in a 6 trillion dollar economy! But there is a design flaw. A firm will now have an incentive to reclassify a $4 worker as a $3 worker and put in a claim for an extra dollar of subsidy to be able to continue the employee's wage at $7. The employee will not be hurt, and might not even be informed, and the firm will go on enjoying the employee's services, but for an increased profit at the expense of the government and, therefore, must be presumed infeasible. (We are farther than ever from being able to operate the economy on an honor system.)

The optimal wage subsidy scheme must be compatible with the incentive of firms to abuse it by false claims of large numbers of workers in their employ who are not worth paying much out of their own pockets. If not cheat-proof it must compromise with first-best principles in order to dampen the degree of cheating. It will illustrate the form that an optimal wage subsidy scheme takes, I believe, to consider the example in which, descending to lower and lower paid employees, with each decrease of one dollar in the out-of-pocket pay per hour to a worker the government responds with an increase of only *one-half* of a dollar. Since the government is not making up the whole of the difference in the firm's out-of-pocket expenditure, the firm does not gain an addition to profit (per hour of this category of workers) equal to the whole of the reduction in its expense; the firm gains only the one-half dollar paid by the government. (Had the government responded, instead, with three-quarters of a dollar, the firm would have instead gained that much.) But, to achieve a genuine gain the firm will have to claim that its out-of-pocket expense is less by one dollar an hour, to obtain the increased subsidy, while, at the same time, it will have to make some maneuver to benefit the employee if, as I suppose, it continues to be necessary to ensure that the employee receives the same total compensation (including what comes indirectly from the government) as before. One such maneuver is a *sub rosa*, under-the-table, wage payment to the employee to make up the shortfall in total compensation that would otherwise result, since the government itself has not made up the whole of the one dollar reduction claimed; while claiming to be paying one dollar less, the firm would actually be paying one-half dollar less and defrauding the government on one-half dollar in order to come up with the same total wage to the employee as before. It may be supposed that sufficiently strong penalties, taken with the fact that the gain is only one-half dollar for a whole dollar of misstatement, would be sufficient to deter all or most such cheating. The other maneuver that the firm could make would be to create nonpecuniary benefits worth, precisely, the missing one-half dollar of wages to the workers involved in the reclassification. 'I am being paid less, but the improved choice of lunches and the new flexible hours makes up for it,' workers might say. This maneuver has the advantage of legality, but if the firms were already offering the optimal package of pecuniary and nonpecuniary benefits to employees, the cost of a half-dollar of benefits per hour might considerably exceed one-half dollar; the distortions thus introduced would serve to limit the reclassification of workers.

How much would this hypothetically optimal plan cost the government per year? I will confine my calculations to the limiting case in which the deterrents to reclassification of employees just discussed, the penalties and the distortionary costs, actually serve to block all such reclassification. Then there will still be 5 million workers in the $3 category and they will still occasion a subsidy of $4 an hour for 2000 hours a year to sustain their new target wage of $7; the annual cost to the government is $40 billion as in the previous calculation. The next tranche of wage earners, those costing the firms $4 an hour, will now receive a subsidy of $3.50 per hour, not $3 as under the unworkable scheme; the annual cost to the government here is $35 billion. The next category will receive a subsidy of $3 an hour, not the $2 called for by the incentive-in-compatible scheme; the annual cost is $30 billion. The series is $40, $35, $30, $25, $20, $15, $10, $5 billion. The total cost per annum to the government is $180 billion. That is hardly a daunting figure in a 6 trillion economy, either. But, it has to be remembered that it is a lower bound on the true cost, in one respect, because it assumed that firms did not find it optimal to reclassify workers in view of the penalties and other costs of doing so. On the other hand, wage earners receiving as much as $9 an hour occasion some subsidy to their employers and, hence, receive some increase in their wage under this graduated subsidy scheme; so, the nation's taxable income would be significantly increased and, as a result, some of the government subsidy outlay would find its way back in the treasury as tax revenue.

Clearly, a subsidy scheme in which the subsidy rate tapers off less gradually with higher and higher wage rates would, on a calculation such as the above, cost less. But that cost reduction has to be weighed against the cost increase that would come about from the consequently increased incentive of firms to reclassify employees into lower paying categories.

Calculations such as mine, in the eyes of some, foreclose any possibility of enactment of an employment subsidy scheme to lift the rewards of the working poor for their contributions to the economy. 'This economic justice of yours and the others',' they seem to say, 'costs too much.' Certainly, deficit-financing an expense like this, on top of the already substantial deficit, would be a hard sell – Congress is now requiring tax financing or expenditure substitution – and it is hard to imagine the increased tax or decreased expenditure that would meet political acceptance. Yet the wage subsidy, I believe, is an idea whose time is coming.

References

Drazen, A. (1986) 'Optimal Minimum Wage Legislation,' *Economic Journal*, **96(3)** (September).

Hammond, P. J. (1977) 'Axioms for the Maximin Criterion,' *Econometrica*, **45**: 853–70.

National Conference of Catholic Bishops (1986) *Economic Justice for All: Pastoral Letter on Catholic Social Teaching and the U.S. Economy* (Washington, DC: US Catholic Church).

Phelps, E. S. (1986) 'Legislating Economic Justice for the Working Poor' (New York) (December) (unpublished typescript).

Phelps, E. S. (1985) *Political Economy* (New York: W. W. Norton).

Rawls, J. (1971) *A Theory of Justice* (Cambridge, MA: Harvard University Press).

Vining, R. (1956) *Economics in the United States of America* (Paris: UN Educational, Scientific and Cultural Organization).

Comment

Thomas Karier

Edmund Phelps' chapter deals with the broad question: why worry about poverty and inequality in the first place? The fact that not enough attention has been given to these issues in the past few decades is at least one of the reasons for this book. The alarming statistics on poverty and growing inequality have reached a point where these issues deserve to become a national priority.

But why are we concerned about it? Conventional economics does not give us much encouragement. Unless poverty reduces total production, there is little reason to change it under the rules of Pareto optimality. The reasons that poverty and inequality should be redressed have very little to do with maximizing output, growth, or personal freedom. They are based on another value, economic justice, as pointed out in this chapter by Phelps.

Economic justice is neither an objective nor a quantifiable concept. For these two reasons it seldom penetrates the core of economic analysis. It is not measured in the Census Survey, and you cannot run regressions with it. But it nevertheless underlies many of our objections to poverty and the increasing inequalities in income and wealth. And it cannot be ignored in a discussion like this one.

There can be little doubt that the concept of economic justice is subjective and varies between individuals. From his perspective Phelps considers the recently increasing disparity between rich and poor to have had a negative effect on justice. On the other hand, he acknowledges that it would be possible to go too far. If the level of equality is too extreme, the result may leave all participants worse off. The problem of having an income distribution that is too equal seems to me to be extremely remote based on the current political moods and the person occupying the White House.

When is the income distribution too unequal? How much income should be redistributed from the elite to the poor, as Phelps suggests? These are important political questions on which economists do not necessarily have any more insight than the general public. However, economists can deal with such questions as why income inequality has increased, why the poverty rate remains high, why increasing numbers of children and single female-headed households are falling into poverty. These are critical questions to address before effective policies can be formulated which improve the current state of economic justice.

In this regard Chapter 3 in this volume makes an important contribution. In it, Joan Rodgers discusses the increasing importance of female-headed households in the overall poverty rate. Mishel and Frankel (1991) refer to the fact that only 18 percent of the poor came from such families in 1959, compared to 37 percent in 1989. The growth can be attributed not so much to increasing poverty rates of these families, but primarily to the increasing percentage of the population in these families, from 8 percent of the total population to 13 percent over the same time frame.

This raises the question of why the relative numbers of female-headed households have increased. Mishel and Frankel point out that for 1989, in 36 percent of these families the woman is divorced, 24 percent widowed, 23 percent never married, and 17 percent were married to absent husbands. This suggests that divorce, death, having children out of wedlock, and absent husbands can largely explain the growing incidence of female-headed households, in that particular order.

There is also the important question of why these families are poor. According to Joan Rodgers, the feminization of poverty draws attention to the relationship between poverty and household type, but to a large extent is misdirected. Her argument is that perhaps these families are poor for reasons other than household structure, such as education, discrimination, low job experience, disabilities, or more children.

Mishel and Frankel argue many of the same reasons for poverty of female-headed families. The heads of these families have lower education levels, less training, are disproportionately black, and have more children than male-headed families. But one should be skeptical that these factors alone could explain the high incidence of poverty among female-headed families. There is clearly an advantage to having more adult workers relative to the total family population which includes infants and other dependents. Therefore one would expect women-headed families to be poorer for all of the human capital reasons as well as family structure.

Rodgers applies a statistical test to see if any of the differences in family income can be attributed to family structure once other factors are controlled. The answer is, yes. One surprising result is that the return to many measures of human capital are lower for female-headed households. Much of this difference can probably be attributed to the fact that women heads of households are more frequently compelled to work part-time, which reduces pay for otherwise comparable abilities. In general, the results are consistent with the belief that women-headed households are poor because of poor skills and education and because they are women-headed households.

One problem with Rodgers' study is that it focuses on the supply side of the labor market ignoring the demand and institutional sides. Large businesses pay more than small ones, manufacturing pays better than services, and union jobs pay better than nonunion. These could all reasonably be counted as 'omitted variables' in the income regressions, which casts doubt on the results.

I would question, however, the assumption that if the utility from being married exceeds the utility from being single, then the person marries, otherwise he or she remains single. I think there should always be room for unrequited love in any economic model.

Finally, I would like to emphasize one other reason for the poverty of female-headed households noted by Mishel and Frankel which does have an obvious policy alternative. 'Only 55 percent of divorced mothers, 33.7 percent of separated mothers, and 13.6 percent of never-married mothers received any child support in 1987.' Some of these cases may be excused if the father is in dire poverty, but there are many cases where child support could be and should be improved. This would be a significant contribution to economic justice.

Reference

Mishel, L. and D. M. Frankel (1991) *The State of Working America*, Economic Policy Institute (Armonk, NY: M. E. Sharpe).

8 Growing Inequality as an Issue for Economic Policy

Paul S. Sarbanes

There have been a number of studies of inequality, but what one encounters in these studies is that they are undertaken by clearly demarcated advocacy organizations. In this regard, there is always the suspicion that the facts are taken in a manner so as to serve a particular advocacy position. I think the essays in this volume, and the conclusions drawn, allow the establishment of an objective common base.

My own view is that the growing inequality of wealth and income is a real danger and threat to our society. Everyone knows that income inequality in the United States has risen steadily in the 1980s. Despite an expansion since 1982, and contrary to the usual historical pattern in the United States we have experienced a diminishment in income equality. In fact, inequality of income stands at its highest point since 1947, when the Census Bureau began keeping statistics. We know a lot about the rising inequality of income, but less about the disturbing rise in inequality of wealth. The IRS has completed a study which found a marked increase in the concentration of wealth at the very top of our society. In 1986, the top 1.6 percent of adults, that is, 3.3 million people with gross assets of more than \$500 000, had total gross asset holdings of \$4.3 trillion and net worth of \$3.8 trillion and they controlled 28.5 percent of the nation's personal wealth, which was up from 23 percent in 1982. This is a very sharp increase over a four year period in terms of the concentration of wealth.

In what follows, I want to review and assess the manner in which the problem of growing inequality is coming into focus and in the policy debate in Washington, and which facts and approaches about inequality seem to carry the greatest weight in the discussions; and the perspectives that are most easily grasped by people in the political arena. One of the reasons that Washington is interested in inequality is because there is a lot of important data that the Census

Bureau reports and which finds its way into the political debate. The debate has now shifted from answering the question of 'what is happening to the very wealthy and the very poor' to the question of the growing gap of inequality between the richest quintile of families and the rest, and the poorest quintile and the rest. Obviously, this shift changes the political dynamic in a very significant way. This very different sort of debate and political dynamic deals with the situation of the 1980s in which the very wealthy experienced incredible gains; those in the top 5 percent have seen a 45 percent increase in their average real income and, even more dramatically, the top 1 percent had an average real income 75 percent higher than at the beginning of the debate, although the average household real income had increased only about 3 percent overall. Furthermore, during the same period, we have seen a stagnation in real compensation per hour. The real average weekly earnings for production and non-supervisory workers have plummetted, from $200 in 1971 to less than $165 in 1990. What we have experienced is that inequality and the distribution of wages have been growing not only between groups with some obvious differences in education, but also within groups of similar education. These inequalities seem to be increasing, and they have put tremendous pressure on families to develop new ways of making ends meet. For many families, this means they can only sustain a higher or their existing living standard by working longer hours or by putting more family members into the workforce. Thus, the number of workers per family increased over the 1980s for families at all income levels, but the increases were greater for low and middle income families. At the same time, the growing number of family members at work often has very hidden costs to the families themselves, the employers, and society. Two-earner families have more work expenses than single-earner families, so they may be worse off even at the same level of earnings. Families in which both parents work, especially those with relatively low incomes, may find it difficult to invest much time and effort in child rearing, which raises the need for social services. Furthermore, even if they are not needed, there is some concern about how much working parents can devote to helping their children become the future productive workers, since there may be pressure for teenagers to work as well. Often, when visiting a McDonald's restaurant, one wonders about this kind of pressure, the drawing of young people away from really preparing themselves for tomorrow's job market and for the future.

One of the consequences of this growing inequality is, therefore, the impact it has among the young. The reported data are alarming in terms of the number of young people in poverty; 20 percent of children are in poverty in 1990 as opposed to 14 percent in 1973. The group in the population that was usually most in poverty was the elderly, but this is no longer the case. In fact, as a society, we have made very significant advances in moving the elderly out of poverty and although there is much more to be done, particularly in the health care area, to assure them of a reasonable life in their retirement, it is the young – who are after all the future of the country – that we find in poverty. We have had, in effect, a 50 percent increase in the number of children in poverty over the 1973–90 period.

The increasing inability of the labor market to provide adequate earning opportunities puts an enormous strain on public programs. We have this question of the working poor. We can no longer assume that if one has a job that it will be adequate to meet one's needs; instead, we have a situation in which people who have a job and are working cannot meet their housing needs, and other requirements of the family, and become dependent on social programs because their earnings are not sufficient. Another serious problem is the increase in the proportion of the population without health insurance or unable to deal with the astronomical increase in the costs of emergency, and the uncompensated care needed to patients who become sick. The costs of health care put an enormous strain on the budgets of hospitals, state and local governments, paying patients, and their insurance companies which in turn raise the health care premiums that employers and employees pay. The increases in premiums affect the competitiveness of United States firms in the international arena. This is so significant a problem that the management of some of the major companies in this country have joined with labor organizations to push the idea of comprehensive national health insurance. This coalition one finds, particularly in those companies and unions that are involved in international competition, because the cost of health care of companies in other countries that are competitors is met generally through some social program and not directly in an employer–employee relationship. In my view, this issue of health care exacerbates economic inequality. I believe that economic growth and economic equity are not conflicting or competitive values, except at the extremes. In the reasonable ranges, however, the two can work together and reinforce one another. Contrary to the assertion that is made by some, in this country, we have moved to the point where economic inequality is, in fact, hampering economic growth.

Let me, now, turn to the root causes of the growing inequality. This examination often leads to a very intense and partisan debate, but it is an important debate because it may well hold the key to our future. Any phenomenon as fundamental and as pervasive as the distribution of income is likely to have multiple overlapping causes. I do not think a single explanation would be adequate, especially for such a large, vastly complicated and heterogeneous country as the United States. It is very important, I think, that we look at the contributions which public policy has made to the increasing inequality. Some have sought to explain a lot of it simply on the basis of demographics. While that may be a partial explanation, the trouble with it is that it tends to treat the rising inequality as a purely natural phenomenon. This assertion treats inequality like the weather, as something over which one has no control. My own view is that bad policies play a major role in reversing the trend of the income disparity. Furthermore, I believe that good policy is essential if we are going to reverse these trends. It was bad policy that got us where we are and we are going to need good policy to get us out of it. There is, of course, some value for a demographic explanation of the rising inequality, but the largest increase in baby boom workers and single-parent families occurred in the 1970s and not the 1980s. This is very important to keep in mind. The policy changes, instead, that were put into place during the so-called Reagan revolution, really represented a deliberate effort to give a greater return to the top of our society and less to the bottom. The policies were explicitly against high marginal tax rates on the wealthy and against transfer payments to the poor. President Reagan moved aggressively on that front, and his policies had enormous consequences for income inequality. First, the tax policies, put into place with the concurrence of the Congress, sharply reduced the progressivity of the tax code. The usual point of view that we had been confronted with was that, 'If you increase taxes and redistribute the money to the poor, that will take away the work incentive from the poor and, similarly, that from the rich to build motels and businesses that provide jobs and health benefits.' This was really the sort of trickle-down theory that we were given in the 1980s. However, empirical evidence shows that there was no trickle from the trickle-down theory. Thus, we have the two divergent points of view on the same issue.

The evidence shows that the reduction of the marginal tax rates, the increases in payroll and excise taxes that resulted during the decade of the 1980s, the percentage of income paid in taxes by the poor fifth of households, increased by about 16 percent while the percentage paid by the richest fifth declined by about 6 percent. Moreover, the very wealthy, those in the top 1 percent, experienced an even greater decline of the share of income they paid in taxes, which declined by about 14 percent.

A second point that needs to be made is that public spending priorities were shifted sharply away from domestic programs to the military. Since 1980, federal spending on all programs, other than social security and defense, has fallen from 9.7 percent of GNP to 7.3 percent, representing a 25 percent decline. Thirdly, fiscal monetary policies produced a macroeconomic environment that was characterized by a sharp recession in the early 1980s followed by a recovery which had been marked by high real interest rates, an overvalued dollar and an exploding trade deficit. The high real interest rates directly bolstered the income of those with money to lend, outstripping inflation by a wide margin. Interest incomes soared as a share of personal income at the beginning of the decade, contributing markedly to the income inequality of the 1980s. The high interest rates also caused the exchange value of the dollar to soar, which contributed to the deterioration of the US trade balance and subjected US industries that are international to much more intense competition. The more intense competition resulted in wages in those industries being held down. Many of those industries were in the goods producing sector which has ordinarily been the trend setter for wages throughout the economy.

A fourth point to be mentioned is the wholesale deregulation of the financial system, which contributed to a series of changes in the financial markets that also helped shift the distribution of income. Corporations took on enormous amounts of debt at high costs of servicing it which forced these same corporations to apply enormous pressures for lower wages and which also affected their level of profits.

What, then, is to be done? It seems to me that reviewing federal policy in relation to its effect on the growing income inequality, we need to follow certain guidelines. First of all, it needs to be noted that the United States is faced with an investment deficit which is in addition to the budget and trade deficits. In my view, it is essential that we increase public investment in those programs which enhance the ability of our citizens to be productive. These include education, research and development, public capital stock, transportation and other physical infrastructure, and health care, particularly preventive health care. All of these that our international competitors have been investing in, are necessary, if we are to have a more competitive and productive economy in the future. It is absolutely clear that we need to come to grips with the issue of developing the human capital at the bottom end of the income distribution. This is not only a humanitarian concern, but also one of self-interest, because our society can no longer simply carry it. We can no longer have a situation, as it might have been in the past, where we could say that since most of the members of our society are productive, we will simply carry the burden of those who are not. The dimensions of this problem have grown to such an extent that, unless it is addressed, carrying this burden will eventually drag down our economy. In my judgment, first, the progressivity of the tax code, an issue that is currently debated in Washington, needs to be restored. Second, the supervision and regulation of the financial structure, which is an arena that has been allowed to run wild and which has cost dearly, needs to be addressed, as well. And, third, another factor that affects the rising income inequality is the growing internationalization of the world economy, with capital and technology flowing across borders, and which also needs to be addressed.

We face global competitive pressures on what we must pay our workers. Our less skilled workers, especially, are increasingly in direct competition with huge numbers of unskilled workers in other countries and without an effective countervailing response from public policy, there is a danger that internationalization will further increase the disparity of income and wealth which we have seen started in the 1980s. The North American Free Trade Agreement (NAFTA) needs to be evaluated in terms of the impact it will have on the distribution of income in this country.

Robert Reich, referring to the fortunate fifth of the US income distribution ladder which held both wealth and human capital, noted that 'It is now possible for the most fortunate fifth, to sell their expertise directly in the global market, and thus maintain and enhance their standard of living and that of their children even as that of other Americans decline.' Architects, engineers, lawyers and others, and many increasingly functioning in the global environment, are very competitive, can go all over the world and draw a recompense out of the world economy. As the other Americans' fortunes decline, there is less and less basis for a strong sense of inner class, inner dependence because the relationship is not vertical. Meanwhile, the fortunate fifth have been able to insulate themselves from the less fortunate, by living in suburban enclaves far removed from the effects of poverty. Neither patriotism not altruism may be sufficient to overcome these realities yet, without the active support of the fortunate fifth, it will be difficult to muster the political will necessary for change.

We Americans need to draw some comparisons with what is taking place in other countries and try to move some of the myths we had out of our minds. We are convinced that we are a severely overtaxed society. In some absolute sense, I suppose, we can reach that conclusion. In any relative sense, however, if we look at the tax burdens of other industrialized countries, we will observe that we are at or close to the bottom of the list. By the same token, if we look at the services that are provided in other countries, that is, what people have to do in order to finance education, health care, etc. compared to us, we would see that the differences are often very dramatic. Underlying all of this is the unwillingness of people at the top of the distribution ladder to assume the responsibility for the rest. As I indicated, the dynamics are changing because the group at the top is becoming smaller and the groups that are impacted are becoming much larger. These groups are encompassing the middle class, and this gives a different political dynamic. What seems essential to me is attitudinal change, in that we have to overcome and rephrase President Reagan's wrong question of 'Are you better off?' to 'Are we better off?' Are we better off as a community or are we better off as a nation? There has to be some sense, some perception, that no matter how well off we may be personally, we should have an interest and an involvement in the balance of the society. We cannot be insulated, occupying the top of the house in any sort of secure position, if the foundations below are rotting away. My appeal then is for a sense of civic virtue in terms of a broadened perception of responsibility which I think has marked this nation at its best. The time has come to regain what we have lost in the 1980s.

9 Causes of and Possible Responses to the Recent Rise in Income Inequality

Leonard A. Rapping

9.1 INTRODUCTION

The ordinary person, as distinct from the academic economist or the intellectual, judges the performance of our economic system on the basis of its ability to generate an ever-improving standard of living, to maintain our political and economic freedoms, and to distribute the fruits of our material progress in a reasonable, fair way. My concern is with this last matter, fairness.

Space limitations prevent me from considering, in detail, what is meant by the term 'fairness.' As Peter McClelland has recently discussed, most Americans believe in the work ethic, in the appropriateness of the economic race, in the need for income differentials to incite effort, and in the requirement that all able-bodied men and women work. They also have a rough sense that income and consumption differentials can be 'excessive.' The possibility of too much inequality naturally arises when large distributional changes occur in lifetime consumption. This appears to have happened in the 1980s. However, lacking lifetime measures for consumption, I will follow the common procedure of using changes in current income as a crude approximation to lifetime changes in consumption. In choosing to measure income for a single year, I am reminded of the counsel given by the ancient Greek historian, Herodotus, who wrote: 'Count no man lucky until he is dead.'

9.2   STYLIZED FACTS ON CURRENT INCOME DISTRIBUTION

The stylized fact on the matter of income distribution for the 1980s is that measures of family income, based on both Census sample data for self-reported income and internal revenue data based on tax returns, show a sharp increase in income inequality among families. The increased inequality is a market phenomenon and is not the result of the Reagan tax law changes between 1977 and 1986. The compression of marginal tax rates by income class during this period had only a small effect on the distribution of after-tax income. Most of the change in this statistic, about 80 percent of it, was a pre-tax event. In turn, most of the market changes were driven by a decompression of wage and salary income, not by the rise in property income. The proper goal is therefore to account for decompression in the distribution of wages and salaries during the past ten to twelve years.

Concentration on changes in the distribution of hourly earnings has the advantage of providing a better measure of changes in the distribution of living standards than the usual annual income measure (except in periods of excessive involuntary unemployment) because it provides a rough measure of the change in the value of household production and leisure, at least if we are willing to evaluate these magnitudes at the wage rate. According to early estimates by Nordhaus and Tobin (1972) and later estimates by Zolotas (1981), the combined value of household production and leisure is of the same order of magnitude as measured GNP. Since wages and salaries comprise about 80 percent of measured factor incomes, they comprise about 90 percent of income measured to include household production and leisure. The wage rate is, therefore, an especially useful measure of differences among individuals at a point in time, as well as differences over time in the standard of living.

The increasing inequality in the distribution of wages and salaries in the last decade has occurred at a time when growth in the average wage rate has slowed noticeably. This slowdown adds greater importance to the increase in inequality. In a period of normal, *average*, wage growth, increasing inequality simply means less wage growth for those at the lower end of the wage distribution. But, with slow average wage growth, increasing inequality now means an absolute decline, not just a growth slowdown, in wages at the lower end of the distribution.

9.3 STYLIZED FACTS ON RECENT PRODUCTIVITY CHANGES

This brings us to a second stylized fact of considerable importance, the productivity growth slowdown brought on by the first oil price shock in the fall of 1973. While productivity growth has increased in the period 1979–89, having risen from 0.7 percent per year in the 1973–9 period to 1.4 percent per year, it still remains below its long run growth over the past 125 years of 2.1 percent per year.

While productivity growth does not track wage growth on a one-to-one basis, a fact resulting from adjustment lags, as described by myself and Professor Lucas (Rapping 1988), the two variables are closely associated over long time periods as reported in the historical studies of Stanley Lebergott (1984). The current wage slowdown appears, in substantial part, to result from the productivity slowdown. However, in the past seventeen years, this long term relationship has been partly masked by the rise in the Consumer Price Index relative to the GNP deflator, probably a reflection of the exceptionally poor performance of productivity growth in the service sector. As a result, measured productivity growth (using the GNP deflator) has exceeded growth in average hourly compensation (using the CPI deflator).

9.4 FALLING THEN GROWING INEQUALITY

The late Simon Kuznets referred to the years 1929–46 as the period of the Income Revolution. Over these years, income inequality fell dramatically. The share of income received by the upper 5 percent of the income units fell from about 31 percent to about 20 percent. Lindert and Williamson (1980) account for this development primarily as a compression in the distribution of wages and salaries, not as a change in the share of income going to the owners of property. With only small additional changes, this compressed income distribution persisted until the late 1970s. Then decompression began.

The evidence suggests that we do not have a U-turn as Barry Bluestone and Bennett Harrison contend, but, rather, an 'inverted staple' or an 'upside down table'. While the distribution of income changed only slightly over the period 1949–79, it began to decompress in the late 1970s. According to estimates by the Congressional Budget Office (which are not fully comparable to the figures cited above since they include government transfers), the share of income received by the top 5 percent of families has grown from 21.5 percent in 1977 to 25.1 percent in 1988. Data from household surveys reported by Frank Levy (1987), and tax data, reported by the late Joseph Pechman (1990), indicate a similar trend in recent years, although exact magnitudes differ depending on the data source which is used.

It is difficult to judge whether the compression during the New Deal was greater than the decompression during the Reagan period. The above data suggest that the changes during the period 1929–46 were greater than the reverse changes during the more recent period, but other data suggest that we have returned to the degree of inequality that existed during the 1930s. For example, during the 1930s, the share of income going to the upper 1 percent of tax reporting units was estimated by Kuznets (Lindert and Williamson, 1980) to have averaged about 14 percent. It then fell to about 9 percent by the years 1945–8. In comparison, Pechman reports that during the 1970s, this statistic averaged about 8 percent, then rose to almost 15 percent in 1986.

9.5 ACCOUNTING FOR RECENT CHANGES IN INCOME DISTRIBUTION

The matter of unemployment, especially as it affects those in poverty and the underclass, has been stressed in a number of studies; it thus seems appropriate to begin by exploring briefly the link between unemployment and the recent rise in inequality. There is no doubt that the business cycle impacts on income distribution. Alan Blinder and Rebecca Blank (1986) have documented that inequality increases in a downturn. I do not dispute this observation; but, my concern here is with the secular rise in inequality in the 1980s, not with its relationship to the trade cycle. On this matter, the effect of unemployment cannot be inferred from the trade cycle relationship. Quite the contrary, it does not appear to be an important explanation for the *secular* trend in inequality.

Rough evidence in support of this assertion is contained in Table 9.1. Table 9.1 shows decade averages of the unemployment rate and the share of income going to the top 1 percent of income receiving units for the years 1910–89. There is no relationship between these two variables. In particular, the Great Depression, while it created much economic distress, did not bring about a sharp increase in measured inequality. Nor were the high unemployment rates of the 1970s, which were comparable to the rates of the 1980s, associated with increasing

Table 9.1 Average annual unemployment rates by decades and associated average annual share of income received by the top 1 percent of income receiving units, 1910–89

Years	Average annual unemployment rate (%)	Average annual share of top 1% (%)
1910–19	5	14.0[a]
1920–29	5	13.5
1930–39	18	12.6
1940–49	5	9.4[b]
1950–59	5	8.7[c]
1960–69	5	8.8[d]
1970–79	7	8.0[e]
1980–89	7	14.7[f]

Notes:
[a] Average for 1913–19 only.
[b] Average for 1940–8 only.
[c] 1953 figure only.
[d] Average for 1963 and 1967 only.
[e] Average for 1972 and 1977 only.
[f] 1986 figure only.

Sources:
Unemployment:
1910–80, Lebergott (1984), p. 497.
1981–9 *Economic Report of the President, 1990*, p. 330.

Income Shares:
1910–48 data Simon Kuznets' work as reported in Williamson and Lindert (1980), p. 3.

inequality. Although these data suggest that the explanation for the secular raise in inequality is not to be found in the secular behavior of unemployment, I would not totally eliminate the possibility that unemployment plays some, albeit a modest, role in the secular behavior of inequality. However, before returning to this matter, let us consider briefly other explanations for the recent increase in inequality.

In the 1980s the American economy became more internationally competitive than in earlier years. Import penetration increased, while both legal and illegal immigration continued at high levels. While there were clearly American gains from this movement of goods and people, these gains were not equally shared among the population. Indeed, some Americans were harmed by this process. Of particular relevance is the possibility that foreign labor, who migrated to the United States and competed directly with American labor, or who competed indirectly through the shipment of their products to the United States, might have driven the wage of American labor below what it otherwise would have been. In this event, those workers directly in competition with foreign workers have not been beneficiaries of expanded trade and migration.

The available evidence presented in a series of studies by the National Bureau of Economic Research by economists including John Bound, McKinley Blackburn, David Bloom and Richard Freeman, George Johnson, Lawrence Katz, Kevin Murphy and Ana Revenga suggests that, at most, about one-fifth of the increased inequality in the 1980s can be attributed to the factor price equalization process. This leaves much to be explained.

The decline in unionization might also be a factor in this process of expanding wage differentials, but again evidence presented by Blackburn, Bloom and Freeman (1991) in one study, and Ferguson (1989) in another, indicate that the accelerated decline in union membership as a proportion of the labor-force – from about 20 percent in 1978 to about 13 or 14 percent in 1988 – cannot account for very much of the increased inequality in this decade.

The only explanation that seems to be quantitatively significant is one based on an acceleration in the rate of growth of the unskilled labor supply relative to that of the skilled. If we are willing to assume a secular and steady decrease in the relative demand for unskilled workers, based on a presumed skill-enhancing bias in technological chance, then this increase in relative supply can account for a considerable part of the increase in inequality.

9.6   MACRO AND MICRO POLICY IMPLICATION

Were a lower unemployment rate to moderate the degree of inequality in the system, there would be an additional incentive to propose public action to reduce unemployment. With unemployment rates now rising, this is an especially timely issue. Of course, even if unemployment has little to do with the secular increase in inequality, it is still desirable to moderate the rise in unemployment. The question is: can it be done?

Much of the debate in the last seven years has revolved around the issue of 'crowding out' and the proper mix of monetary and fiscal policy. Jim Tobin, Franco Modigliani and others have argued for balanced fiscal budgets so as to permit the Fed to lower the interest rate and thereby facilitate an increase in the rate of investment. It is presumed that increased investment would enhance productivity. The appeal of this macroeconomic proposal is its operational simplicity, at least as compared to the available microeconomic proposals for improving productivity. Such proposals include increased expenditures on government sponsored R&D and increased spending on education and training.

I have never been convinced by this macroeconomic proposal. First, there are many historical periods in which the relationship between investment and interest rates is very weak. We might, currently, be in such a period. Moreover, I do not think that lowering the federal funds rate or creating more bank reserves will necessarily lower the long rate of interest which is, after all, the goal of monetary policy. Expectations as to the future course of interest rates might not be easily changed by simply lowering the current short rate.

More generally, one might wonder whether a combination of expansionary fiscal and monetary policy can offset the current depressionary forces that are now in motion. In the often-heard plea for policies to generate a lower unemployment rate, William Vickrey stresses the economic constraints on policies designed to lower unemployment rates. In particular, he highlights the problem of inflation. The alleged tradeoff between inflation and unemployment has always been emphasized by Paul Davidson and other post-Keynesians. Many years ago, for example, Davidson, along with Abba Lerner and Sidney Weintraub, proposed ingenious income policies to escape this tradeoff dilemma. These policies were potentially effective in an economy in which 'key' industries were dominated by unions and monopolists. However, in the past two decades, foreign import competition has all but eliminated product market monopoly in these key industries, and the decline of unionism has greatly extended the domain of competitive labor markets. The institutional basis for an effective incomes policy no longer exists.

Let me turn now to a few concluding comments on several microeconomic policies that might be proposed as a means of reducing income inequality. Two general approaches to the growing inequality in earnings among workers should be mentioned. With the growing spread between the wages of those with lots of schooling compared to those with little schooling, it would seem that an appropriate action is to compress the differences in educational attainment among workers. Americans have always been committed to policies which make the economic race fairer. Free public education has been the main policy vehicle to offset the financial and motivational advantages of those fortunate enough to have been born into advantageous economic and/ or cultural backgrounds. Unfortunately, in recent years, our educational system seems to be performing less effectively than it once did, especially for those who choose not to continue on to college. Evidence concerning both the poor performance of American students compared to foreign students, and compared to earlier generations of American students, are quite suggestive on this matter. Additional federal and state expenditures on public schools may not ameliorate this situation. Instead, major institutional surgery may be required.

Leaving aside the complex issues arising in the debate over the public school system, direct assistance to low wage workers is another possible response to widening wage differentials, especially if the expanding differential is a result of the internationalization of the economy for, in this case, those who gain from trade should compensate those who lose. This assistance can take many forms: a reduction in social security taxes, an earned income tax credit or some other form of wage subsidy, such as that recommended by Edmund Phelps in Chapter 7 of this volume. Choosing among the various options involves matters of political feasibility, as well as economic efficiency. Of particular concern, on the question of efficiency, is whether large transfers are feasible without large disincentive effects. This is an important matter, but I will not consider it here. Instead, let me restrict myself to the political issues which become more dramatic as the magnitude of the transfer being considered grows.

Consider the problem of providing quantitatively meaningful economic support for the working poor, say, those who earn between $4.00 and $8.00 per hour. This involves about 30 million workers. A large scale program would comprise the transfer of about $90 billion per year (an average transfer of $3000 per worker). To provide a fix on what magnitudes of this size mean, recall that our current earned income tax credit – a program in support of the working poor – costs about $5 billion a year. On the other hand, 'welfare' for those who do not work (excluding the elderly and unemployed) costs about $150 billion a year (including Medicaid, food stamps and housing subsidies). Assistance to the elderly in the form of Social Security and Medicare costs about $350 billion a year. Support of public education costs about $300 billion a year.

It is difficult to judge whether we are entering a period when government support for the working poor can successfully compete with the elderly, the nonworking poor and families with school age children for government support. We should note, however, that there is an ebb and flow in which groups occupy a preferential position in political debate over nonmarket transfers of income.

Support of the young, through government-financed education, has remained the major redistributive program for the past 175 years. Until relatively recently, the government did not have a major transfer program. However, with the passage of the Wagner Act in 1935 and the subsequent rise of the CIO unions, attention was directed to industrial workers. For 30 years, concern centered on what might be termed the mandated benefits (i.e., improved wages and working conditions financed by employers) which derived from government-supported collective bargaining. Collective bargaining began declining in quantitative importance starting in the mid-1950s. In the early 1960s came the Civil Rights movement and then came the social rebellion of the late 1960s. In response, government attention turned to blacks and women. The political system promoted a new mandated benefit program, Affirmative Action. This program was coupled with direct government financing of the welfare roles. At about the same time, the government introduced Medicaid and, shortly thereafter, indexed Social Security benefits to the inflation rate. Now it was the elderly who were the beneficiaries of direct government support. By the early 1980s, the government's direct and indirect economic support of blacks and women waned. However, the elderly have maintained their special position as beneficiaries of government support. Perhaps the working poor are next in line for government support.

References

Blackburn, M., D. Bloom and R. Freeman (1991) 'An Era of Falling Earnings and Rising Inequality?' *The Brookings Review*, **9(1)**: 38–43.

Blank, R. and A. Blinder (1986) 'Macroeconomics Income Distribution and Poverty' in S. Danziger and D. Weinberg (eds), *Fighting Poverty* (Cambridge, MA: Harvard University Press).

Bluestone, B. and B. Harrison (1988) *The Great U-Turn: Corporate Restructuring* and *The Polarization of America* (New York: Basic Books).

Ferguson, W. (1989) 'Declining Union Bargaining Power and the Rising Wage-Productivity Gap in the US Economy since the late 1700's', unpublished PhD dissertation, University of Massachusetts.

Lebergott, S. (1984) *The Americans: An Economic Record* (New York: Norton).

Levy, F. (1987) *Dollars and Dreams* (New York: Russell Sage).

Lindert, P. and J. Williamson (1980) *American Inequality: A Macroeconomic History* (New York: Academic Press).

Nordhaus, W. and J. Tobin (1972) 'Is Growth Obsolete?' in Milton Moss (ed.) *The Measurement of Economic and Social Performance* (New York: National Bureau of Economic Research).

Pechman, J. (1990) 'The Future of the Income Tax', *American Economic Review*, **80**, 1–20.

Rapping, L. A. (1988) *International Reorganization and American Economic Policy* (New York: New York University Press).

Zolotas, X. (1981) *Economic Growth and Declining Social Welfare* (New York: New York University Press).

10 The Widening Wage Distribution and its Policy Implications

Rebecca Blank

My comments in this chapter will be more general than specific about the topic at hand. I want to discuss what I think are the major causal theories about why wage inequality has risen so much over the 1980s, and then make a few comments about the policy implications of this trend.

I spent the year 1990 in Washington, DC working for the Council of Economic Advisers. One thing that I did frequently during that year was to suggest to my colleagues and to others in the Administration that they ought to be paying attention to the issue of widening wage inequality. I cannot say that I was very successful in persuading anyone.

The reasons are probably obvious. First, discussion of rising inequality over the past decade is typically seen as at least an implicit criticism of the Reagan administration, something that the Bush administration was sensitive about. Second and more important, however, any discussion of rising inequality that presents it as a problem that people in Washington, DC should be concerned with immediately raises the question: 'what should we do?' And right now those of us who study inequality are far better prepared to talk about the facts of the problem than we are prepared to talk about the appropriate policy response. I learned that it is not useful in Washington to raise a perceived problem unless one can also talk coherently about its policy solutions. And I do not think there is currently any clear sense of what we should do about rising inequality, or even that we should do anything at all.

I want to start by presenting a few of the most frequently discussed theories about why rising inequality has occurred in the 1980s. I shall focus entirely on the issue of rising wage inequality, which I think is the primary issue of concern. And I want to emphasize before I start

185

that most of what I am going to talk about here is *theory*. While a growing body of research literature is now available to describe the facts of wage equality over the past decade, far less work has looked at this issue in a causal way. I plan to tell you what I think the primary hypotheses are, and to lay out some of the research questions that need to be pursued before we can claim to understand this inequality phenomenon.

THEORY 1

I shall call this theory the *sophisticated sectoral shift* argument. Its antecedent, the simple sectoral shift argument, has been clearly shown to be inaccurate. That simple argument, which many people believed a few years ago, claimed that the rising inequality was due to the shift of jobs in the macroeconomy away from manufacturing and toward services. People were leaving middle income manufacturing sector jobs and becoming re-employed in low wage service sector jobs. Hence, inequality rose.

Unfortunately for this theory, if you look at the distribution of wages within manufacturing and within services, they look virtually identical. Shifting people between these two sectors is not, in and of itself, going to produce very much in the way of changing wage inequality. In addition, if you look within each of these sectors, you find that there are increases in wage inequality within manufacturing and within services, and that these within sector increases are the primary reason for overall widening inequality. The simple sectoral shift story simply does not fit the data.

That does not mean that these sectoral shifts in employment are not related to rising inequality, as the more sophisticated sectoral shift story attempts to explain. A basic summary of the more sophisticated story might go as follows: changes in world markets, combined with changes in the domestic labor market, have placed US manufacturing at a comparative disadvantage, leading to a loss of jobs in the US manufacturing sector. In particular, the middle income unionized jobs that have provided good wages to a substantial number of less educated blue collar workers for many decades, are disappearing. The result is rising inequality in the manufacturing sector, as the higher paying white collar jobs and the lower paying blue collar jobs make up a higher share of overall manufacturing employment. At the same time, as the displaced workers from manufacturing flood the service sector, their lack of formal education places them in competition for less skilled and lower wage jobs. The increased number of people seeking these jobs in the service sector drives down the wages of less skilled service sector jobs, thereby leading to rising inequality in the service sector as well. The result is a dynamic process, in which inequality grows in both sectors because of the underlying sectoral shift occurring in the US economy, but the immediate causes in each sector are different. (The story I have told here is, of course, a bare bones version. Included in this story are frequently detailed discussions of immigration, trade balances, world labor mix, and a variety of other related forces.)

THEORY 2

I shall call this theory the *new industrial relations* theory of rising wage inequality. It is not unrelated to the story about sectoral shifts. This theory claims that a fundamental change over the past decade has occurred in the way that firms are dealing with workers. This shift in the industrial relations system is typically demonstrated with a wide variety of anecdotes about changing firm behavior: firms are increasing their use of temporary workers, they are engaging in less labor hoarding, they are distinguishing more between workers hired into long term jobs with substantial on-the-job training and workers to whom they do not want to make long term commitments, etc.

These changes are often related to the economic environment of the 1970s and early 1980s, when firms were hit by a series of price shocks, high inflation, and two back-to-back recessions in the late 1970s and early 1980s. Firms may have changed the way they utilize labor simply to protect themselves against such an uncertain economic environment. These changes may also be related to new technologies, which require firms to maintain a small pool of highly trained and skilled labor, but no longer require long term commitments to less skilled workers. Finally, these changes are also clearly correlated with the ongoing decline in unionism in the US economy.

THEORY 3

Next is the *it is the fault of the politicians* theory. There are two ways to tell this. First, it can be told as an intentional political choice: in the 1980s, the Reagan administration made a conscious effort to redistribute government resources away from certain groups in this economy and toward others. The widening distribution seen today is merely the result of a series of cuts in such areas as low income assistance and anti-discrimination enforcement, that were designed to lessen the political and economic power of certain groups. At least one problem with this version of the story is that it is not necessarily those who lost government assistance in the early 1980s who have seen their market opportunities fall most.

The second way to tell this story is the unfortunate and unforeseen result of a variety of policy decisions made in the past. Contributing factors include the deregulation of certain industries, tax changes, and the recent mix of monetary and fiscal policy. These, combined with a changing world economy, produced the widening inequality that the United States is currently experiencing.

THEORY 4

This is the *labor supply* theory. It claims that the problem is declining productivity among a certain segment of the work force. At an extreme, this theory talks about those often referred to as the 'underclass', claiming that a growing segment of the population is less willing to work in mainstream jobs, less willing to invest in education, and less willing to follow the norms of success in mainstream America. But this theory also can be applied much more broadly, through references to the declining effectiveness of the public school system, producing a higher number of poorly educated or illiterate low skilled workers, rising numbers of immigrants with poor language skills and little knowledge of how the US labor market works, and rising returns to black market activity in drugs, which pulls people out of mainstream jobs.

The crux of this theory is that the supply of labor is changing, for whatever set of reasons. Some group of workers is less productive, leading inevitably to a decline in their wages, and rising wage inequality. Of course, this story explains only why wages might have fallen among certain groups. It says little about the marked wage increases among more skilled workers that occurred during the 1980s. For that, we need to turn to our final theory.

THEORY 5

This is the *skill shift* theory. This was first articulated in a major way a few years ago by the US Department of Labor in their *Workforce 2000* report. Their claim was that the demand for skilled workers in the US economy was rising and would continue to rise faster than the supply of skilled workers available, producing skill shortages. Of course, one of the inevitable results of such a shortage is an increase in the real wages of those workers with the skills in high demand. Thus, this theory says the problem is not just that some group of workers may be becoming less productive (as Theory 4 claims), but that not enough workers are trained for the jobs that are open. The result is a skill mismatch: too many less skilled or inappropriately skilled workers for the jobs that businesses have available. This theory is often related to changing technological demands, as firms move to more and more automated production processes that require less 'muscle labor' and more 'smart labor'.

While all of these hypotheses may be plausible in one way or another, there is little work within the academic community testing these theories as causal hypothesis. There are of course some exceptions to this, but the bulk of the literature is focused on trying to understand the facts. This is an important endeavor and one that should necessarily precede hypothesis testing. But it is clearly time for the next wave of research to focus on explaining the underlying causes of rising inequality. I leave this as a challenge to the reader. We are in need of creative and good empirical work in this area. My guess is that like most areas there is no 'single cause' to these inequality trends. All of the above theories may well be true to a certain extent.

I am particularly concerned with the question of why the macro-economic expansion of the 1980s produced such unexpected micro-economic effects, and specifically, why it is that the aggregate economic growth of the past eight years has produced very little in the way of poverty reductions. Between late 1982 and late 1990 the US experienced the second longest expansion the country has ever seen. But quite unlike the longest expansion, which occurred in the 1960s, little of this has 'trickled down' to the poor. For example, in 1988 real GNP grew by more than 4 percent. Yet, the decline in poverty over that year was statistically insignificant. Historically, this is quite astounding.

Alan Blinder and I did some work in the early 1980s analyzing the relationship between the macroeconomy and poverty. We estimated the determinants of the poverty rate, based on aggregate data since 1959, which is when US official poverty numbers start. It is clear in these estimates that the macroeconomy matters to the poverty rate. You can take the coefficients from those equations and forecast, on the basis of what actually happened in recent years, what the expected poverty rate in 1989 should be. The answer is about 9 percent. But poverty in 1989 was 12.8 percent. The interesting research question is why poverty was so much less responsive to overall economic growth in the past decade than it has been in earlier decades.

There are at least three possible causes for slower declines in poverty over the last decade. First, there is evidence that the poor are a definably different population in the 1980s than they were in the 1960s. In particular, there is a substantially higher percentage of female-headed households among the poor, and this is a group that is much less able to take advantage of economic growth. When job and employment opportunities expand, women who head families may not be able to take advantage of those expanded opportunities because of child care responsibilities and constraints. The rise in female-headed households should clearly decrease the responsiveness of the poverty rate to the overall macroeconomy.

Second, however, policy toward the poor changed in the early 1980s. We restricted a number of programs to be less generous. Of course, there is a timing issue that has to be addressed in this story: Why should one-time changes in program parameters in the early 1980s substantially change the response of the poor to macroeconomic changes later in that decade?

In a joint research with Maria Hanratty (1992) I have been investigating differences in poverty rates in Canada vs. the United States. These two countries provide a fascinating comparison because they are so similar in many ways; they have similar populations and are impacted by very similar macroeconomic events. Yet, over the 1980s, poverty in Canada declined while poverty rates in the United States actually rose slightly. The underlying causes of this difference are quite clear: pre-transfer income in both countries moved in an almost identical way. Income transfer programs to the poor expanded in Canada, however, thereby decreasing the Canadian poverty rate, while they contracted in the United States. At best, one has to conclude that the overall rise in poverty rates in the United States was not inevitable in the 1980s, and clearly had some relationship to overall public policy efforts.

Finally, the third explanation for sticky poverty rates in the United States over the past decade is a changing macroeconomic environment.

The expansion of the 1980s seems to have been definably different from other recent economic expansions. For example, there was much greater variance across regions in their economic indicators than in previous expansions. Some areas had 2.5 percent unemployment rates for two to three years while others were still struggling with unemployment rates around 10 percent. In addition, all of the effects mentioned above might have occurred: more use of temporary workers, changes in the demand for workers at different skill categories, etc. These changes in the larger economic environment clearly not only widened the wage distribution, but were also crucially linked to the unexpectedly small declines in the poverty rate.

But let me move away from the specific question of poverty and return to the larger question of widening wage inequality. I suggested at the beginning of these remarks that not everyone was convinced that widening inequality constituted a problem. One might care about the lack of progress against poverty because of a concern about the well-being of the poor. But is inequality, *per se*, a valid public policy concern? Some might propose that only academics worry about the income distribution.

I think the question of 'Why should we care about income and wage inequalities?' is an important item for everyone's research agenda. We know very little about the effects of rising inequality on a country. I might note that economists may not have a comparative advantage in addressing this issue; it may be better addressed by those who study social psychology. It is certainly a question that provides an opportunity for good interdisciplinary research. Among the questions I would like an answer to are: (i) what is the long-term political impact of greater income inequality between different groups? (ii) What is the effect on individual and social consciousness of regularly seeing homeless people sleeping on the sidewalk? (iii) How does our sense of well-being change if our relative position in the income distribution changes? These are interesting questions, that both economists and noneconomists need to look at. (The only empirical research I know that addresses these questions has been cross-country studies of whether certain types of political events, such as government coups or civil wars, are more frequent in countries with wider income distributions.)

The question: 'why should we care about widening income differentials?' is closely linked to the question: 'what are the public policy implications of widening income differentials?' If the issue is the well-being of those at the extreme end of the income distribution – the poor – I think there are a number of clear policy agendas linked to the problem of poverty. One sees regular discussions about which set of new programs or reformed programs should be implemented to better fight poverty in this country.

But the policy agenda relating to the larger question of widening inequality is far less clear. Few people have articulated what I consider a coherent policy framework that would attempt to halt or reverse the rise in inequality in recent years. While there is a growing awareness of inequality as a potential political issue, the window of opportunity created by that awareness will not be translated into real political action until a clear linkage is drawn between the facts of inequality and a particular set of policies that can be used to address those facts.

I am perhaps the wrong person to put together that political agenda because, as I noted above, I am pretty convinced that there are multiple causes and we should probably do a whole range of things. That might be a good academic answer, but it is not very appealing in Washington, DC. Political effort and budget monies are limited, and in these circumstances a person who is willing to stand up and say 'Here is one program that will substantially offset the widening inequality in this country' will get far more attention than those of us who say 'Well, maybe you should do a little of everything.'

But, in the end, unless these concerns about inequality are clearly linked with a few seemingly do-able public policy options, I am not sure the 'inequality debate' will get the attention in Washington, DC. There are a number of such policies available, just waiting for a spokesperson: Edmund Phelps has already talked about wage subsidies in Chapter 7 of this volume; Isabel Sawhill mentions the EITC, and job training opportunities in Chapter 11; others are talking about school reform, changes in the minimum wage, further changes in the child care credit, and other related issues. It remains for someone to effectively and publicly link one or two of these policies with the inequality issue.

I think the greatest concern confronting us as a result of these inequality trends is the effect of worsening labor market opportunities on low skilled workers. In the midst of an eight year expansion, people with high school degrees have seen their real wages decline. This is an appalling fact for anyone who worries about incentives. For years we have tried to tell our children that there are certain things they ought to do: stay in school, get at least a high school degree, and once you leave school, get a job. It is hard to give that advice with a straight face when you know that for the past decade people who have followed that advice have earned less and less each year. An effectively functioning economy must provide the incentives for people to take school and work seriously, and the wage inequality trends of recent years that threaten those incentives. For this reason, if for no other, we should care very much about the widening wage distribution. This is an issue that I think deserves the utmost attention among those who care about the future well-being of the United States.

References

Blank, R. and A. Blinder (1986)   'Macroeconomic Income Distribution, and Poverty,' in S. Danziger and D. Weinberg (eds), *Fighting Poverty* (Cambridge, MA: Harvard University Press).

Blank, R. and M. Hanratty (1992)   'Down and Out in North America: Recent Trends in Poverty Rates in the United States and Canada,' *Quarterly Journal of Economics*, **107**(1).

11 Income Inequality and the Underclass

Isabel V. Sawhill

For the last several years I have been doing some work on the underclass and I want in this chapter to discuss a particular aspect of that work. How, you may ask, does the underclass differ from the poor? The underclass is engaged in behaviors that are individually and socially harmful. These behaviors include crime, substance abuse, dropping out of school, early childbearing and irregular attachment to the laborforce. We estimate using a behavioral definition of the underclass that in 1980 there were 2–3 million people living in neighborhoods where these behaviors have become so prevalent statistically as to constitute a way of life and possibly a new set of social norms in those communities. We could eliminate income poverty amongst this group for about $5 billion a year but I believe it is doubtful that $5 billion would eliminate the behaviors that concern us or the inner generational cycle of poverty that those behaviors tend to produce. Other solutions are in other words needed, and of all the behaviors that have produced and are perpetuating this permanently disadvantaged group probably none is more serious than early childbearing. I would like to explore some of the possible solutions to that problem.

In the order in which I will discuss them, they are: first, more jobs for either women or men, although most of the discussion recently has been about jobs for men; second, a reform of the welfare system; third, better child support enforcement; fourth, financial incentives for good behavior, in other words bribing people not to get pregnant; fifth, better contraception.

Some argue that if we want a return to the Ozzie and Harriet family of the past, we need to make sure that Ozzie has a decent paying job so Harriet will want to marry him. Right now the lack of what Wilson (1987) calls marriageable males leaves young women who want children with no choice but to have them out of wedlock. The empirical evidence in favor of this thesis is weak at best. The most recent empirical work has been done by Ellwood (1990), at Harvard, and most studies have not found a strong relationship between male employment opportunities and marriage. During the depressed 1930s for example, marriage rates among young black males were not only much higher than they are now, but also higher than those of whites. If the empirical evidence does not convince you, the logic should. Why should Harriet react to a lack of marriageable males by having a baby before she reaches adulthood? Why does not she postpone childbearing until she herself is better prepared to handle the responsibility? In the meantime, she might also become a more attractive marriage mate if she wanted to be. If the problem is too few men to go around, women might be expected to compete for those who are available by not tying themselves down with young children, but the most important point is that no matter how bleak a young woman's marriage or job prospects may be they are going to be bleaker still when she has children.

What about welfare incentives, are they the problem? The argument here is that welfare has changed the calculus of early childbearing by providing financial incentives for women to have babies. Thus far most researchers have been unable to find a significant relationship between the generosity of the welfare system and out of wedlock childbearing. But even if such evidence existed it is not clear we would know what to do about it. One cannot take away a mother's benefits without harming her children. Extending benefits to two-parent families in all states, a step that was taken in 1988, reduces the bias against marriage somewhat, but past experiments with generous benefits for intact families have not had the stabilizing effects anticipated. The dilemma between perverse incentives and minimally decent standards will not go away. The disincentives in the current system can be eliminated only by reducing the incomes of children in single-parent homes. By keeping welfare benefits well below the poverty line in most states, we are already sacrificing the well-being of children to larger ideological objectives concerning work and family.

Let me turn next to child support enforcement. The argument here is that at the same time that women are provided a means of going it alone by the welfare system, men are relieved of any liability for their behavior. Two-thirds of the birth certificates of babies born to unwed teens contain no information about the father, and only 14% of the fathers of children born out of wedlock provide any regular support to those children. Defenders of the status quo argue: (a) that paternity cannot be established and (b) even if it could be, fathers have no money. Computerized tracking of tax and employment records together with genetic testing have removed most of the impediments to paternity determination. The mother's cooperation is still needed, however, she has little incentive currently to work with the authorities since all but $50 of any child support is offset by a reduction in her welfare check. The 'fathers are penniless' theory is belied by estimates that close to $20 billion in untapped funds would flow to single parents if all fathers contributed a reasonable share of their income to their children. The Family Support Act of 1988 goes a long way toward correcting some of the deficiencies of the current system although most of its provisions have yet to be implemented. Missing, however, is any effort to secure the cooperation of the mother by allowing her to get more of the money collected or by assuring her a government-provided minimum benefit, if the father's income should prove insufficient. Many people believe that the offer of an assured benefit conditional on identification of the father and establishment of an award would go a long way toward eliminating welfare as a form of deposit insurance for irresponsible fathers.

A combination of a part-time job, subsidized child care and supplementation of the mother's wages through a wage subsidy or a more generous earned income tax credit and assured benefit could significantly reduce welfare dependency. It would also refocus more attention on men. Those with the ability to pay would be required to do so, those without such ability could be given job training or other forms of assistance. Most important, the next generation of young men might think twice about fathering children before they were ready to support them.

How about rewards for the mother's good behavior? Child support is clearly the nasty financial stick in the teenage parenting story. Some programs actually now provide carrots as well. A Planned Parenthood Program in Colorado, for example, pays teenage parents $1 a day to show up for weekly counseling and to not get pregnant. A Maryland county has proposed paying teenage parents $30 a month to avoid a second pregnancy. Practitioners claim that such efforts work but good evidence on their effectiveness is lacking; nor is it clear what accounts for any success there may be. Some argue that money is not directly responsible for any change but serves a mechanism for getting teenagers into counseling or a more supportive environment, and that it is the latter that changes their behavior. So far there has been only one rigorously evaluated program in which teenage mothers were provided with intensive services and mentoring although no financial incentives. It had some positive effects on mothers and their children, but it did not reduce pregnancy.

Let me turn finally to what I think is the most important issue of all, birth control. In the past the principle means of birth control was abstinence forced by a set of social norms that would be difficult if not impossible to recreate. By the age of 19, more than half of American teenagers today are sexually experienced. The mean age of first intercourse for males in the United States overall is 16, for inner city males according to some studies it is 12. That is the mean age. Attempts to put this particular genie back in the bottle are doomed in my opinion, to fail. The social controls that used to link sex to marriage no longer operate. European countries which have gone much further than the United States in recognizing this shift in sexual norms have had considerable success in controlling its worst consequences. With rates of sexual activity among young people at least as high as those in the United States, they have managed to reduce teenage pregnancies, abortions and births to a very small fraction to those prevailing here. High rates of teenage pregnancy among black Americans are often suspected of skewing the US figures; however, differences in racial composition across countries explain only a small portion of the excess teenage pregnancy in the United States. European success is due not to the different composition of their population but to the more widespread use of contraception, especially the pill.

The Netherlands is a striking example. If American teenagers were as successful as those in the Netherlands at avoiding pregnancy, 87% of current abortions and a similar proportion of teenage births could be avoided in the United States. That drop would save American taxpayers an estimated $17 billion annually. More important it would greatly enhance the life chances of not one but two generations. The best way to prevent abortions is to prevent pregnancy, and the best way to prevent pregnancy is to encourage contraception. Anti-abortion activists seem to be either unaware of or uncomfortable with this fact. Many are not only pro-life but also anti-contraception on the grounds that it encourages immorality. Yet there is no convincing evidence linking the wider availability of contraceptives to more promiscuous behavior. Those who are truly pro-life ought to focus more of their attention on contraception and less of it on terminating a women's right to end an unwanted pregnancy. It is hard to predict the likely effects of reversing the US Supreme Court decision of *Roe* v. *Wade*. Certainly it would not stop all abortions. Undoubtedly they would remain illegal in some states, and some abortions would be obtained illegally. Equally, certainly it would increase the growth of single-parent families with most of that growth concentrated among the youngest and most disadvantaged women.

European experience most dramatically refutes the notion that little can be done to reduce teenage pregnancy. A great deal could be accomplished by providing more information and services to at risk youth; school based clinics that provide both counseling and contraceptives have proved quite effective at reducing unwanted pregnancies. Much more controversial but worth pondering is the possibility of new contraceptive technology that can routinely protect any adolescent whether sexually active or not against pregnancy. The FDA is currently testing a procedure called Norplant that provides long term contraceptive protection, and such methods are already in use in other countries. Doctors can give women a shot or an implant that prevents pregnancy for an extended period. Imagine a society where all girls at puberty were strongly advised by health care professionals and their parents to seek such protection. If the practice were universally accepted or nearly so, it would carry no stigma and no implication of immoral behavior. It would protect nearly 1 million teenagers from unwelcome pregnancy each year including those who become pregnant by rape or incest. If women were universally protected, the decision to have a child would become a conscious choice, decoupled from the dictates of biology, hormones and peer pressure which are extremely intense in adolescence. Early child-bearing would gradually become less common and as it did social norms would undoubtedly shift as well. A new ethic might emerge, one which places more emphasis on social economic and psychological readiness to care for a child and less on biological readiness to bear one. An Orwellian fantasy, perhaps, but it is a useful benchmark against which to measure present practice. Although the means are controversial the ends are less so. The challenge as I see it is to find acceptable ways of achieving a good family environment for every child. Social norms which used to require delaying marriage until one could afford to support a family and delaying childbearing until after marriage helped to accomplish this goal. These norms have now disappeared. My argument is that we should put something else in their place.

References

Ellwood, D. (1990) 'The Mismatch Hypotheses: Are There Teenage Jobs Missing in the Ghetto?' in R. Freeman and C. Echniowski (eds), *The Black Youth Employment Crisis* (Chicago: University of Chicago Press).
Wilson, W. J. (1987) *The Truly Disadvantaged* (Chicago: University of Chicago Press).

Index